CARMEN POMIÊS

Cover Pictures
Front cover
Carmen Pomiès and Florrie Redford, captains of France and England
Before the kick-off at Herne Hill, South London, June 1925

Back cover
Team photo of Fémina Sport de Paris, February 1920

Artist's impression of women's football in France:
Fémina v Les Cadettes de Gascogne, October 1923

Resistance on the streets of Paris before the Liberation, August 1944. The woman with the gun is 'Nicole Minet' (real name Simone Segouin) but Carmen Pomiès was there too, shouldering her rifle.

CARMEN POMIÊS

FOOTBALL LEGEND AND HEROINE OF THE FRENCH RESISTANCE

CHRIS ROWE

PEN & SWORD
HISTORY

AN IMPRINT OF PEN & SWORD BOOKS LTD.
YORKSHIRE – PHILADELPHIA

First published in Great Britain in 2022 by
PEN AND SWORD HISTORY
An imprint of
Pen & Sword Books Ltd
Yorkshire – Philadelphia

Copyright © Chris Rowe, 2022

ISBN 978 1 39909 170 1

The right of Chris Rowe to be identified as Author of this work has been asserted by him in accordance with the Copyright, Designs and Patents Act 1988.

A CIP catalogue record for this book is available from the British Library.

All rights reserved. No part of this book may be reproduced or transmitted in any form or by any means, electronic or mechanical including photocopying, recording or by any information storage and retrieval system, without permission from the Publisher in writing.

Typeset in Times New Roman 12/16 by
SJmagic DESIGN SERVICES, India.
Printed and bound in the UK by CPI Group (UK) Ltd.

Pen & Sword Books Limited incorporates the imprints of Atlas, Archaeology, Aviation, Discovery, Family History, Fiction, History, Maritime, Military, Military Classics, Politics, Select, Transport, True Crime, Air World, Frontline Publishing, Leo Cooper, Remember When, Seaforth Publishing, The Praetorian Press, Wharncliffe Local History, Wharncliffe Transport, Wharncliffe True Crime and White Owl.

For a complete list of Pen & Sword titles please contact
PEN & SWORD BOOKS LIMITED
47 Church Street, Barnsley, South Yorkshire, S70 2AS, England
E-mail: enquiries@pen-and-sword.co.uk
Website: www.pen-and-sword.co.uk

Or
PEN AND SWORD BOOKS
1950 Lawrence Rd, Havertown, PA 19083, USA
E-mail: Uspen-and-sword@casematepublishers.com
Website: www.penandswordbooks.com

Contents

Acknowledgements		vi
Author's Note: Finding Carmen		viii
Prologue	The Kiss that went around the World	xviii
Chapter 1	Beginnings: Carmen's Paris	1
Chapter 2	Football Féminin Français	10
Chapter 3	Carmen's English Connection: Paris & Preston	24
Chapter 4	North American Adventure, 1922	46
Chapter 5	Successes, Scandals and the Fight for Survival: The 1920s	62
Chapter 6	Keeping the Flame Alive: The 1930s	85
Chapter 7	Carmen's War	112
Chapter 8	Carmen in America	137
Chapter 9	Knowns and Unknowns: The Road to Champcueil	153
Epilogue	What Happened Afterwards?	165
Appendices		
	Carmen's Football Diary	186
	Carmen's Travels	197
Afterthought: Awkward Questions		200
Find Out More: Books and Online Sources		206
Newspaper Acknowledgements		210
Index		211

Acknowledgements

Five friends and colleagues contributed enormously to the writing of this book. Marcel Put and Ian Rowe were there from the very beginning, offering encouragement, expertise and critical evaluation every step of the search for Carmen. Helge Faller has been unfailingly generous in sharing his unrivalled knowledge of women's football in the interwar years; so, too, has Steve Bolton, grandson of Lizzy Ashcroft, always full of enthusiasm and new evidence and one of the handful of historians as interested in Carmen Pomiès as I am. Without the inspiration from Petra Landers when we first met at a Football Makes History conference in Eindhoven in January 2020, the idea of a book about Carmen might never have gotten started at all.

I am also indebted to Pen & Sword Books for accepting my proposal of such a book and then bringing it to fruition. Claire Hopkins, Laura Hirst and Sarah-Beth Watkins have guided me through the ups and downs of publishing with clarity, kindness and patience.

History books have deep roots. Since I left classroom teaching behind in 2002, my outlook on history and history teaching, especially on issues such as multi-perspectivity, diversity, equality and inclusion, has been shaped in invaluable ways by colleagues at EuroClio and Historiana by Bob Stradling, Steven Stegers, Helen Snelson, Alice Modena, Andrea Scionti, Francesco Scatigna, Sean Wempe and a host of teachers and interns too many to mention. Similarly, the team of enthusiasts at footballmakeshistory.eu led by Jonathan Even-Zohar has been both an endless source of new ideas and a joy to work with. Colleagues such as Martin Liepach, Peter Bijl, Denver Charles and all those who worked with me on more than a hundred football life stories have given me in equal measure energy, ideas and friendship.

Acknowledgements

Long before I had ever heard of Carmen Pomiès, colleagues, friends and family were already influencing my understanding of twentieth-century history. I owe much to the outstanding history department at Liverpool University, where scholars like David Quinn, Joe Shennan and Henry Mayr-Harting inspired me to be a historian. I owe similar gratitude to David, the two Ruths, and the many wonderful colleagues who made the staffroom at Winstanley College my second home; and to the friends like Alan Midgley, Mike Tillbrook and Sally Waller who for so long have shared the unique life led by senior A level examiners.

Closer to home, Tess, Joanna and Jasmine, Mark and Alison, John, Sicily, Thomas and Jessica may never realise how much they mattered, how much their energy and optimism has kept a pensioner young. In the wider family circle, the same could be said of Ian and Carolyn, Neil and Gina, Jane, Ellie and Lily, Kate, Simon, Mira and Gregory Beth, Dave and Sophia, and a host of cousins and second cousins. They, like me, all remember the older generation who lived through the twentieth century: Alec and Jean Rowe, Auntie Jen, Auntie Mary, Dorothy and Joan, Arthur and Roy. All of them, and so many others, were history teachers without knowing it, passing on wisdom, values and lessons for life.

As for errors, omissions or missteps along the way to writing this book, they are nobody's fault but mine.

Author's Note

Finding Carmen

Carmen Pomiès was a child of the twentieth century. She was born in Paris in 1900 while the Exposition Universelle was displaying the glories of French culture to the world; she died in 1982 at Champcueil, Essonne, a few miles south of Paris, on her eighty-second birthday. As a young girl in a well-to-do family, Carmen witnessed the sights and sounds of Belle Époque Paris in a time of industrialisation, urbanisation and progress, but also a time of dislocation and hard living at lower levels of society. Carmen was thirteen when France went to war. She was eighteen when the armistice brought a kind of peace to a ravaged, exhausted nation.

In the 1920s, Carmen lived through *Les Années Folles* (The Crazy Years), a time of rapid social change and vibrant, adventurous, often disturbing new cultural trends. Carmen had a front-row seat from which to observe the new culture. Her younger brother Georges became a famous modern dancer and a film star. Through football, Carmen travelled far and wide, to Britain, Spain, Portugal and the United States. In the 1930s she became an important roving ambassador for women's football while, in the background, Europe was assaulted by economic depression, dangerous new ideologies and the rise of dictatorships.

Then, after barely twenty years of peace, France went to war again; what began as a now almost forgotten European war morphed into the vast sprawling conflict we call the Second World War. In 1940, France suffered humiliating defeat and fell under German occupation. French democracy fell apart, replaced by the oppressive, pro-German Vichy regime. For four years, the French people lived in a twilight zone, trapped between passive acceptance, collaboration and resistance. Carmen was at the centre of these moral complexities. Often, she was a brave activist committed to the resistance. At other times, like almost everyone, she was compelled into silence or compromise with the occupiers in order to survive. When liberation finally came in August 1944, Carmen was there, a résistant with her rifle on the streets of Paris.

Liberation was followed by peace but not by tranquillity. Like most of Europe, France was ruined economically and deeply divided politically by the war. Dealing with the legacies of defeat and occupation was difficult and painful. This may help to explain why, in 1946, Carmen decided to emigrate to the United States, lured by the dream of a new life in a country that had not been torn apart by war and was a beacon of hope, prosperity, abundance and national confidence. By now, aged forty-five, Carmen's football days were over. In America, her love of sport would have to focus on tennis instead.

For at least the next fourteen years, Carmen lived the American Dream, first in Rochester in Upper New York State, then in New York City. These were the years of the emerging Cold War, with the division of Europe, Communist revolution in China, and the hysteria of McCarthyism. Once again, Carmen had a close-up view of world events. From 1950 to 1953, during the war in Korea, Carmen worked as a translator at the United Nations. She set about becoming an American citizen. But she did not completely turn her back on France.

While living in America, Carmen made many return crossings of the Atlantic. She was still linked to Paris by her parents, her sisters, old friends and news from home. Carmen observed, if only from a distance, what was happening in post-war France: slow economic recovery, the painful colonial conflicts in Indochina and Algeria, the return of Charles de Gaulle to found the Fifth Republic in 1958. But then, after 1960, Carmen's story faded into the mists of time.

We know very little of her life after the age of sixty, only that she eventually returned to France and died there in 1982.

Carmen's twentieth century was my century, too. I lived through sixty years of it; and what went before me was the time of my parents, aunties and uncles. For a historian of my generation, much of Carmen's life and times seems very familiar, even though for the first seventy-eight years of my life I had never even heard of Carmen Pomiès.

When I began teaching, I was not likely to pick up Carmen's trail. My special field was the Age of Discovery and the world outside Europe. Lectures on Portuguese Africa, Aztec Mexico, India, the Spice Islands and Japan were never going to include references to a female footballer from France. It was only years later that the focus of my teaching switched to twentieth-century Europe, especially the years before, during and after the Second World War.

Carmen's century took over my life, in my teaching, in the exam papers I set and in the textbooks I authored on Britain, the United States, Stalin's Russia, Italy and Mussolini, Hitler's Germany. One topic I taught and wrote about was France under German occupation and the Vichy regime. I had no idea of this at the time, but teaching students about the complexities and ambiguities of collaboration and resistance in occupied France was bringing me closer to Carmen's life and times.

It is worth noting, too, that when I began, twentieth-century history was seen almost entirely through the lens of international affairs and high politics: the world wars, the Cold War, revolutions and dictatorships. Over time, however, social and cultural history became much more central. Looking at how social change affected the lives of ordinary people through issues such as class, the status of women, popular culture, sport and society, became more and more important for historians like me.

Seeking ways to get young people to engage with these issues led me towards the possible connections between football, history and citizenship. In a chapter I wrote on society and culture in post-1945 Europe for a textbook, *Years of Division*, one way to explain patterns of social change was through the lives of three iconic footballers of different generations: Nat Lofthouse, Ferenc Puskas and Ruud Gullit.

Nat Lofthouse was a legendary centre-forward for Bolton Wanderers and England, but it did not make him rich. His wages were low, held down by a rigidly-enforced maximum wage. He was a 'one-club man' who stayed with Bolton all through his career, with no transfer to a bigger, richer club. Lofthouse belonged to the 1940s and the 1950s, to an age when few players drove a car, or owned their own house.

Ferenc Puskas was rigidly controlled in a different way. He was a star player for Honved and Hungary's 'Golden Team' but he was supposedly an amateur, playing 'in his spare time' as an officer in the Army. He was famous but he was neither rich nor free. Then came the Hungarian Rising of 1956. Puskas and several players in the Golden Team escaped to the West. Puskas signed for Real Madrid, played for Spain and became what would nowadays be called a *galactico*, a different kind of superstar far away from the very different football world he had known on the other side of the Iron Curtain.

Ruud Gullit was never a 'slave' to a system like Lofthouse or Puskas. Gullit became a star in the Netherlands, Italy and England, first as a player, then a coach, finally a TV pundit. Coming from an immigrant background (his father was from Surinam) Gullit was also a shining symbol of modern multiculturalism, at least on the surface. He was never controlled in the way Lofthouse always was and Puskas was before he left Hungary. Confident, assertive, sometimes described as a 'stroppy Dutchman', Ruud Gullit knew his own worth; and that worth was measured in millions.

Although it was only one part of one chapter, the idea of analysing social change through the life stories of footballers took root in my mind. Years later, I came back to the idea with a more ambitious plan, to present a range of football lives from all over Europe in order to illustrate the whole history of the game. A lot of things happened to push this plan along. In 2002 I left college teaching behind to be a freelance consultant, travelling around Europe to work with history educators for the Council of Europe, EuroClio and Historiana. These projects all had similar objectives, promoting a transnational, multiperspective approach in order to make history more inclusive and strengthen values for living in a democracy.

Working with historians and educators from many countries divided by recent conflicts, such as Cyprus, Northern Ireland and the Balkans, was instructive, opening contacts with new colleagues from countries like Croatia, Italy, Germany, Norway, Spain and the Netherlands who were interested in 'weaponising' football to engage young learners. This was not to be a 'Hall of Fame' feeding enthusiasm for football for its own sake. It was using football as a 'hook' to get people learning about big themes like politics, migration, identity, diversity, discrimination and equality. The result was *footballmakeshistory.eu*, based in The Hague, a website offering online resources and learning activities. One of my tasks was to produce 100+ football life stories; when I got going on this, one of my chosen footballers was Carmen Pomiès.

By this time, I had been forced to re-think many of the ideas and assumptions I grew up with. I'd learned a lot about discrimination and the hidden barriers to equality. It was clear that my football lives should include individuals affected by many forms of racism, such as anti-Semitism, Islamophobia and discrimination against people of colour. My list would have to include lives relating to LGBT issues, disabled people, the problem of depression; and it was obviously essential to include a substantial number of women. I was getting closer to finding Carmen.

All this required me to get past my own blind spots and learn as much as possible as fast as possible about the history of women's football. I bought a lot of books, talked to a lot of colleagues in Football Makes History and got to work. I found there were three main episodes: the first beginnings of the game in Scotland and England in the 1880s and 1890s; the interwar years between 1918 and 1940; and the 'third wave' that brought about the gradual revival and expansion of the women's game from about 1970 up to the present day. All three episodes were fascinating, providing lots of women to choose from; but it was the interwar years that caught my attention most vividly, because so many women and girls were attracted to the game at that time and because the backlash against them was so powerful and oppressive.

I already knew a bit about this, especially the surge in football for 'munitionettes' in war factories and about the legendary Dick, Kerr Ladies of Preston. It was easy to select for my life stories the great Lily Parr and the dashing centre-forward Florrie Redford. I knew that women's football was strong in France in the 1920s and that Alice Milliat, the 'Suffragette of Sport' who did so much to promote women's sport in France, had to be on the list along with the wildly controversial Violette Gouraud-Morris. What I did not yet realise was how closely Carmen Pomiès was connected to all these great names of women's football.

It became clear that Carmen was a special friend of Lily Parr and Florrie Redford, that she lived in Preston for a year in 1921-22 and was part of the Dick, Kerr Ladies tour to North America in 1922, that she led French touring teams to England almost every year in the 1930s. It was a revelation to discover how closely her life was intertwined with famous names like Violette Morris and how important Carmen was as a player, captain, tour manager and ambassador, fighting to keep women's football in France alive. So Carmen's was one of the first life stories to go online, followed by a couple of articles about Carmen's life and about her special friendship with Florrie Redford. This was the autumn of 2019. The search for Carmen had really begun.

As I got going, I was lucky to find willing helpers. At a Football Makes History seminar in Eindhoven in January 2020 I was lucky enough to make friends with an authentic star of women's football,

Petra Landers, who had won trophies with Bergisch-Gladbach and played many times for Germany. I learned a lot from Petra about the sexist attitudes of the German Football Association; about the great adventure of the Climb to Equality in 2017, when Petra was one of the troupe of international players who took part in the Level Playing Field football match 5,700 metres high near the summit of Mount Kilimanjaro; and about her annual trips to Lusaka in Zambia to coach young African girls in the townships. Petra's story made it plain how much women and girls playing football were involved in a fight for equality.

From inside the Football Makes History team, I got terrific support from Marcel Put, from Heerlen near Maastricht. Marcel is a real bloodhound in historical research and helped me to dig out a huge amount of information and ideas about Carmen. A lot of the evidence we collected, including three books by Carmen's older sister Hélène, was in French, so I had to lean on my older brother, Ian, a teacher of French who has travelled more widely around France than anyone I know. It helped that Ian became as keen as anyone to learn everything that could be found about Carmen's story.

Through Football Makes History, I also became acquainted with Steve Bolton, a historian who is the grandson of Lizzy Ashcroft, one of the key players in the story of Dick, Kerr Ladies and a close friend to Carmen. Steve was already convinced that Carmen is one of the most important personalities in the history of women's football in the interwar years. He also has a wonderful archive of pictures and documentary evidence. Steve has been exceptionally generous in sharing his knowledge and resources. So has Helge Faller. Based in Germany, Helge is the leading authority on women's football in France, Belgium and Austria in the interwar years and acquiring his many fascinating books proved invaluable. Helge has been unfailingly helpful in sharing information and expert guidance. My quest to find Carmen would not have got very far without the contributions from these five marvellous helpers.

As my researches took me deeper into Carmen's life, it was remarkable how many parallels and connections between her story and my own came to light. Like Carmen, I was madly enthusiastic about sport. Cricket was an obsession from the age of eight and was the only sport where I got to play on the same field as superstars like Sonny Ramadhin and my idol, Brian Statham. I was a half-decent goalkeeper, played rugby union, a bit of tennis, quite a lot of golf. I was hopeless at swimming and on skis. So it was easy for me to identify with Carmen's love of sports, even though I had to accept she came from another planet in terms of athleticism and natural ability.

I also shared with Carmen a love of sport that went beyond just playing. Like Carmen, I was often captain of teams I belonged to. Like Carmen, I was often an organiser, arranging fixtures, or finding replacement players at the last minute, or arguing in committees. I could identify with Carmen on her 1937 tour of England when she managed an inexperienced squad full of high school girls. Although they often got slaughtered, sometimes by scores in double figures, it was easy to imagine Carmen encouraging them, keeping them determined to do better next time, because I had started a girls cricket team at the mixed grammar school where I taught in the 1970s. They never won a game either but got a lot of fun and pride out of a new challenge.

There were other connections with Carmen. She was twenty-two when she first crossed the Atlantic, out from Liverpool with the Dick, Kerr Ladies football tour and back home from New York. I was twenty-three when I sailed to New York on *Queen Elizabeth,* with the same sense of a once-in-a-lifetime experience as Carmen had forty years before me. Liverpool was my home city and seeing ocean liners at the Pier Head ready to depart for Canada or New York was part of my youth. The Pier Head still has its iconic buildings, the 'Three Graces', but is now a heritage waterfront. My Liverpool in the 1950s was much closer to the city Carmen knew in the 1920s than to the present day. That's also true of the terraced houses, trams and trolley buses in northern towns like Preston, Chorley and Bacup that Carmen came to know so well on her football tours and were familiar to me in the 1950s. Nobody can visit them now, except in their memories, through historic photographs, or by time machine.

There was also an American connection. My study year in 1965-66 was at Brown University in Providence, Rhode Island. In three of her matches on the 1922 tour, Carmen was the goalkeeper playing against men's teams at Pawtucket, New Bedford and Fall River. All of these places are very close to Providence and I knew them well. Then, in 1967, I went to live and work in North America (in Western Canada) as Carmen had done in 1946. Like Carmen and like so many European migrants to America, I did not stay forever but eventually came back home again to Europe.

These parallels and connections made finding Carmen an ever more desirable goal but tracking Carmen's life outside sport turned out to be unexpectedly difficult. Many episodes in Carmen's life story, especially her football career, are well documented. Carmen's connections with Preston are a big part of the story of Dick, Kerr Ladies, told in loving detail by Gail Newsham in *A League of Their Own!*. The context of women's football is analysed in depth by Professor Jean Williams in *A Game for Rough Girls?* and *The History of Women's Football*. Three books by Carmen's older sister, Hélène, provided vivid insights, especially about the brief career of their film star brother Georges. A terrific collection of photographs and memorabilia edited by Patrick Brennan appears on his Donmouth.com website. For large parts of Carmen's life, however, the trail of evidence remains amazingly thin for a woman who led such a colourful life and was so important for football and equality.

So finding Carmen remains a quest far from finished. History is often a work in progress, full of uncertainties and provisional judgements. It has been said often that writing history is like doing a jigsaw puzzle. Well, yes, but the task has to be done with no picture on the lid of the box as a guide, with lots of pieces missing, and with a sprinkling of pieces that belong to a different puzzle. The picture that is put together can be partial, perhaps with gaps too big to even guess what's missing.

Then, too, there is the Covid Factor, the pandemic that has placed people like me under house arrest for almost two years. In normal times, I would have been out and about searching for more on Carmen's story. Given the chance, Ian and I would have been to Paris to find more about Carmen and the Pomiès family in the streets of Montparnasse or in the National Library of France. We would have gone to the high mountains above Grenoble to trace Hélène's first-hand experiences of the Vercors Rising in 1944. We would have gone to Champcueil, where Carmen died in 1982. Sadly, the pandemic decreed that our travels could only be virtual.

Without the pandemic, I might have been able to visit Rochester NY to find out more from the *Democrat & Chronicle* newspaper, or from the Rochester historical society. I would be able to meet Steve Bolton and Helge Faller in person, not just by phone and email. As things are, it seems as if the search for Carmen might never reach a definitive end.

So the balance between what we know and do not know about Carmen is tantalising. Sometimes, gaps in the story lead toward what historians are supposed never to do, to speculate about what lies hidden from the historical record. Speculation can indeed be a dodgy business, but there are times in Carmen's life where nothing else will do. Even so, enough evidence is visible for us to know what an adventurous, fascinating, historically important story is told by the life of Carmen Pomiès.

Prologue

The Kiss that went around the World

DAMEN FUSSBALL – WETTKAMPF MIT KÜSSEN
[Ladies Football - Sporting Contest with Kisses]

International Competition in London: In a new fashion, instead of shaking hands, the lady captains kiss each other before the kick-off. Ball in hand, French captain Carmen Pomiès leads her team out onto the field of play with enthusiasm for the battle to come.

Some pictures tell a big story. This German postcard, with its twin pictures of the captains before the kick-off and Carmen leading the

French team out onto the field of play, was derived from press photos taken at an international women's football match played at Herne Hill, South London, in May 1925. The picture on the left shows the captain of the France team, Carmen Pomiès, greeting the England captain, Florrie Redford, before kick-off. Their little kiss could easily be seen as just polite sportsmanship between two people who might be strangers, like a handshake between male captains. But at Herne Hill in 1925, there was more to it than that.

The two women were already the closest of friends. Carmen and Florrie had played against each other many times before, the first time at Preston in April 1920. They had also regularly played together as teammates, and for months at a time had stayed at each other's homes. In 1921, Carmen moved from Paris to live in Preston and play for Florrie's hometown team, Dick, Kerr Ladies. In the autumn of 1922, Carmen and Florrie were together for Dick, Kerr's football tour of the United States.

In 1923 and 1924, Florrie was living in France, playing with Carmen's Fémina team as it won trophy after trophy. A photograph of the Fémina team after clinching victory in the French league championship, with Florrie and Carmen sitting together in the middle of the front row, reflects the friendship and camaraderie between them. The two would remain friends long after 1925, part of the close links between Paris and Preston that were so important in women's football in the interwar years.

The original picture of Carmen and Florrie at the kick-off of that match at Herne Hill in 1925 is possibly the most widely circulated and enduring image in the history of women's football. This version, from the magazine *Picture Post* was only one of many taken by press photographers and newsreel cameramen at the time. Their images spread all around the world. A few weeks after the match, it reached Argentina via the magazine *El Grafico,* published in Buenos Aires. The captains' kiss also appeared in *The Brisbane Courier* in Queensland, Australia, in the United States, in British and French cinema newsreels – and on the German postcard.

The worldwide publicity was not accidental. Since December 1921, when the English Football Association imposed an official ban on women's football being played at grounds under FA jurisdiction, the women's game had been struggling against powerful and pervasive influences attempting to obstruct and suppress it. So the Herne Hill match was launching a deliberate campaign to revitalise the women's game. It was the grand opening of an ambitious tour of Britain, with an intensive schedule of ten matches taking the players from London to Burnley, Blackburn and Manchester, to Kilmarnock and Dumfries in Scotland, to Belfast and Dublin in Ireland and back again to London, to prove that women's football was still alive and kicking.

The longer-term impact of this orchestrated 'propaganda tour' is hard to assess. Many of the matches attracted large crowds and extensive press coverage, though the publicity could not be sustained on the same scale as for the first game.

Much of the comment aroused by the match, and by the picture of the captains' kiss, was ill-informed, misogynist, or just silly. There had been a surge of women's football during and after the First World War, and the notion of women and girls playing the game really should not have seemed so strange and exotic. But it did. The obsession with the captains kissing reflected this; it had to be re-staged for the cameras over and over again, like wedding photographs, or handshakes between world leaders at a summit meeting. Women's football was forever having to fight back against such attitudes, and against more direct attempts to denigrate, marginalise or ridicule the women's game.

All in all, then, France v England at Herne Hill in 1925 was no ordinary football match; and Carmen Pomiès and Florrie Redford were no ordinary football players. Tracing the story of the eventful life of Carmen Pomiés illuminates a neglected but important episode in the history of football and of Europe in the twentieth century.

Chapter 1

Beginnings: Carmen's Paris

Carmen Charlotte Marianne Pomiès was born in Paris on 29 September 1900. Her father, Charles Pomiès, has been described as a dentist, but this underrates his wealth and status. He was an orthodontist who owned a business that manufactured dentures and dental equipment. Carmen's mother, née Adèle Guignard, came from the Indre region, south of the Loire. The family home was at No 4 Rue de la Gaîté, an elegant street just to the east of the Gare Montparnasse, running past the Theatre Montparnasse, crossing over the Boulevard Edgar Quinet to the bustling shops, stylish cafés and glitzy nightlife of the Boulevard du Montparnasse.

Carmen was born into a well-to-do, educated, cultured family. Before he went into business, Charles Pomiès had studied Fine Arts in Le Havre. Charles's father Félix, born in Bruges, had been a musician. Carmen also had Spanish blood in her veins: her grandmother, Marie Incarnation Lucile Garcia Lopez ('Lucie'), born in Madrid in 1840, had been a dancer and actress.

Lucie Garcia seems to have made a particularly deep impression on Carmen's eldest sister Hélène Marie Lucile, born in January 1897, who became a writer, translator and editor. In 1937, Hélène's mastery of Spanish would make her a key contributor to a book, *Nouvelles Espagnoles* (Stories from Spain), translated into French by Hélène and edited by a noted left-wing intellectual, Jean Cassou. Another older sister, Yvonne Clementine Louise, born in August 1898, seems to have been a talented pianist, much admired as accompanist to singers. Carmen's younger brother, Georges Félix André (taking his middle name from his grandfather as Hélène did from her grandmother), was very close to Hélène, with similar aspirations to be a writer and poet. But Georges had other talents, too.

In the 1920s, Georges embarked on an artistic career, first as a *chanteur,* singing in clubs and music halls before he was persuaded that he had even greater potential as an 'interpretative' dancer. Georges became internationally famous for his 'modern dance technology' and his flair for mime and comedy. By 1928 he was launching his career as a film star, taking one of the three lead roles in *Tire Au Flanc* (The Sad Sack), a silent movie directed by Jean Renoir.

Carmen seems in some ways to be the odd one out in this cultured family. Highly intelligent and multilingual though she was, Carmen's passion was for sport. After leaving school, Carmen was briefly a student at l'école odontechnique (dental college). This seems not to have been her own idea; her father wanted one of his children to have expertise in dentistry to help the family business. Carmen decided otherwise. Charles Pomiès next tried to persuade Georges to become a dental student. That did not work either. Georges was drawn away towards singing, dancing and acting, just as Carmen opted for athletics and football.

Carmen's real passion was sport. Fit and strong, with apparently boundless energy, she loved swimming and diving, skiing, tennis and athletics – both middle-distance running and throwing the javelin. She loved even more the physicality and team spirit of women's football. This passion for sport was not only part of Carmen's youth. She played football at a high level until her late thirties; she was a serial winner of tennis tournaments in America at fifty. Her father's dream of Carmen becoming an expert in the technical aspects of the orthodontics business was never likely to come true.

Carmen was a child of the twentieth century. When she was born in September 1900, Paris was hosting the Exposition Universelle, or World's Fair, Not far from the Pomiès family home, imposing buildings like the Grand Palais had been specially constructed for the event. Close by was another symbol of the new Paris, the Eiffel Tower, completed a few years earlier, in 1889. Alongside the Exposition Universelle was the Olympic Games, following on from the revival of the Olympic movement in Athens in 1896. In 1900, however, the Paris Olympic Games were a sideshow, of less importance and less well attended than the World's Fair. Not until 1908, in London, would the Olympic Games become a dominating world event in its own right.

The Great Exposition lasted from May to October and was a showcase for Paris as a world city, at the cutting edge of high culture, haute cuisine, haute couture and progress in science, technology and medicine in the age of the Second Industrial Revolution. Paris was the 'City of Light', already a magnet for international tourism, a hub of the globalised, interconnected world, an imperial city with links to North and Central Africa, to Indochina and the South Pacific.

This was the Paris of the Belle Époque, of art nouveau architecture, fashionable hotels and restaurants, world-famous museums and art galleries, of motor cars and café society. This was the Paris often visited by the Prince of Wales before he became King Edward VII, a city of sophistication, glamour and opulence, But there was another Paris in 1900, a city of factories, overcrowded poor-quality housing, gritty working-class lives, social and political divisions, and culture wars. The social upheavals of rapid urbanisation pushed and pulled many people towards political extremes. After the French monarchy was overthrown following defeat in the Franco-Prussian War of 1870-71, France became the Third Republic, a liberal constitutional democracy; but the 'Bourgeois Republic' had dangerous enemies.

On the Right were monarchists, extreme nationalists and Catholic conservatives. On the Left were radical socialists, anarchists, pacifists and 'Syndicalists', trade unionists less concerned with improving the conditions of the workers than in mobilising political revolution against the state. By 1900, these dividing lines in French politics and society were sharp-edged and raw.

Since 1894, the Dreyfus Affair had convulsed the nation, opening deep and wide divisions between Dreyfusards and Anti-Dreyfusards.

Notionally, the Affair was all about the fate of Alfred Dreyfus, a staff officer in the French Army who was convicted of passing sensitive military secrets to the Germans. Dreyfus, who happened to be Jewish, was publicly disgraced before being imprisoned at the notorious penal colony of Devil's Island in French Guyana. His case led to a storm of nationalist outrage, strongly flavoured with anti-Semitism.

This was already enough to raise the political temperature in France but it was only the beginning. In 1898 and 1899, campaigning by supporters of Dreyfus forced a re-investigation of his case. It was proved beyond reasonable doubt that Dreyfus was innocent. By then, however, partisan loyalties had become entrenched and immovable. Anti-Dreyfusards insisted that the honour of the Army was of higher importance than the fate of one Jewish officer. Even when Dreyfus was released from Devil's Island, his health ruined as well as his career, it was due to a grudging pardon for a crime he had never committed, not rehabilitation of an innocent man.

The fight for and against Dreyfus continued to divide politics, friendships and families in France. Dreyfusards claimed they stood for liberalism, social justice, democracy and the separation of Church and State. Anti-Dreyfusards claimed they were defending Church, Army, and Nation against 'godlessness'. Some yearned for the return of the monarchy. Dreyfus himself was finally declared innocent. He was rehabilitated at a symbolic, very public ceremony in July 1906.

Temporarily at least, the Dreyfusards and the Republic had triumphed, but French politics remained turbulent, menaced by lasting grievances on the Right. *Action Française* was founded in 1899 at the height of the hysteria over Dreyfus, as a far-right political movement backed by a daily newspaper of the same name. Its ideological mastermind was Charles Maurras, moved by virulent anti-Semitism, Catholicism and a hatred of parliaments and modern liberal values – all symbolised by his hopeless dream of a restoration of the French monarchy.

Another hostile right-wing nationalist group was the League of Patriots, led by Paul Déroulède. In February 1899, when President

Félix Faure died in scandalous circumstances, romancing his thirty-year-old mistress in the Élysée palace, Déroulède attempted to use the death of the president to spark revolution in the streets and a military coup d'état. The coup was amateurish, without planning or direction. It ended in a humiliating failure, closer to farce than high political drama, In 1905, the right-wing enemies of the Republic suffered another defeat when the government forced through the Separation of Church and State. It was a victory for anti-clerical liberals and a setback for Catholic conservatism. Even so, threats from the Right did not disappear. Charles Maurras and *Action Française* kept up their attacks. They would come back to the forefront of politics in the 1930s.

Exactly where the Pomiès family stood in relation to these fractures in French politics and society is difficult to know, though there is some circumstantial evidence to go on. Although a wealthy businessman, Carmen's father was arrested three times after the German occupation of France in 1940, which seems to suggest he was suspected of liberal or Leftist sympathies. Georges Pomiès was a leading figure in the daring artistic life of 1920s Paris, part of a cultural freedom of expression that challenged traditional society. Hélène Pomiès was in the Association of Revolutionary Writers, originally founded in Moscow in 1927 (Georges joined the ARW in 1932, probably influenced by his sister). Hélène collaborated on literary projects with noted left-wing intellectuals like Jean Cassou and Henri Barbusse.

Thus it appears that Carmen grew up in a family in tune with modern social and political ideas. Carmen was perhaps less 'political' than Hélène, but she was a warrior for female equality through her passion for football and athletics. We know Carmen fired the starting pistol at a Socialist Youth Games in the late 1930s, for a race dedicated to the memory of her brother Georges. We also know Carmen and Hélène were involved in the Resistance during the Second World War, and that, after the war, Carmen had an idealistic view of her work for the United Nations.

The Pomiès family lived at a fine address close to the elegant Paris beloved by tourists and the well-to-do. Nearby were the Luxembourg Gardens, the Eiffel Tower, Notre Dame cathedral. This was the Paris of the Belle Époque, of style, wealth and progress. But in streets not far away from the Rue de la Gaîté was the Other Paris, an ever-expanding, rather chaotic urban underworld of poverty, struggle and grinding hardships. In busy streets like Rue Immeubles-Industriels and Rue St Julien de Pauvre, all the social problems that were the price of urbanisation and progress were on display: damp overcrowded housing, poverty, hunger, alcoholism, prostitution, domestic abuse and petty crime. It was a breeding ground of rent strikes, radical socialism and the rising anxieties of the middle classes.

Carmen was a schoolgirl growing up in comfortable surroundings. Her life had little or nothing to do with the Other Paris. But it was part of her youth. Her home in Rue de la Gaîté was in the heart of Montparnasse and the 14th arrondissement, an area with many poor districts alongside the bourgeois affluence. The young Carmen was able to observe the sights and sounds of streets crowded with beggars, rag-pickers, soup sellers, letter writers for the illiterate, the tired faces of people with hard lives. How much Carmen noticed of this Other Paris, how it made her think and feel, we cannot know. But she knew it was there.

Carmen's high school was the École des Filles, in Rue Huyghens. Walking to school took her from Rue de la Gaîté to the other end of the Boulevard Edgar Quinet. Nowadays, Carmen's old school has been absorbed into the coeducational Lycée Paul Bert but in her time single-sex schools were the norm. Her brother Georges went to an elite boys school, Lycée Lavoisier. In 1914, the École des Filles hosted a special event, a huge 'dance instruction' for 300 girls led by Raymond Duncan, famous brother of the even more famous dancer and choreographer, Isadora Duncan.

The event had interesting connections with Carmen's later life. The Duncan dance dynasty extended beyond Isadora and Raymond to the 'Isadorables', six young dancers who were the adopted daughters of Isadora. In the late 1920s, when Georges Pomiès became an international star, his long-term dance partner was Lisa Duncan, one of the 'Isadorables'. Also, two of the girls involved in the dance instruction at the École des Filles in 1914 were the Brulé sisters, Thérèse and Jeanne. Both joined the Fémina sports club around the same time as Carmen. From 1920, the Brulé sisters played alongside Carmen in countless football matches for Fémina and for teams representing France.

Paris, like all of French society, was deeply affected by the First World War. When the war began in August 1914, it was greeted by an outpouring of patriotism and national unity, the so-called 'Union Sacrée' bringing together all the divided strands of French society. But the war gradually descended into a deadly stalemate that put the entire nation under terrible strain. There were shortages, strikes and demonstrations. The awful costs of the war became more and more visible. Casualty lists posted in public places recorded countless numbers of 'Nos Mutilés', the war-wounded who had lost legs, arms, eyesight, or suffered lung damage in gas attacks. These legacies of war were to have strong connections with Carmen's later life in women's football. Dozens of matches she played in were to raise funds to support wounded ex-servicemen.

Already by 1910, when Carmen was a little girl, the district of Montparnasse was famous for its theatres, elegant café society and vibrant nightlife. In the years that followed, especially just after the war, Montparnasse was even more a hub for new artistic and intellectual trends in entertainment and freedom of expression. Patrons overflowed across the pavement outside cafes like La Closeries des Lilas, famous for being patronised by artists, or La Dome. Trendy bars and restaurants like La Rotonde and La Coupole were famous night spots, places to dance, watch floor shows by stars like Kiki, the 'Queen of Montparnasse', and feel part of the action.

At night, this cultural life on Carmen's doorstep in Montparnasse, a milieu in which her brother Georges would launch his artistic career just after the war, was raffish and edgy, attracting noisy crowds, exhibitionism, and criminality. In Rue de la Gaîté, for example, was a dance hall called Bal Grateau, 'where dances were nothing but battles, fisticuffs, obscenely swaying women unbuttoned down to their waists, and hiccupping drunks'. Yes, Montparnasse was a milieu of glamour and excitement but it also had its ugly side: petty crime, exploitation, broken glass and broken dreams.

In the early 1920s, many Americans regarded Paris as the most wonderful city in the world to visit or live in. Famous names such as Ernest Hemingway and Josephine Baker added to the buzz. Postwar France was very pro-American, with squares in Paris named after President Wilson, General Pershing and others. American jazz, cinema and lifestyle, such as cocktails at the American Bar, were all the rage.

All this made a lasting impression on Carmen Pomiès; her feelings about America would later have a significant influence on her life. In November 1918, Carmen was one of thousands of subscribers who donated money to a fund for a commemorative quill pen to be used by the American President, Woodrow Wilson, to sign the final treaties at the Peace Conference. In the book of donations, Carmen identified herself as 'une jeune Parisienne, admiratrice de Wilson et de son pays, terre de liberté'. Carmen gave 1Fr 50. In 1919, her sister Hélène sailed to the United States to study there. In 1922, Carmen would herself travel to America, as a player with the Dick, Kerr Ladies football tour. After the Second World War, Carmen would choose to live there, first in Rochester NY then in New York City. In 1954, she would become a US citizen.

French society was deeply affected by the First World War. When the war began in August 1914, there was an outpouring of patriotism and national unity, the so-called 'Union Sacrée'. France was roused to a great collective war effort, but the hopes of a 'short victorious war' turned to ashes in a deadly stalemate that seemed never-ending. Social change was already happening in France in the years before the war, but the rate of change was dramatically accelerated by the strains of war. One among many of these most important aspects of change was feminism.

Carmen was thirteen when France went to war supported by wild public enthusiasm. She was fifteen when France endured the Battle of Verdun in 1916, a cataclysmic siege battle that lasted five months and cost France half a million killed or wounded soldiers. Carmen's life was far from the front, but she knew all about the daily public notices of war deaths, and the anxieties of civilians who received, or feared, terrible news of loved ones. Carmen was sixteen when France struggled through the crisis year of 1917, rocked by mass casualties, army mutinies and fears of revolution on the home front. She was still only eighteen when the war was ended by the armistice of November 1918, and when world leaders started arriving in Paris in 1919 for the post-war peace conference. The war was, to say the least, a formative experience.

Carmen did not fight at the front, of course, nor did her immediate family. Her father was too old and her brother was too young. Also, although the war cast a huge dark shadow over France, civilian life in wartime is often remarkably 'normal'. Even though France suffered the highest casualties of all the Allied powers during the war, for Carmen, life in Rue de la Gaîté went on: school, friends, family occasions, time for leisure activities. And, for Carmen, leisure meant above all things sport.

Carmen Pomiès was a girl with natural athletic ability, a sociable personality and energy to burn. Whether she was consciously motivated by politicised concepts of female equality we cannot be sure but it seems safe to say she wanted to run free on the sports field, just like boys did. Carmen was exactly the kind of girl Alice Milliat was looking for.

Chapter 2

Football Féminin Français

French society was deeply affected by the First World War. When the war began in August 1914, there had been an outpouring of patriotism and national unity. The 'Union Sacrée' called France to a great collective war effort but the dreams of heroic victory were lost in the grim realities of total war. The long war quickened the pace of multiple revolutions, political, economic, social and cultural, that were transforming France and the world. One among many strands of social revolution was feminism. In the vanguard of the feminist movement was Alice Milliat, the 'Suffragette of Sport'.

Alice Million was born in Nantes in 1884. She was a teacher, who for a time lived and taught in England, where she met and married Joseph Milliat. In 1908, however, Joseph died unexpectedly and Alice returned to France. She was already a keen sportswoman, outstandingly good in rowing and single sculls. Energetic and imperious, a good networker and fierce campaigner for female equality, Alice had a passionate belief in sport for women. As a widow, she also had a special status, able to do things that would have been out of reach for any single girl or married woman. She used her social position and her talents as an organiser to become the dominant personality behind the rise of sport for women in France. In 1911, Alice Milliat began her involvement with Fémina Sportives, a new sports club in Paris running a wide range of activities for women and girls.

By the time she was seventeen, Carmen Pomiès had become one of many enthusiastic recruits to Mme Milliat's sporting empire. Carmen's talents included swimming, diving, tennis and football as well as running 1000m races and throwing the javelin. But in the end, what she loved best was football.

Mme Milliat's two driving ambitions were to achieve votes for women and to increase female participation in sports, especially in athletics. Above all, she dreamed of winning recognition for women's events at the Olympic Games. In 1896, with enthusiastic support from France, the Olympic movement had been revived by the first modern Games, in Greece. Paris had hosted the Games in 1900, though only as a sideshow to the Exposition Universelle. The only events for women were sailing, tennis and golf. The 1904 Games took place far away from Europe in St Louis, Missouri, again as an appendix to the World's Fair. The London Games in 1908 allowed women to compete in archery and figure-skating.

Small progress was made at the 1912 Games in Stockholm, where forty-seven women were able to compete in new events such as swimming and diving, but Alice Milliat wanted much more. It was a major frustration that the 1916 Olympics, scheduled to take place in Berlin, had to be cancelled because of the war. In 1919, it was another major disappointment that the Inter-Allied Games, when athletes from eighteen nations came to Paris for a sporting celebration of unity in victory, was for men only. At the 1920 Olympics, held in Antwerp, women were still excluded from track and field events. Tired of waiting for concessions from male-dominated committees, Mme Milliat threw herself into organising the *Olympiad Féminines* (Women's Olympiad), a championship for female athletes only, first held at Monte Carlo in March 1921.

Carmen was there at Monte Carlo for the inaugural Women's Olympiad. Now twenty years old with a powerful physique, Carmen won the bronze medal in the two-handed javelin, in which competitors threw both right-handed and left-handed, with the longest aggregate distance counting. This was one of many times Carmen competed against (and was usually beaten by), Violette Gouraud-Morris, who won gold medals in the javelin and shot putt. They had competed before, in the championships of Paris and of France. There would be many parallels in the lives of Violette and Carmen.

Seven years older than Carmen, married and with a distinguished record of service in the First World War as an ambulance driver, and as a runner taking messages along the front line at the Battle of Verdun, Mme Violette Gouraud-Morris was a versatile and intimidatingly powerful athlete, famed for her prowess in swimming and running as well as power events such as weightlifting, discus, shot-putt and javelin. Violette was also a formidable footballer, one of the foremost players for the Fémina de Paris team, though she later moved to a rival team, l'Olympique.

In 1922, again at Monte Carlo, another international tournament for female athletes only, now called the Women's World Games, was staged to build on the success of the 1921 Women's Olympiad; it was announced that the new tournament would take place every four years, the next one scheduled for Gothenburg in 1926. Carmen did not compete at Monte Carlo in 1922. Still only twenty-one, her athletics career was ending. Football had taken over her life instead.

From 1919, Alice Milliat was president of the Fédération Féminine Sportives de France (FFSF) an umbrella organisation established in December 1917 to promote women's sport in France. Throughout its history, until it disbanded in 1936, Mme Milliat was the dominant personality in the FFSF. Athletics and Olympic recognition were always at the top of her agenda but Mme Milliat's ambitions ranged widely. The FFSF coordinated many sports; women's football was high on the list.

In the early days at least, Alice Milliat supported women's football with energy and enthusiasm. Later, from 1925, she started to waver in the face of the conservative social backlash against it but, in the beginning, she played a crucial role in attracting women and girls to the game. From 1918, the Fémina team was one of the leading women's football teams. From 1919, it was the FFSF under Mme Milliat's leadership that organised the structure of league and cup competitions providing the women's game in France with strong foundations.

Football and feminism were closely related. For girls like Carmen, there may not have been an overtly political consciousness. Perhaps it was just a carefree enthusiasm for sport, a simple desire to play games for fun, but in the prevailing social climate of the times female infiltration of sport, especially a 'men's sport' like football, was unavoidably a political act.

The rise of sport and feminism in France, as in countries like Britain and Germany, fitted wider social trends affecting issues of employment, education, leisure activities and the right to vote. The French Union for Women's Suffrage was formed in 1909 to demand voting rights for women. Campaigning for women's rights took many forms, militant and moderate, with aims ranging beyond just suffrage. Just like English women of the Rational Dress Society, many Frenchwomen wanted to wear looser, more practical dress. They wanted to ride bicycles, to be free of social constraints and double standards. These trends were accelerated by the First World War.

One example of connections between sport and feminism in Carmen's Paris was the rise of 'Les Midinettes', the young women who worked in the booming fashion industry, sewing the clothes that set trends for the rest of the world to follow. The Midinettes were famous for their habit of going out together for lunch, dressed to kill and carrying their sewing boxes like samurai swords. In some ways, the Midinettes did not really fit the feminist mould. The public perception (at least partly true) was that they were out to catch the eye of potential husbands, preferably from a higher social class. Social conservatives warned against these 'dangerous' modern women. Anxious liberals worried about them being 'in moral danger' and proposed the opening of women-only restaurants where they would be safe.

Yet the feminist connection was real. Radical newspapers of the time like *L'Humanité* applauded the Midinettes as assertive, independent females fighting for their rights. Modern journalists and historians with leftish sympathies have defined them as 'the forgotten avant-garde of working-class women', arguing that the feminist movement in France was not exclusively dominated by articulate middle-class women.

The Midinettes did indeed have a fierce *esprit-de-corps*, a sense of solidarity and togetherness. They also provided important links between women and sport. In 1903 the Midinettes began what was to become a famous Paris tradition: a twelve-kilometre race from the Place de la Concorde to the village of Nanterre on the northwest edge of the city. Dressed in strikingly varied outfits of loose-fitting clothing, competitors wore numbers, like marathon runners. The first race caused a public sensation. Huge crowds brought traffic to a standstill and delayed the start by nearly an hour. The event was widely reported in the press and the race of the 'Catherinettes' was instantly established as an annual event every 25 October, St Catherine's Day.

The traditions of the 'Course des Midinettes' involved political consciousness as well as sport, weaving together elements of a modern-day city marathon race with those of a proud trade union parade like the Durham Miners Gala. In 1917, at a time of crisis and national soul-searching about how badly the war was going, the authorities ruled that all workers must make sacrifices by 'donating' half a day in unpaid work, to help the war effort. The Midinettes refused, demanding acceptance of the 'English Week', with a half-day Saturday as leisure time, and no loss of pay. Then they went on strike, gaining support from significant sections of public opinion. The government felt compelled to give in. Victory was a proud moment for the Midinettes and attracted noisy approval from voices on the Left.

The Midinettes left a lasting legacy connecting politics and sport. As the Fémina football team took shape in 1919-20, along with bourgeois secretaries, students like Carmen and two factory workers, the players included several seamstresses and dress makers.

In 2017, one hundred years after their wartime strike, the links between the Midinettes and the birth of women's football in France were celebrated by an exhibition held at the Centre Hubertine Auclert, Ile de France. The four themes of the exhibition drew together past and present, sport and equality, feminism and football:

> Pioneers of sport for women: from the 'Course des Midinettes' in 1903 to the flowering of women's football in France in the 1970s
>
> Alice Milliat and the fight for international recognition of women's sport
>
> Suzette Robichon, militant feminist and player for the Dégommeuses
>
> The incredible history of the women footballers of FCF Reims

These historical connections were made plain in the introduction to the exhibition:

> The advance of women in France was as difficult in sport as in anything else. Paradoxically, the mobilisation of men to fight in the First World War was favourable for the rise of interest in women's sport in Europe. National championships of women's football, and also basketball, hockey and water polo, were put in place soon after the end of the war. The highlight of football's development was the first-ever international match between representing England (Dick, Kerr Ladies of Preston) against a selection of the best players in France, which took place in Manchester, watched by 25 000 spectators, 29 April 1920.
>
> It was a Frenchwoman, Alice Milliat, who was the guiding hand establishing the legitimacy of women's

sport on the international scene. But the physical nature of competitive sports seemed in the eyes of many to be a dangerous element in the emancipation of women. Strong resistance came from those who used pretended concerns about medical dangers to women as an excuse for their opposition. By the 1930s, this anti-feminist reaction against women's football was succeeding. It was only much later, from about 1968, that there was a renewal of the women's game; a renewal personified by the exploits of the female players who made PCF Reims the leading team in France.

Women's football was new to France but it did not come from nowhere. The women and girls who eagerly joined in football games at Fémina Sportives from 1917 were part of a wider picture. From the early 1880s, there had been a surge of enthusiasm in Britain fostered by pioneers like Helen Matthews, leader of 'Mrs Graham's XI', and 'Nettie Honeyball' co-founder of the British Ladies Football Club, formed in 1895.

These ventures were in tune with feminist aspirations. Helen Matthews was both a Scottish suffragist and a keen supporter of the Rational Dress Society. The BLFC received influential backing from an aristocratic patron and committed feminist, Lady Florence Dixie. Women's football attracted considerable public interest, much of it positive, but also an orchestrated campaign of disapproval and ridicule. There were good reasons why 'Mrs Graham' and 'Nettie Honeyball' chose to play the game under false names. Women's football also faced difficult problems of organisation and finance; the brave efforts of Helen Matthews culminated in a sad anti-climax, losing a court case about unpaid bills for her team's travel and accommodation.

Elsewhere in Europe, there were small signs of the game's potential appeal to women and girls. In August 1911, a federation to support women's football was launched in Tsarist Russia. A 1914 team photograph captures the exuberant optimism of Las Spanish Girls

Club of Barcelona. In France in 1910 and Belgium in 1911, there were instances of schoolgirls experimenting with playing football, alongside other sports such as tennis, basketball and hockey. It was only later, however, in the special social conditions of the First World War that women's football began to take off. One example of the way the war pushed football forward was a match between teams representing France and Belgium, organised to raise funds to help refugees displaced by the fighting.

Staging special wartime football matches to keep up morale and to provide financial help for wounded servicemen or displaced civilians played a significant role in the story of football in the Great War. There were many such matches by men's teams, not least because so many top-level footballers had been called up to fight. The women who played in the France-Belgium charity match in 1918 were following the example of the Front Wanderers, a team founded solely for that purpose by Armand Swartenbroeks, a Belgian international player who was serving at the front in West Flanders as an army doctor. Armand became deservedly famous, often known as the 'Red Doctor' but he was only one example of a widespread trend.

It was in Britain that women's football advanced furthest and fastest as a result of the war. The mobilisation of women for work in war industries had a revolutionary impact on women's place in society in all countries but especially so in Britain. When the war began, other great powers already had huge standing armies, whereas Britain was obsessed with empire and sea power. The introduction of conscription in 1915, combined with the exponential increase in demands for munitions, caused massive social dislocation as women were conscripted for the war effort on the home front.

In this shifting social landscape, women became amongst other things postmen, firemen and policemen. From 1916, vast numbers of young women worked as 'munitionettes' packed into factories converted from peacetime operations to war production. The work of the munitionettes was vital for the national cause; it was also demanding and dangerous. On the other hand, it brought women together in new and unfamiliar ways, often inspiring a new sense of collective solidarity and self-worth.

Munitionettes came together to play football in their spare time, sometimes with or against male work colleagues. Some industrialists began to see football and other sports as something useful for maintaining morale and improving the health of their workforce. The backing from factory owners and managers was important because it solved, in wartime at least, some of the problems that had bedevilled earlier attempts to promote football for women by providing organisation and financial support, time off for matches and access to pitches to play on. Perhaps just as important, the girls enjoyed a sense of acceptance and approval for what they were doing.

These favourable circumstances enabled the rapid spread of 'munitionettes football' across industrial Britain. Many of the new teams were in areas that were already hotbeds of football: the North West, the North East, Scotland, the industrial Midlands. There were also teams in the London area and the South West. The roots of these teams in specific war industries were reflected in their evocative names: the Vulcan Shell Girls based on a historic railway works in South Lancashire, Wallsend Slipway Ladies based in Tyneside shipyards, the Mossband Munition Girls, Woolwich Arsenal Rockets FC and the exotic Government Rolling Mills Ladies XI in Southampton. The giant armaments empire of Armstrong Whitworth sponsored teams all over Britain.

The story of wartime women's football in Britain is well told in *The Munitionettes,* a fine book by Patrick Brennan, who has also curated a website, Donmouth.com, that contains fascinating visual evidence about women's football, in France as well as Britain, including several galleries of team photographs. One striking feature of these images is how rapidly team uniforms progressed from standard working clothes to full football kit (striped shirts were particularly popular). Their football matches were frequently watched by large crowds of spectators, raising a lot of money for good causes. For the women workers, it was great fun and also a step along the road leading toward greater independence and equality.

In 1917, women's football in Britain even went international. 'England', based on teams in the North East, with five players from Wallsend Slipway, played against an 'Ireland' team from Belfast and towns in Northern Ireland. Well-publicised in advance, the match was arranged in aid of the Lord Mayor's Relief Fund. It attracted a sizable crowd of spectators and confirmed the effectiveness of the 'business model' for charity football matches. The model would be followed over and again in the future, as was shown by the France-Belgium 'international' in 1918.

By the time the war came to an end, in Western Europe at least, in November 1918 Britain had more than one hundred women's football teams, from Plymouth to Newcastle, from Cardiff to Stoke, from Belfast to Preston. The team that achieved the most famous place in history, and was to have the greatest impact on the life of Carmen Pomiès, was Dick, Kerr Ladies of Preston. The team's meteoric rise was typical of 'munitionettes football'. Before the war, the Dick, Kerr Company factory on Strand Road in Preston produced rolling stock and electric motors for trams and light railways; from 1915, production switched to shells and other war materials.

In keeping with the nationwide trend, the girls employed at Dick, Kerr began playing kickabout football in lunch breaks. They played their first organised match in 1917, helped by Alfred Frankland, a middle manager at the factory, who was the organiser and facilitator of the team, arranging fixtures, providing team kit, and finding money to meet expenses. These 'expenses' included regular payments to his best players, which made it easier for Mr Frankland to recruit new talent from other teams.

At the end of the war, the massed armies of female workers in Britain's war industries began returning to 'normal' life. Many women were more than happy to do so but there were many others whose outlook and sense of self had been transformed by their wartime experiences. Women had at last gained the right to vote. Traditional social attitudes towards women were challenged; about dress, smoking cigarettes, female education and employment. And women's football received a shot in the arm.

So there was no slowdown in football activity after the war ended, partly because the consequences of war were so visible everywhere in the thousands of men who had lost limbs, sight, mental equilibrium or their jobs. In December 1918, Dick, Kerr played a series of matches to raise funds for wounded ex-servicemen and other war charities. On Christmas Day, a crowd of 8,000 spectators watched them win against Bolton Ladies at Deepdale, home of Preston North End.

Women's football was catching the public imagination. In March 1919, 35,000 spectators filled Newcastle United's ground, St James's Park, to see Dick, Kerr Ladies play Newcastle Ladies. By the end of 1919, Dick, Kerr Ladies were widely known as an elite team. Their fame spread far beyond Preston and the North West. It even reached Paris, where women's football was growing in strength and ambition.

The rise of women's football in France played out differently from the story of munitionettes football in Britain. In France, the game developed later, and rather more slowly. At first, women's football in France was watched by small crowds, partly because men's football was, too. In England, the leading professional clubs were already part of the social fabric, with large crowds and loyal fanbases, and this made it easier to attract interest, if only curiosity, in women playing the game. In France, there was relatively little press coverage in the early days, though *L'Auto* did report quite favourably on the women's international match between France and Belgium in April 1918.

In many ways, however, the women's game in France developed with a more secure organisational structure than was achieved in Britain. According to the historian Laurence Prudhomme-Poncet, 'the true birth of women's football in France was in 1917 in Paris'. The sports magazine *L'Auto* reported in September 1917 on 'the first time girls played association football'. Fémina took the lead. At first, matches were played by teams drawn from within the club because, as yet, there were no other women's teams to play against. One way to find suitable opposition was to play against schoolboy teams. The Fémina girls did not often win but they learned valuable lessons in how to play the game. In February 1918, one such game between Fémina and the boys of Lycée Carnot was watched by people intending to form a new women's team. It led to the founding of En Avant! (Forward!) Fémina's first great rivals for pre-eminence in Paris. When the two clubs competed in the first-ever championship in 1919, Fémina won the final 2-0 on aggregate.

The emergence of competitive women's football fitted well with Alice Milliat's campaign for female equality in sports and with her talents for organisation. The Fémina club was ideally positioned for the expansion of the game. The re-structuring of the FFSF in 1919, with Mme Milliat moving up from treasurer to president, provided a way of by-passing male-dominated committees. It also ensured there would be an efficient vehicle for regulating league and cup competitions between clubs.

Fémina managed to secure firm foundations for women's football when a wealthy donor, Julien Bessoneau fils, offered financial support. His idea was to equip all club members with uniform sports kit but club officials said they would rather see the money spent on acquiring a sports ground. M Bessoneau agreed and Fémina took proud possession of Stade Elisabeth. According to Fémina club records, the new sports ground was, tactfully, named after M Bessoneau's wife. In reality it was named after Elisabeth Gabriele, Queen of the Belgians (Julien Bessoneau fils never married).

The career of Julien Bessoneau fils did not run smoothly. He was the adopted son of Julien Bessoneau père, a rich industrialist from Angers, who built a prosperous business empire but died suddenly in 1916. Julien fils rapidly expanded the business, especially its operations in Paris, which enabled him to be a wealthy benefactor to French women's football. He was also a politician, elected to the Chamber of Deputies in 1919. But he used what the courts called 'hazardous business practices'. In 1923, he was convicted of fraudulent dealings in shares and dividends and was sent to prison for four months. Despite his disgrace, Bessoneau's legacy to women's football was benign. Stade Elisabeth proved a precious asset for the game throughout the interwar years.

For the 1919-20 season, a new club, Academia de Paris, was ready to challenge Fémina and En Avant. Subsidiary competitions were introduced for the 'farm teams' of the major clubs. More new teams were being launched, including Les Cadettes de Gascogne, Les Sportives and Olympique. The press began to take more notice; a match between Fémina and Academia in February 1920 figured prominently on the front cover of *Le Miroir des Sports*.

The timing was perfect for Carmen Pomiès. Until 1921, she was heavily involved in athletics, especially the javelin, but almost from the start of team games at Fémina (which included basketball and hockey), Carmen was one of the girls with special enthusiasm for football. By early 1920, she had moved up from the junior teams to appear regularly for Fémina in league matches, usually as left-sided defender. A team photograph from that time shows Carmen sitting on the front row, to the left of goalkeeper Louise Ourry, looking utterly delighted to be involved. Carmen was to feature in countless such team photographs throughout the interwar years.

Alice Milliat thought the timing was right, too. The growth of women's football in France seemed assured. Mme Milliat wanted to challenge the best, and the best was in Preston. She contacted Alfred Frankland, the guiding hand of Dick, Kerr Ladies and a promoter as determined and ingenious as herself. They arranged for a French team to tour England in the spring of 1920. It was to be a celebration of the bonds between France and England as allies in the Great War.

It was announced with some fanfare by *L'Auto* magazine that there would be four matches in April and May. France would be represented by seventeen players, nine from Fémina, including the agile little goalkeeper Louise Ourry, the Brulé sisters and Carmen Pomiès, and seven from En Avant, including the Laloz sisters and the captain, Madeleine Bracquemond. The team would play in a special new kit: blue shirts with a tricolour badge, black shorts and socks, and wear black berets. Alice Milliat would travel with the touring party as manager and chaperone. All the players selected were instructed to meet under the clock at the main entrance of the Gare du Nord at 08.45 on the day of departure.

The stage was set for a long-lasting French Connection between Paris and Preston that defined the history of women's football in Europe through the interwar years. Carmen Pomiès would be part of that history, from the beginning to the end.

Chapter 3

Carmen's English Connection: Paris & Preston

When they travelled from Paris to Preston in April 1920, the girls in Alice Milliat's touring party were taking on a big foreign adventure, visiting a very different cultural world to test themselves against stern opposition. Of all the women's football teams that grew up in England during and after the First World War, Dick, Kerr Ladies of Preston had already established their reputation as the best. Still only nineteen, Carmen was venturing into alien surroundings destined to become very familiar. She can hardly have realised it at the time, but during the next twenty years the Dick, Kerr team would be more friends than rivals and Preston would be her second home.

Dick, Kerr's rise had been astonishingly quick. In later life, Alice Norris, a pillar of the team in its early days, looked back at the informal and haphazard beginnings of the women's game during the war: 'We used to rival the boys, shooting the ball at the windows. If the boys beat us we had to buy them Woodbines (cigarettes); if we won they had to buy us a Five Boys (a bar of chocolate)'. The ringleader of the women footballers was Grace Sibbert, whose husband was a prisoner of war in Germany after being captured at the Battle of the Somme in 1916. The idea of an organised team was first put forward by Grace, though she might not have been so successful without the helpful support she got from Alfred Frankland, who worked as one of the managers in Dick, Kerr's office.

The determination and organising abilities of Alfred Frankland were at the heart of the rise of Dick, Kerr Ladies between 1917 and 1920; and for the entirety of the team's history. From the beginning,

Mr Frankland aimed high. He arranged for the team's first game, on Christmas Day 1917, to be played at Deepdale, home of Preston North End, then one of England's leading professional clubs. This was a big occasion in more ways than one. It was the first match at Deepdale since 1915, when the Football League had stopped its operations because of the war, which helps to explain why the match attracted 10,000 spectators.

The Christmas Day match was also significant because of its 'business plan'. Alfred Frankland and Grace Sibbert were able to ensure financial viability for the game by making it a charity match that would raise funds for Moor Park, a local hospital where many wounded soldiers were cared for. Mr Frankland did not invent this financial model, which was adopted widely during and after the war by men's football as well as women's; but he applied it as skilfully as anyone, not only in the special circumstances of 1917-1920 but for many years afterwards.

Dick, Kerr Ladies won that first match 4-0 against Arundel Coulthard Foundry. A contemporary report in the *Daily Post* described the match:

> Dick, Kerr's were not long in showing that they suffered less than their opponents from stage fright, and they had a better all-round understanding of the game, Their forward work, indeed, was often surprisingly good, one or two of the ladies showing quite admirable ball control.

In addition to the satisfaction of a winning start and the generally favourable perceptions of the quality of the football, the game was a big success in terms of fundraising; Alfred Frankland was able to cover the expenses of staging the match and to donate £200 to Moor Park hospital. The foundations were being put in place for Dick, Kerr Ladies to go beyond the special conditions of wartime and continue into the future.

By 1918, Dick, Kerr Ladies already had a core of excellent players including the captain, Alice Kell, a strong defender, Lily Jones, and a lethal goalscoring centre-forward, Florrie Redford, one of the 'ladies with quite admirable ball control' picked out in newspaper reports. In addition to her exceptional dribbling skills, Florrie had lightning speed and the innate composure in front of goal that sets the best finishers apart from the rest. She and her teammates played numerous matches against factory women's teams in 1918. When the war ended in November 1918, and factories switched back to peacetime working, they were determined to carry on playing.

The Dick, Kerr girls were not alone. Enthusiasm for the women's game remained high, with wide support for charity matches raising funds for wounded ex-soldiers and other good causes. There was opposition from social conservatives but also a positive response from many sections of society. Big crowds came to watch and there was a lot of encouragement from the men's game. Many professional players and ex-players spoke admiringly about the skills and athleticism of the best female players. Many helped out with coaching and physical training. Dick, Kerr Ladies received valuable backing from Preston North End, not least in being able to play some matches at Deepdale stadium.

Along with the successes on the football pitch, the rapid rise of Dick, Kerr Ladies fostered strong feelings of collective solidarity. As is often the case with a winning team, there was a good spirit of togetherness. Remembering it all two generations later, the players who had lived through it as teenagers commented on how they had looked up to older team leaders and 'minders' like Alice Kell and Florrie Redford.

Good though his team already was, Alfred Frankland was always on the lookout for new players to improve it. On several occasions, he recruited opposition players who had impressed him. Four joined from Lancaster, including Jessie Walmsley and Molly Walker. He signed Alice Woods, who had twice scored the winning goal against Dick,

Kerr. Most important of all was signing Lily Parr, a fourteen-year-old left-winger from St Helens. Despite her young age, Lily was already an exceptional player; before long she would be widely regarded as perhaps the best female player in the world.

So when the French team arrived in Preston in April 1920, they knew they faced a daunting challenge against elite opposition. But their tour was not just about football rivalry. It was primarily a celebration of victory and peace by wartime allies. The idea of strengthening Anglo-French friendship through football was not new. It had first been floated in 1917, but nothing came of it. The surge of enthusiasm for women's football after the war, and the huge success of charity matches raising funds for ex-soldiers, opened the way for Femina's tour, which was to be in aid of the National Association of Discharged and Disabled Soldiers and Sailors.

Alice Milliat and her players arrived in Preston on 28 April 1920 in a glare of publicity. The French tourists had been met at Dover by Alfred Frankland. At Preston railway station they were welcomed by large, excited crowds. There was extensive coverage in local newspapers, with much talk of the 'Entente Cordiale' between France and Britain, and of the bonds of friendship forged during four years of joint struggle and sacrifice. The French team knew they were not just footballers, here to play and to enjoy themselves, but also ambassadors bringing together two cultures.

There was also a bond between the two organisational masterminds. Despite their very different social backgrounds, Alfred Frankland and Alice Milliat were two of a kind. Both were energetic and skilful promoters who made things happen. Both were constantly seeking new opportunities to recruit players, arrange fixtures, attract spectators, and find ways of paying for it all. They combined forces so effectively that the French tour of 1920 was no one-off event but the beginning of an enduring football friendship between Paris and Preston.

Most of the French players were city girls, from a bourgeois background far removed from Preston. There were two factory workers and a couple of seamstresses but the rest of the squad were middle-class: several shorthand typists, one philosophy student and Carmen Pomiès, described as a dental student, though she would never complete her studies. To the Dick, Kerr girls and the good people of Preston, these *jeunes Parisiennes* seemed impossibly sophisticated and 'posh'.

In taking on Dick, Kerr Ladies, the French team faced a huge challenge in unfamiliar surroundings. In the 1920 season as a whole, Dick, Kerr would play thirty matches, winning twenty-five, scoring 133 goals against fifteen. Not only were the French girls up against intimidating opponents, they were also in for an exhausting tour, with four matches in seven days, starting in Preston and finishing in London, at Chelsea's Stamford Bridge stadium. The team stayed at the Bull and Royal Hotel in Preston. This meant intensive travel as well as twice playing two matches in two days. It's just as well most of the players were young.

The first match, at Deepdale, was watched by 25,000. Carmen was there, as she was for all four matches on the tour, playing as a left-sided defender. Like the rest of the team, she was aware of being the centre of attention. Alfred Frankland had worked hard to arouse interest from the press and there was intense advance publicity before the game and high-profile match reports afterwards. The French line-up was:

> Goalkeeper: Louise Ourry (Fémina))
>
> Georgette Rigal (En Avant!); Carmen Pomiès (Fémina)
>
> Jeanne Janiaud (Fémina); J. Trottman (En Avant!); R. Viani (En Avant!)
>
> Thérèse Brulé (Fémina); Germaine Delapierre (Fémina); Alice Trottman (En Avant!)
>
> Madeleine Bracquemond (captain, En Anant!); Thérèse Laloz (En Avant!)

The home team won that first match at Deepdale 2-0. As usual, Florrie Redford scored one of the goals. For the French, in addition to Carmen in defence, the captain, Madeleine Bracquemond, was noted as an elegant playmaker, and the goalkeeper, 'Mademoiselle Ourry', attracted a lot of attention partly because she was so small but also because she was impressively agile and alert. Some French players said afterwards they were taken aback by the 'rough, tough, physical' play of the English girls but the match was played in a friendly competitive spirit. The extensive and enthusiastic press coverage included a humorous but kindly full-page cartoon drawing headlined *FRENCH LADIES v DICK, KERR'S LADIES AT DEEPDALE.*

The next day, at Stockport, south of Manchester, 15,000 spectators watched Dick, Kerr win the second game 5-2. Florrie Redford scored twice, while Madeleine Bracquemond was again deemed to be outstanding; she scored one of the French goals.

After two games in two days, the teams got a short break. There was a tea party at Alfred Frankland's house. On the Monday, there was a group excursion to Blackpool on a day when the wind was strong enough to blow a French hat into the sea. But the 'exotic' Parisian visitors bonded well with their northern working-class hosts. The story of the hat blown into the sea became a legend and a Girls Day Out at Blackpool would be an enduring tradition for all future touring teams, Belgian as well as French, right down to the last summer before the war. The last of numerous photographs of Carmen on tour in England was taken on one of these day trips to Blackpool in 1938.

The day in Blackpool was part of a cultural exchange that made a powerful impression. The Preston that Carmen Pomiès encountered for the first time in 1920 was a long way from Montparnasse and doubtless something of a shock for her and for her Parisian teammates. Preston already had a long history, with many fine buildings and much civic pride, but the immediate post-war years were hard times for northern England, and especially for the textile industry, so vital for Preston's economic well-being. In a town of terraced houses and limited horizons, the French tourists might well have seemed visitors from another world.

Despite the outward differences, the French girls, especially Carmen, established close bonds with Preston. Many of them came back again on later tours or made personal visits. Carmen lived in Preston in 1921-1922 and visited many times more in the years that followed. Visiting Preston was almost an annual event for Carmen through the 1930s and it was not just Preston she came to know so well but the whole of northern England. In all, Carmen played football in at least forty different towns across the North. Her last known visit to Preston was in 1945.

The tour ended with two games in two days. The third match, at Manchester City's ground, was a 1-1 draw; the French team might have won but for several fine saves by Dick, Kerr's goalkeeper. On 6 May 2020, the 100th anniversary of the match, *The Guardian* re-published the original report of the game from the *Manchester Guardian*. Unlike many such reports in those times, it managed to avoid being trivial or prurient. Sadly, however, the tone adopted by the reporter reflected many of the ingrained, patronising assumptions of pre-ordained female inferiority that dogged women's football throughout the interwar years:

> It is not in vain that women offer to the public an exhibition of their skill at football. Some men's league matches would not have drawn a bigger crowd than gathered yesterday at the Manchester City ground to watch a game played between French and English women. Even a beauty chorus might sigh in vain to attract so many spectators in one afternoon. In the crowd there must have been many who had made up their minds beforehand that football is a game that ill becomes women.

Even the description of the wintry weather that prevailed seems to reveal surprise that delicate women might be able to cope with wind and rain on the football field, or that bourgeois girls from Paris might manage to cope with such alien surroundings:

> The weather probably went some way to strengthen such prejudices. It would be painful to imagine worse conditions for a game. No one, it might be supposed, would play unless paid to do it. The skeletons of the incomplete stands helped to etch more deeply the impression of bleakness and dinginess.

Once it came to the football, however, the *Manchester Guardian* reporter managed to supply well-informed and fair-minded analysis of the game:

> The Frenchwomen were perhaps least affected by the oppressive surroundings. Meeting their opponents for the third time, they escaped defeat for the first time by achieving a draw. The fourth and final match of the tour they are making in England takes place today at Chelsea's ground. Despite the gathering weight of the ball in the rain, the game was played with a good deal of ardour on both sides.
>
> The Frenchwomen were incomparably faster than the English, but they were also lighter and less powerful in shots and clearances. As a team, they had the half-back manner to perfection. Intercepting the ball with sprightliness, they made plenty of openings, but their forwards were ineffective in front of goal. A fall by one of the English backs allowed the French to open the scoring in the second half. Whenever the English forwards attacked they seemed to be dangerous. Their shots at goal were strong and their attacks from the wing were always likely to produce a goalmouth scramble. It was from a wing movement the equalising goal was scored.

> Although the French women had neither the weight nor the power of the English, their zest for the game seemed inexhaustible. In the second half, as the rain thickened and the ball became even more heavy, the French were visibly less weary than their opponents.

After such an expert and professional dissection of the technicalities, it was a pity that the report concluded with familiar condescension:

> The teams devoted as much energy to the game as women are ever likely to. But, obviously, there is something in the character of football which will always keep it as a definitely masculine pursuit.

The final match, in London at Stamford Bridge, home of Chelsea, was watched by a crowd of 10,000. The French team finished on a high note, winning 2-1. It was clear the tour had made a good impression, with four closely-contested matches, watched by large, appreciative crowds and favourably reported in the press. A lot of money was raised to help the war-wounded; a press photo shows a smiling Louise Ourry standing on the touchline alongside amputees and other disabled ex-servicemen.

The tour was clearly a great success, both in football and in building amity between nations. Before the team set off for home, there was a farewell civic reception given by the Lord Mayor of London at the Mansion House. When they arrived at the Gare du Nord, crowds of well-wishers were there to greet them. Arrangements were already in place for Dick, Kerr Ladies to make a reciprocal tour of France later in the year. Alice Milliat said at the Gare du Nord: 'Our girls played well and everybody was so friendly to them. We were overwhelmed by kindness. We must give the English girls a welcome to match when they arrive here in the Autumn'. Contacts were maintained through the summer to prepare for this.

For Carmen there was time for a return to athletics; she was soon busy training for the women's athletics championships. As ever, Alice Milliat was the organising genius behind the championships. The 1920 Games was one of many occasions between 1917 and 1921 when Carmen competed with the ferociously powerful Violette Morris in the javelin; Violette won the gold medal, Carmen won silver.

Anne Sebba, author of *Les Parisiennes: How The Women of France Lived, Loved and Died Under Nazi Occupation,* wrote of Violette:

> She was a colossus. Her biceps had a circumference of 14 inches, about the size of an average woman's neck. But she was only 5-foot-5, so a solid hunk of a woman and very, very strong. Morris was a natural athlete. As a girl she excelled in boxing, javelin, discus, shot putt and swimming. As a schoolgirl, she coined the motto 'anything a man can do, Violette can do, too'. She really was the first female all-round sports person France had produced.

In Preston, Dick, Kerr Ladies kept playing, and winning, through the summer. As they got ready for their tour of France, they stepped up their training, helped by ex-players from Preston North End. They had French visitors, too. Louise Ourry, the Fémina goalkeeper, was so enthused by her time in England that she returned to Preston that summer, in order to train with and learn from the Dick, Kerr girls; Louise played in three charity matches at Morecambe, Harrogate and Burnley.

When Dick, Kerr's sixteen-strong squad set out for France in November 1920 they were sent off with a flourish. There was a civic reception the night before and enthusiastic crowds to see them off from Preston railway station. The first match of the tour, in Paris, was well publicised. A crowd of 22,000 came to watch the game. The match programme trumpeted the claim it was *The First International Match of the 1920-21 Season, between France and England.*

That first match in Paris was a close affair, ending in a 1-1 draw. One day later, the teams played again, at Roubaix, a textile town north of Lille, not far from the border with Belgium. Barely two years since the guns went silent on the Western Front, this was a war-ravaged landscape of ruined towns and villages, of fields scarred by trenches and littered with the debris of artillery bombardments.

The Roubaix match sparked lively public interest in the English visitors. There was a crowd estimated at 16,000 to watch 'England' win 2-0 after Florrie Redford scored twice in the second half. The day after the match, the English team attended a wreath-laying ceremony at the war memorial in Roubaix. It was an indication of how much the tour, and women's football in general, had been shaped by shared experiences and legacies of the Great War.

After two matches in two days, there was time to see the sights of Paris. Lily Parr became one of very few teenaged girls from St Helens to be given a guided tour of the Palace of Versailles and to climb to the top of the Eiffel tower. There was a celebration dinner for both teams, nights out at the circus and the theatre and free time to go shopping. It was a time for strengthening new friendships and Carmen, with her language skills and gregarious nature, played a leading role in interactions between the teams.

Perhaps the most important achievement of the reciprocal tours of 1920 was in the many enduring friendships that were forged. The Paris-Preston connection was to be lasting; so was a special attachment between Carmen and Florrie Redford. By the time the English girls were getting ready for their farewell matches at Rouen and Le Havre, it had already been arranged that Florrie would come back to Paris before Christmas, as a guest of the Pomiès family. The bond between the two stayed strong for the next twenty-five years and shaped both of their lives.

The game at Le Havre was very one-sided, an English win by six goals to nil. The last match, in Rouen the next day, was much closer but 'England' won again by 2-0. At the final farewell party for his team, Alfred Frankland said the French team's play had improved markedly since their tour of England in the spring; though the results of the matches did not actually reflect this. Dick, Kerr team enjoyed a happy homeward journey, including an overnight stay in London and a triumphant reception when they reached Preston. Their tour of France was a springboard for two big events that were typical Alfred Frankland productions, showing his flair for fundraising and publicity.

The match against a 'Rest of the World XI' at Deepdale, was notable for being played under floodlights. The Ministry of Defence had given special permission for military searchlights to be used for the game. There was intense publicity in the press and on Pathé News. As usual, it was to raise money for charity, for the Unemployed Ex-Servicemen's Fund. Florrie Redford scored one of the goals in a 4-0 victory.

The second big occasion, Dick, Kerr against St Helens, was played at Goodison Park, home of Everton, on Christmas Day 1920. This match attracted 53,000 spectators, with 14,000 more locked out because the ground was full. This was a landmark in the rise of the women's game but, sadly, for Florrie, she was not on the pitch this time. The return journey from her pre-Christmas stay in Paris did not go as planned and she got back to Preston too late to be selected for the match. Florrie would have been gutted to watch rather than play but, even without her, Dick, Kerr won easily 4-0.

The wave of success that women's football was riding at the end of 1920 surged even higher throughout 1921, when Dick, Kerr Ladies played sixty-seven matches, winning all of them and scoring 448 goals in the process. Lily Parr scored 108 goals, Florrie Redford scored 170. And for at least twelve of the victories in this *annus mirabilis,* Carmen Pomiès was an important player in the Dick, Kerr team.

1921 was a hectic sporting year for Carmen. It began with a defeat: Fémina lost the French cup final against their keen rivals En Avant! by five goals to four. They did not win the league championship either, failing to qualify for the play-off finals.

In May, Carmen was getting ready for a new French tour of England, playing for the Probables against the Possibles in a trial match. The players selected were all from Fémina, En Avant! and Les Sportives, with Madeleine Bracquemond as captain. Carmen played in all four matches on the tour, losing 5-1 to Dick, Kerr at Longton but winning the other three: 1-0 against Huddersfield Atalanta, 3-1 against Stoke Ladies at Stoke City's Victoria Park and then 1-0 over Plymouth Ladies, watched by a crowd of 11,000 at Plymouth Argyle's Home Park. By this time, Carmen had already made up her mind to come back to England in the autumn to live and play in Preston.

The success of the French visit to Plymouth in May 1921 led to a reciprocal visit to Paris at the end of October. The redoubtable Mrs Boultwood led a tour party based mostly on Plymouth Ladies, strengthened by a few guest players. Two matches, both goalless draws, were played at Stade Pershing. A French photograph from the time shows the two teams mixing happily together, with the captains, Mrs Boultwood and Madeleine Bracquemond, centre stage.

L'EQUIPE DU PLYMOUTH LADIES AFC ET L'EQUIPE FEMININE DE FRANCE

Janiaud, Lewis, Levéque, Ford, Guille,
Bevan Massabreu, Wilcox, Rigal, Griffiths-Jones,
Pomiès, Hatherley, Gisciard, Tiller,
Thackery, Laloz, Boultwood, Mr Reeves (referee),
Bracquemond, Duncan, Viani, Jeanniot

Among them was Carmen, who had taken a break from her new life with Dick, Kerr Ladies to come back to Paris for the occasion. After the tour of England had ended in May, Carmen had returned to France for a busy summer of athletics. Already in March 1921, before the football tour of England, Carmen competed in the first

'Women's Olympiad' staged in the gardens of the Monte Carlo Casino. It was a triumphant moment for Alice Milliat. As usual, Carmen did well, winning a bronze medal in the javelin. As usual, Violette Gouraud-Morris finished ahead of her.

In June, in the Paris Athletics Championship, Carmen came third in the 1000m race and third in the javelin. A week later, at the French national championship, Carmen was fourth in the 1000m and again third in the javelin. Despite her successes, the summer of 1921 was the end of Carmen's time winning medals in athletics. After 1921, there is no record of her in competitions, though she may have attended the Women's World Games in Paris in 1922; and in the 1940s she told people in Rochester NY that she had been at the Women's Games in Prague in 1930, and London in 1934.

There was one more link to Carmen, the javelin thrower. From the start of her association with Lancashire, Carmen became firm friends with Lily Parr, even though Lily was five years younger and from a totally different social background. A famous press photograph taken in the 1930s shows Lily throwing the javelin as to the manner born; the temptation to believe it was Carmen who taught her how to do it is irresistible. But by 1921, football was taking over Carmen's life

Carmen's lasting friendships with Lily Parr, Florrie Redford and so many others who played for Dick, Kerr Ladies raise interesting questions about the life of Carmen Pomiès. What drew her so close to these friends? Why did Preston become virtually her second home? In her book *The Dick, Kerr Ladies: The Factory Girls Who Took On The World,* Barbara Jacobs dwells on the class differences that might have separated Carmen from Lily but did not:

> In 1921, Carmen decided to live in Preston for the foreseeable future. Immediately, and perhaps surprisingly, she formed a close friendship with Lily which would last a lifetime. Carmen was one of the few people Lily ever took back to St Helens with her, to visit her family. Goodness

knows what the educated middle-class Parisienne thought of the St Helens welcome and the bacon and eggs with black pudding.

One plausible answer is that Carmen seems to have been untroubled by class consciousness. Her later life shows Carmen apparently at ease with well-connected bourgeois elites: film stars like Renée Saint-Cyr, the cultured friends of Georges and Hélène, the well-heeled members of the tennis clubs of Rochester and Genesee Valley. On the other hand, Carmen's easy camaraderie in football, with teammates and opponents alike, seems to show she loved the democracy of the dressing room and the mutual respect between gifted sportswomen.

It is also clear that Carmen was happy to be living at Florrie Redford's mother's house, and taking temporary jobs in Preston as teacher of French, or shorthand typist. In later photographs of days out in Blackpool and mixing with friends in Preston, Carmen looks as relaxed and happy as can be. A letter Carmen sent to Preston from Spain in 1941, at a time when she felt hopelessly cut off by the war, reveals the passionate emotional bonds tying her to her English friends. Carmen had an unusual capacity to be at home wherever she was and whoever she was with. Perhaps she came to feel more at home in Preston than anywhere, even Paris.

From August 1921, Carmen was living in Preston as an integral part of Dick, Kerr Ladies during the final run of victories of their triumphant year. Her first game was a 3-0 victory over St Helens in an exhibition match played at Port Erin on the Isle of Man. Sixteen-year-old Lizzy Ashcroft was in the St Helens team. She married in 1935 and became Lizzy Bolton. By then, Carmen and Lizzy had become old friends. After the Isle of Man, came two matches against Coventry Ladies, a 4-0 win at St Andrew's, the home of Birmingham City, then a 3-0 victory at Derby.

In September, Carmen was in Scotland, where Dick, Kerr won 6-0 in Aberdeen and 6-1 against Dundee Ladies. Next came a narrow

2-1 win over Yorkshire Ladies, played in Rochdale, followed by a 4-0 win in Blackpool, against Wales. One week later, the team was in Bristol to win 5-0 against South of England. Three weeks after that, it was back to Scotland for an 8-0 win over Dumfries, and then across the Irish Sea to beat Ireland 6-1 in Belfast, raising £500 for Belfast's hospitals. The year ended on Boxing Day 1921 with a 3-1 win at Fleetwood.

The Dick, Kerr team, and women's football in general, seemed in perfect health (if very tired after so many games and so much travelling). But by the time of the match against Fleetwood, the women's game had received a crippling blow. Earlier in December, the men who ran the English Football Association had passed a resolution that removed official recognition from women's football:

The FA Council ruling of 5 December 1921 stated:

> Complaints having been made as to football being played by women, the Council feels impelled to express their strong opinion that the game of football is quite unsuitable for females and ought not to be encouraged. Complaints have also been made as to the conditions under which some of these matches have been arranged, and the appropriation or receipts to other than charitable causes. The Council is further of the opinion that an excessive proportion of the match receipts has been absorbed in expenses, and that an inadequate percentage devoted to charity. For these reasons the Council requests clubs belonging to the FA to refuse the use of their grounds for such matches.

The FA ruling is often referred to as a ban on women's football, but this is not quite right. Women and girls could not be banned from playing if they were keen enough and if they could find somewhere suitable to stage their matches. But organising women's football became immeasurably harder. No pitches could be used that belonged to clubs affiliated to the FA; there could be no more prestige matches at Deepdale, or Newcastle United, or Everton, or Chelsea.

Women's football already existed on rather unstable organisational and financial foundations. The FA ruling, and the blizzard of anti-female propaganda that accompanied it, made these foundations even shakier. The FA 'ban' was to stay in place for another fifty years. It did long-term damage to the women's game. It also coincided with other adverse factors. The age of football for munitionettes was over; women's teams were no longer supported by benevolent employers and the urgency of fundraising for war charities was slackening. From a historical perspective, the threat to the survival of women's football seems clear. From the historical perspective, the threat to the survival of women's football seems clear. Preventing women's matches from being staged at any sports ground affiliated to the FA was destined to be a shattering blow. Its harmful impact was to last for fifty years, though it took time for people to realise how damaging it was to be in the long term.

Even at the time, however, there was a storm of protest from those who were sympathetic to the women's game; briefly, there was some optimism that the ban might be reversed.

On 9 December 1921, four days after the FA ruling, the *Daily Mirror* posted a report from Liverpool setting out the trenchant views of two leading female footballers, 'Miss Florrie Redford, Dick, Kerr's vice-captain and centre forward, who is probably the greatest goal scorer among girls, having scored 368 times in five seasons' and 'Dick, Kerr's wing-half, Mlle Carmen Pomiès'.

Under the headline, HEALTH GIVING KICKS, the *Mirror* informed its readers of the 'chorus of indignation from girl footballers' against the FA's decision to ban women's matches from grounds under their control.

Leading the chorus was Florrie Redford, who 'ridicules the suggestion that physical harm is caused to women by taking part in the sport. She says the only time she was attended by a doctor was when a dog bit her ankle during practice'.

As for Mlle Carmen Pomiès, the *Mirror* reporter announced: 'she told me that girls in France are allowed to play whatever games they like', with the official approval of the President of the Republic.

It was not only women footballers like Florrie and Carmen who argued their case against the FA ruling. Influential men strongly supported them. One such voice was Major Cecil Kent, whose letter was read out at the meeting of the FA on 5 December and widely reported in the press. Educated at Westminster School and Trinity College Cambridge, Cecil Kent had the privileged background and assertiveness of a man to be listened to. (It's not quite clear why he was always referred to as 'Major Kent' – during the 1914-18 war Cecil Kent had served in the Royal Navy Reserve as a Lieutenant Commander. Either way, he was a man of influence).

One argument used to justify the FA ruling was that women footballers were paid 'excessive' expenses without due regulatory procedures. Cecil Kent's letter directly rebutted the concerns over expenses, providing substantive reasons why the expenses paid were necessary and reasonable. He argued that he had often met and travelled with the players and that he had heard nothing but praise for their charitable work and the high standard of their play. 'Why,' Cecil Kent demanded to know, 'have the FA got their knives into women's football? What have the girls done other than raise large sums for charity and play the game?' But the majority of FA councillors was unwilling to accept Kent's views. Though unsuccessful in December 1921, Cecil Kent continued to give his support to the women's game. Later, he would play a large part in organising the French tour of 1925.

In December 1921, however, the extent of the threat to the survival of women's football was not yet fully understood. Plans were already in place for not one but two French football tours of England early in 1922. Strenuous efforts were already being made in 1921 to form a new English Ladies Football Association (ELFA) which would provide a framework for the more than one hundred women's teams in existence. The ELFA planned to launch a national women's cup competition equivalent to the FA Cup. It took a long time for people in the women's game to realise how damaging the FA ruling of 1921 was going to be.

In France, the women's game seemed stronger than ever as the 1921-22 season got going. Fémina won seven out of nine matches and finished second in the league but were knocked out of the playoffs in the semi-final. Along with Fémina, six other clubs competed for the championship: En Avant!, Les Sportives de Paris, Ruche Sportives Féminine, Amicale, Asnieres-Fémina, Les Cadettes de Gascogne. Numerous other clubs were on the rise, including Academia, Olympique, Sportives Reims, Navarre AC and La Clodo. There were dozens of matches for junior and 'farm' teams; and several 'propaganda matches' by which the Paris clubs took the game to regions outside Paris, as far as Perpignan and even Algiers.

The French-British connection was still alive and well, At the end of October 1921, Plymouth Ladies had made an enterprising tour of France, with matches in Paris and then Le Havre. In 1922, there were two separate French tours to England. Carmen had little involvement in the first, in March, by Olympique, captained by Violette Gouraud-Morris including three of the four Laloz sisters, Geneviève, Marguerite and Thérèse. Olympique played five matches and lost all of them, four against Dick, Kerr Ladies, at Cardiff, Preston, Liverpool and Manchester, and one against Hey's Brewery of Bradford. The Hey's team was a real force in the English women's game at this time, and won a famous victory on their reciprocal visit to Paris later that year.

Carmen was in the squad for the second French tour, to South West England in April, by a team representing several Paris clubs. Carmen was one of seven Fémina players, the captain was Madeleine Bracquemond.

> Départ de l'équipe de France pour l'Angleterre le 3 avril 1922.
>
> Goal: Lévêque (Sportives)

Arrières: Janiaud (Fémina), Guille (Sportives)

Demis : Rillac (Sportives), Pomiès (Fémina), Gisclard (Sportives)

Avants: Contesse (AS Amicale), Bracquemond (Sportives, cap), Baldracchi (Fémina), Puisais (Sportives), Goynard (Fémina).

Remplaçantes : Chapoteau (Fémina), Darreau G (Fémina), Darreau A (Fémina).

The French team played three matches, in Plymouth, Exeter and Falmouth, against a 'British XI' based mostly on Plymouth Ladies, captained by the formidable Mrs Jessie Boultwood. strengthened by guest players from Fleetwood, St Helens and Swansea. Mrs Boultwood had enlisted Frank Zanazzi, a coach with innovative ideas about physical training, to improve her players not least in overcoming their reluctance to head the heavy football. Sadly, the venue for the match was small. In 1921, 11,000 spectators had filled Home Park, the stadium of Plymouth Argyle, to see Plymouth Ladies take on the French; now the FA ruling of December 1921 made that impossible.

Jessie Boultwood's verdict on the FA ban was typically trenchant: 'The controlling body of the FA are one hundred years behind the times and their action is pure sex prejudice', she said. 'Not one of our girls has ever felt any ill effects from participating in the game'. One interesting feature of the 1922 match at Plymouth was a report in a local newspaper making special mention of 'Carmen Pomiès of Dick, Kerr Ladies'.

The tour generated lots of goodwill and the renewal of friendships but the different 'English style' of football did not meet unqualified French approval. After returning home, Madeleine Bracquemond had some grumbles that seem familiar even one hundred years later:

> As to the matches themselves, that's another story and my memory of them is not one of the happiest. The roughness of the English players was a great surprise to

the French. However, they did their best to defend the honour of the colours they were wearing. I would not be going too far in saying we should have won two of the three matches. The referees were against us and never ceased to blow for non-existent fouls. Moreover, during the game they often gave advice to the English players, even though their duty required them to be completely impartial.

Carmen spent some time back home in Paris during the summer. She probably attended the annual Women's World Games at the Stade Pershing in August, although she was no longer involved in competition. Football was her sport now and Preston was, at least for the time being, where she lived and worked.

The two French tours of England in spring 1922 seemed to show women's football carrying on as before, but this was not the case. After playing sixty-seven matches in 1921, Dick, Kerr Ladies played only a handful of matches against English opposition in 1922, while the development of the English Ladies Football Association stalled. Led by Stoke Ladies, more than fifty women's teams had supported the ELFA when it was founded in December 1921, though, perhaps surprisingly, Dick, Kerr Ladies were not involved. A national cup competition was inaugurated, won by Stoke Ladies.

Ambitious plans were announced for the governance of the game, possibly with a new code of laws for women's football, but the clubs in the ELFA found it hard going. Crowds were small and the FA ruling of December 1921 created huge difficulties in finding suitable grounds to stage matches. Although more than fifty teams were represented at the meeting where it was agreed to launch the English Ladies Cup, only twenty-three actually competed in the first round. Even more disappointingly, some of the teams who won through to the later rounds were then unable to fulfil their fixtures, allowing their opponents to win by default.

Three of the strongest sides, Doncaster & Bentley, Huddersfield Atalanta and Stoke Ladies made it to the semi-finals. In the final, played at Cobridge, Stoke-on-Trent, Stoke Ladies defeated Doncaster, 3-2. Symbolically, the final had originally been scheduled to be played on the ground of the Bradford Rugby Union club but permission was refused because of hostility from other Yorkshire rugby clubs. The outcome of the ELFA Cup in 1922 revealed the organisational problems of the women's game at that time, especially the impact of the FA ruling barring access to suitable grounds. The ELFA slowly withered and died.

Even Dick, Kerr Ladies, who could play on a pitch they owned, found life hard. Women's football was facing a steadily worsening crisis. Alfred Frankland was ready to fight back. For months he had been planning his most ambitious enterprise yet, to take Dick, Kerr Ladies on a football tour of North America in the autumn of 1922. The tour was to be one of the greatest experiences in the young life of Carmen Pomiès.

Chapter 4

North American Adventure, 1922

In the autumn of 1922, at a time when women's football in England was struggling to come to terms with the consequences of the 'ban' that had been imposed by the Football Association in December 1921, the nine-match tour of the United States by Dick, Kerr Ladies was a bold statement of the values and ambitions of the women's game. Unlike the triumphant year of 1921, it was now increasingly difficult to stage regular fixtures in England. Alfred Frankland knew how important it was to keep women's football moving forward by special initiatives such as international tours.

The origins of his plan for a tour of North America went back many months. It evolved into a massive undertaking, overcoming complex logistical problems of passports, travel, accommodation and finance, not to mention the scheduling of fixtures, match officials, advance publicity and so on. All this had to be negotiated and confirmed in an age of letters by post or the odd telegram; no mobile phones, fax machines, emails or satellite communications. Negotiating with the Brooklyn Football Club, Alfred Frankland planned an ambitious schedule of more than twenty matches including Toronto and Ottawa in eastern Canada, St Louis, Chicago and Milwaukee in the American Midwest as well as Washington, New York, and New England

Alfred Frankland proved many times in his long stewardship of women's football in Preston that he was a resourceful operator and a great improviser, but the North America tour tested his ingenuity to the limit. Major adjustments to his plans had to be made even after the team sailed out from Liverpool. Throughout the tour, there would be moments of financial crisis and last-minute changes to the schedule.

On 15 September, fourteen Dick, Kerr players, with Alice Kell as captain, boarded the Canadian Pacific liner *SS Montclare* at Liverpool, bound for Quebec and Montreal. For the players, it was a once-in-a-lifetime experience; for most, it was the first time they had needed a passport or been away from home for more than a week or two. As they sailed out through the Irish Sea into the Atlantic with a sense of high adventure, Carmen Pomiès was on board with them. It was two weeks before her twenty-second birthday. Perhaps she felt she was catching up with her sister, Hélène, who had sailed from France to the United States three years before.

By the autumn of 1922, Carmen was an integral part of the Dick, Kerr team and utterly at home in Lancashire. On the Canadian Pacific passenger list, Carmen appeared as a 'teacher', aged twenty-one, living at 4 Rossall Street, Preston. This reflects the fact that she had been helping out with French language classes at a local high school. On the homeward crossing seven weeks later, however, Carmen was listed as 'shorthand typist', perhaps in line with secretarial work arranged by Mr Frankland, who often found employment for his lady footballers.

The Atlantic crossing strengthened the togetherness of the tour party. In particular, it brought the friendship between Carmen and Florrie Redford even closer. Two years older than Carmen, Florrie was not just an outstanding player but also a natural leader within the team, regarded as a 'big sister' by the younger players. Florrie and Carmen had become friends as well as rivals during the reciprocal tours of 1920. Since then they had shared their enthusiasm for football, been teammates in Preston and stayed with each other's families. Now they were out in the world together, sharing in a great team experience. Snapshots taken on board *SS Montclare* during the voyage reveal the high spirits and close friendships among the players.

By the time *Montclare* berthed at Quebec on Friday 22 September, however, it was clear the team had arrived in the wrong place. The Dominion (Canadian) Football Association had come under heavy pressure from the English FA to follow its 1921 ruling against women's football. Meeting in Winnipeg early in September, a few days before the Dick, Kerr team set out for Canada, the Dominion FA passed a resolution blocking their tour. The curt resolution read: 'We do not approve the proposal of Ladies Football'. Another reason for the collapse of plans to play matches in Canada was that Canadian women's teams of a suitable standard did not exist. So arrival in Canada was an anti-climax, merely a lengthy detour on the way to the United States.

There were also significant complications threatening to undermine the schedule of fixtures originally planned. It became apparent that the Brooklyn Football Club had promised more than it was able to deliver, especially in terms of finance. The tour might have gone hopelessly wrong without financial and organisational help from the United States Football Association (USFA). In addition to this restructuring of the tour, at that time very few women played soccer in the United States. The only way the USFA could compile a worthwhile fixture list was to have Dick, Kerr Ladies play against men's teams. Plans to play matches in the Midwest had to be abandoned.

Despite all the changes of plan, the tour opened on 24 September, only hours after the team arrived in New York from Canada, with a match against the men of Paterson Football Club in Clifton, New Jersey. This began a demanding sequence of matches, mostly against professional teams in the American Soccer League, with exhausting travel: New York, Clifton, Pawtucket Rhode Island, New York City again, Washington DC, New Bedford and Fall River in Massachusetts, Baltimore and Philadelphia.

Financial worries were ever-present, despite the invaluable support from the USFA. Arrangements for travel and accommodation had to be altered as circumstances changed. As always with Alfred Frankland's schemes, much depended on the matches bringing in substantial income from sponsors and paying spectators. Mr Frankland also had to cope with the failings of his supposed business partner, David Brooks, who had convinced people he was a rich man with good contacts in America. In reality, Brooks was a fantasist who had no money at all and was not above scrounging money from the girls in the team. Finances were always on a knife-edge. Apart from Alice Kell, the captain, most of the team was only partially aware of the organisational problems. For them, the tour was just an epic sporting challenge.

After their sea voyage, Carmen and her teammates had experienced the 330-miles train journey to New York City, passing through the Adirondack mountains, past Lake Champlain and down the Hudson River. It is possible that the forested hills and green valleys of Upper New York state made an especially strong impression on Carmen. Twenty-four years later, when she decided to live and work in the United States, Carmen chose to settle in the city of Rochester NY, on the shores of Lake Ontario.

A few hours after arrival in New York, the team was crossing the Hudson to Clifton, New Jersey, ready to face Paterson Silk Sox in front of a crowd estimated at 5,000. In the light of travel-weariness and coping with unfamiliar surroundings, it is perhaps not surprising the men's team won by 6-3, though a report in the New York Times praised the skill and dash of the women players, especially Lily Parr. After this game, however, there was a six-day break between matches, allowing time to acclimatise and to see the sights of New York.

For visitors, from abroad or from other parts of the United States, as for migrants arriving from Europe, the New York of 1922 was a city of dreams. This was an age before television, before talking pictures. Though not yet the legendary city of skyscrapers (the Empire State Building and the Chrysler Building did not go up until the 1930s), the sights and sounds of the city had a visceral impact, bigger, brighter, newer than anywhere else. The neon lights of Times Square boldly advertised the choices for cinemagoers: the desert epic *Blood & Sand* with Rudolf Valentino, or Douglas Fairbanks starring in *Robin Hood.*

That first week in New York ended with Carmen's twenty-second birthday. As a teenager, she had demonstrated her pro-American leanings at the end of the First World War. Later in her life, Carmen would sail many times into New York on liners from Le Havre or Boulogne; from 1950, Carmen would live and work for several years in Manhattan. It is not fanciful to make a connection between Carmen's new life from 1946 and her first impressions of 1922 amid the sightseeing, the shopping and all the excitement of a young woman grasping at new experiences far from home.

Soon it was time for the football to take over again. The team travelled 200 miles north to Pawtucket in Rhode Island, where 8,500 spectators came to see Dick, Kerr Ladies play out an eventful 4-4 draw with the men of J&P Coats. This game, like all matches during the tour, was a new, deep-end experience for the team's goalkeeper, who was Carmen Pomiès. In her career so far, Carmen's role had been as a robust defender or midfielder; but Dick, Kerr's regular goalkeeper was unable to join the North America tour because of family concerns. So it was Carmen in the firing line.

A famous photograph from 30 September 1922 shows Carmen in her goalkeeper's jersey alongside her teammates just before the kick-off in Pawtucket. The line-up was: Florrie Haslam, Molly Walker, Alice Woods, Jennie Harris, Alice Kell, Lily Lee, Florrie Redford, Jessie Walmsley, Lily Parr, Carmen Pomiès, Daisy Clayton. The next day, they were back in New York to play against a Latino team, Centro-Hispanica. A crowd of 7,000 spectators saw a high-scoring game won 7-5 by the men.

Next, still seeking a first victory, the team travelled 220 miles south to Washington DC, to play against the Washington Stars. This was a big moment for the tour and for the growth of soccer in the capital, where the game was struggling to attract the kind of public attention achieved by the rich industrial factory teams of the North East. Since long before the Dick, Kerr girls set out from England, Washington's daily newspapers had been stoking expectations for the arrival of the famous English women's soccer team 'Newcastle United Ladies Football Club'. It seems that 'fake news' was already part of the scene in Washington DC; something had evidently been lost in translation. Reports confused the women's team from Preston with one of the famous football grounds where they had played. The *Washington Herald* announced that the game was 'one of the most unique international events in the history of DC sportsdom'.

The publicity blitz had to adjust to a late change of date for the match, and to an even later change in the time of the kick-off. The special reason why the USFA insisted on this timetable changes related to America's national obsession with baseball: the soccer match clashed with Game Five of the World Series play-offs between the New York Giants and the New York Yankees. The *Washington Times* was promoting both women's football and special coverage of the World Series. Staging both at the same location on the same day was an attractive proposition for the sponsors.

The Washington Stars match was indeed a special occasion, staged at American League Park as a curtain-raiser to the Pantomime World Series. The real-life baseball, starring the legendary Babe Ruth, was played at the Polo Grounds in New York City, watched by 36,500 spectators. In Washington, US Navy Marines kitted out in baseball uniforms acted out every pitch as it happened, following the live commentary from a dedicated telegraph service. Before that, Dick, Kerr Ladies played their big match against the Stars. Alfred Frankland was not too unhappy about the late rescheduling of the match. Being paired with the baseball ensured a huge crowd was there to see the football and both teams were paid extra money by the *Times* as reward for agreeing to change the starting time.

Despite America's obsession with baseball in general and Babe Ruth in particular, there was genuine interest in the football match, too. Dick, Kerr Ladies were extensively reported in the press before and after the match and the coverage was mostly enthusiastic. *The Washington Times,* of course, as promoter of the whole event, had its own commercial reasons for a positive spin on the women footballers but the match report in the *Washington Post* was both admiring and full of goodwill. The *Post* named Carmen Pomiès player of the match:

> The fair kickers of the Dick, Kerr's women's soccer club of Preston, England, lived up to their reputation yesterday at American League Park when they battled the Washington soccer eleven to a 4 to 4 draw. The women showed a fairly good dribbling game, but their kicking lacked both speed and force. The Washington kickers were extended most of the way. Although the men players got many opportunities they were not successful in registering goals, due to the brilliant defence of Miss Carmen Pomies, the Preston goalkeeper. She checked eleven of the fifteen attempts made by the local booters.

As usual with Dick, Kerr Ladies, Lily Parr attracted special admiration:

> Miss Lilly Parr, at outside left, put up an aggressive, game registering two goals in seven tries she had at the net. The girls were able to penetrate the Washington right wing with success. The District kickers counted first, Green placing one past Miss Pomies after 26 minutes. Miss Parr evened it up shortly before half time. The second half was loosely played by both clubs but the women showed to better advantage with teamwork. They scored twice in the last ten minutes to secure the draw.

Carmen's goalkeeping perhaps merited even higher praise than she received from the *Post*. Not only was Carmen an outfield player doing an unfamiliar job but it should also be taken into account how heavy leather footballs were in that era, especially when they got wet. Saving shots from adult men took courage as well as athleticism.

In many ways, the 4-4 draw in Washington was the game of the trip, even though the first win proved elusive. The women had entered the game with a glowing reputation and they did not disappoint. In front of a crowd of 7,000 they stood up against the men, as they did throughout their American tour. In the end, of course, the game was upstaged by the pantomime re-creation of the New York Giants clinching the World Series against the Yankees, but the soccer received a lot of attention. Having President Harding there to perform the celebrity kick-off was a great moment; and being presented with the match ball signed by the President to mark the occasion would be a highlight in the history of Dick, Kerr Ladies for years to come.

Warren Gamaliel Harding, twenty-ninth President of the United States, was an amiable Republican from Ohio. His presidency coincided with Prohibition in America, a time when the nation was dealing with internal divisions after the First World War. It was said of Harding that his chief interests in life were 'golf, drink and other men's wives'. It was an open secret that Harding's political friends, the 'K Street Gang' regularly attended all-night sessions playing poker and consuming plenty of booze; but in the autumn of 1922, Harding was still popular. It was perhaps for the best that he died in August 1923, before his presidency became tarnished by scandal.

There was personal scandal because Harding had a secret love-child by his mistress Nan Britton. Even worse, there was huge financial and political corruption in the 'Teapot Dome Scandal'. Teapot Dome, a mountain range in Wyoming, had vast oil reserves designated for the needs of the US Navy. Men in Harding's administration defrauded the federal government by selling oil concessions illegally. The Dick, Kerr girls knew nothing of this; to them, Harding was just the kindly president who put an official stamp of approval on their visit and autographed a football for them as a memento.

The Washington match was the springboard for a run of good results. The team went north again to the coast of Massachusetts and won 5-4 against New Bedford Whalers. They won the next game, too, a runaway 8-4 victory over New York FC. A few days later they were back in New England again for a 2-2 draw with the Fall River Marksmen. Local newspaper reports of the match at Fall River make interesting reading. The *Fall River Herald News* noted that a section of the grandstand was reserved for ladies and ladies accompanied by gentlemen. Ladies were charged a special price of twenty-five cents. As for the football match, the *Fall River Globe* reported that:

> Yesterday afternoon, an argument took place between men and women at Mark's Stadium. The women did not win, neither did the men. The score in no way explains how well the English lassies can play the national game of their homeland; and the opposition was from a team of the best men kickers in our country.

The *Globe* also addressed the issue of how competitive the matches were. Reports of the 4-4 draw in Washington suggest both sides were trying hard and the result was genuinely close. The Fall River Marksmen, however, had professionals of a higher quality than the Stars, including one former Chelsea player and one who had played for Kilmarnock. But the Marksmen, the best team Dick, Kerr Ladies faced on their tour, scored only two goals. It seems the atmosphere of the game was rather different from what happened in other matches. The *Globe* wrote of Florrie Redford:

> With bobbed hair and pretty, Miss Redford at centre-forward scored the first goal. Mr Duncan, the Fall River goalie, deliberately let the shot go by him. In the second half, Jock Lindsay twice gave Miss Redford a chance to score. Each time, she passed up the opportunity, indicating she wanted anything she got to be earned, not given free.

The recollections of Pete Renzulli, who had played in goal for Paterson in the first match of the tour, were different again. Renzulli was a serious player; in 1930 he would be goalkeeper for the United States national team at the inaugural FIFA World Cup in Uruguay. Pete's recollections in later life of Dick, Kerr Ladies were highly complimentary: 'I played against them in 1922, for Paterson. We were national champions, but we had a hell of a job beating them'.

It is not easy, therefore, to judge how 'equal' the matches on Dick, Kerr's tour were. It seems that there may have been differences in intensity from one game to another. Some of the better male players may have been more intent on being gentlemanly hosts than hell-bent on winning. It is also notable how many goals were scored; eighty in nine matches, with forty for the tourists and forty by the men, a flood of goals that might fit better with what happens in exhibition matches rather than in cut-throat competition. Then again, the Dick, Kerr girls were going flat out to make a good impression (as they clearly succeeded in doing) and men's teams hated the idea of being beaten by women.

In their final two matches, the women won an exciting game 4-3 against Baltimore Soccer Club and narrowly lost the last match of the tour, 6-5 in Philadelphia. It was a fascinating finale to a remarkable tour. The tourists were based in Philadelphia for a week in which they enjoyed lavish hospitality but also found themselves at the centre of local football politics.

The main source for the story of Dick, Kerr Ladies in Philadelphia was Levi Wilcox, a soccer-mad journalist with the *Philadelphia Inquirer*. On 14 August, long before the tour began, Wilcox was writing articles in the *Inquirer* warning that the 'soccer magnates' of the Football Association of Eastern Pennsylvania were refusing to allow the Dick, Kerr girls to play in Philadelphia as had been arranged by the USFA.

This was partly a bureaucratic dispute between rival football organisations but other issues were involved. Some of the voices against allowing a match between women and men expressed fear 'that a victory for the women players might hurt the sport in our colleges and schools', by turning young male players away from playing soccer. Such fears reinforced concerns that, as has often been the case in its long history, American soccer was struggling to compete with rival team sports.

Levi Wilcox had no patience with such fears. His articles in the *Inquirer* backed the USFA and poured scorn on the local association as he argued for the women's match to go ahead. 'A match of this sort will be a novelty and will be the means of encouraging many a spectator, who probably has never before seen a soccer match, to travel to Disston Ball Park for the purpose of witnessing these women in action'.

On 28 August, Wilcox reported that the Eastern Association was still refusing to sanction the match. On 13 September, still two days before the tourists left Liverpool, a gloomy update from Wilcox informed his readers that 'local soccer fans are to be deprived of witnessing this fine women's team play, unless, of course, they make the trip to one of the other cities where they are scheduled to play'. Six weeks later, however, on 24 October, the *Inquirer* announced that Philadelphia FC would be playing against Dick, Kerr Ladies on 4 November.

The on-off saga of the fixture between Dick, Kerr Ladies and Philadelphia FC throws light on the troubled internal politics of soccer in America as the newly-established ASL (American Soccer League) attempted to secure a foothold for the professional game. It shows, too, that the ingrained social attitudes obstructing women's football in Britain and Europe were as prevalent on the other side of the Atlantic. The saga also illustrates the fragility and uncertainty that surrounded the tour as a whole.

Long before the Dick, Kerr girls set out, there had been doubts as to whether key parts of their itinerary would ever take place. The team's arrival in Philadelphia on 31 October was after their voyage home had been put back by a week until 9 November. Their stay at the Washington Hotel in Philadelphia was just one more last-minute change to add to all the others. It is also worth noting that it had been planned to stage not just the one match while in Philadelphia but three; games against Bethlehem Steel and Wilmington fell through because financial guarantees could not be agreed.

Levi Wilcox was all in favour of the big match scheduled for 4 November. On 30 October he told his readers what they could look forward to:

> Instead of the tourists playing pink tea football as some might imagine, they charge as keenly as the men players, while their combination play rivals that of some of the English league players. They are also exceptionally fast on the ball. Strong as the Phillies might be with rushing and bustling tactics, they will find these women will not give them an inch of ground in that respect. The team is built for speed and is also capable of holding its own when it comes to roughing it.

On the day of the game, 5,000 came to watch an eventful eleven-goal thriller. The women went two goals down in the first few minutes, fought back to level the score at 3-3 just after half-time and finally lost 5-6 after a flurry of goals in the last quarter of the game. By that time, according to several match reports, the crowd was cheering wildly in support of the women. Levi Wilcox felt thoroughly vindicated. His report of the game declared:

> The English team not only gave an exhibition of soccer seldom witnessed on local grounds, but they demonstrated that women can play the game as well as the men.

On 9 November, the day the tourists sailed for home, Wilcox judged their impact:

> From what we have witnessed last Saturday, these English girls, though not as robust as the men players,

as is only to be expected from the weaker sex, have more of the game in their bonnets than any team we have seen in this country – with the exception, of course, of the professional English elevens which have played here.

Levi Wilcox was not an infallible nor an objective observer. His colourful articles were partisan contributions to an ongoing dispute between rival associations running soccer in the United States. They were also full of wishful thinking about how the women's tour might boost the game in America, for men even more than for women. On closer inspection, it also seems clear that Mr Wilcox had a view of female equality that would almost certainly have got him into hot water had he been writing in 2022 rather than 1922.

Even so, the passionate support for their tour from Levi Wilcox and others helped to make the week in Philadelphia an enjoyable time for Carmen and her teammates. Apart from the first week in New York, most places they visited had been one-night stands in between constantly playing and travelling. Eight days in Philadelphia allowed space to enjoy the hospitality from friendly locals, to offer encouragement to the small number of local girls who wanted to become 'soccerettes', or just to absorb the rhythms of American life and reflect upon their tour and what it had achieved.

In football terms, the 1922 tour stands out as a memorable achievement for Dick, Kerr Ladies, and for women's football in general. The final record was three wins, three draws and three defeats. In nine matches against adult men's teams, the Dick, Kerr girls had conceded forty goals and scored forty of their own. They had impressed knowledgeable observers, been watched by appreciative crowds and carved out a place in the history of football. In 2022, a wave of commemorations both in Britain and in America, will give new life to the story of the 1922 tour, rightfully so.

As the team's goalkeeper, Carmen had a big part to play in the success of the tour. Statistically, having to pick the ball out of her net forty times in nine matches might seem less than impressive; such a statistic might well lead to a professional keeper of modern times being replaced by the reserve goalie. On the 1922 tour, however, there was no reserve goalie. Carmen had taken on the role in an emergency. Besides, shipping four goals a game against adult men was hardly a failure. In the 4-4 draw against Washington Stars, Carmen was player of the match. Like all the Dick, Kerr girls, Carmen had much to be proud of.

The length and complexity of the tour drained the energies of the players. It also tested the inventiveness of Alfred Frankland. Finances were shaky, dependent on the size of the crowds and the variable gate receipts. Frankland's partners were also unreliable. The Brooklyn Football Club had been the main American link in organising the tour but proved incapable of living up to its promises. David Brooks, the 'businessman' Frankland relied on as a go-between, proved to be all talk and no money. Without the interventions by the United States Football Association, the tour might have fallen into complete chaos. But, in spite of all the crises, disaster was averted and the tour was carried through successfully.

Though not involved in the details, Carmen was in a position to observe some of the organisational problems, Later, in one of the feature articles about Carmen in the *Democrat & Chronicle* when she was living in Rochester NY from 1947 to 1950, Carmen recalled the stresses and strains of the 1922 tour, including a time when a row about unpaid bills led to the police being called and a sudden change of hotel. Perhaps Carmen was already beginning to learn from Mr Frankland's unique methods of operation. Later in her life, Carmen would be a captain, a tour manager and an ambassador for women's football, often working closely with Alfred Frankland.

Did the tour succeed in its primary objective, to fight back against the bureaucratic obstructionism of the English FA and put new energy into women's football? Well, not really. As a spectacular one-off event, the tour did indeed make its mark but it could not leave a lasting legacy.

Back in England, the same old problems persisted. What women's football in Britain needed above all was the continuity of a stable league structure; a system in which the best teams like Dick, Kerr Ladies, Stoke Ladies and Hey's Brewery of Bradford could compete regularly with self-supporting finances. France had such a structure, England, along with Scotland and Northern Ireland, did not. Periodic special events could not make up the difference.

The 1922 tour was not only about football. Even more than the England-France tours, the North America tour enabled in-depth immersion in a new culture. First in New York and then in Philadelphia, there was time between the matches and the training sessions for the players to see a lot of East Coast America. It would have been a memorable tour without any football at all. One evocative photograph of the team 'off-duty' shows Carmen and Florrie surrounded by Lily Parr, Annie Crozier, Alice Kell, Jessie Walmsley, Alice Mills and Jennie Harris, all of them dressed in stylish long overcoats suggesting they have enjoyed their shopping expeditions. The sense this was a moment of special happiness and togetherness is palpable.

Life-changing experiences alter lives in many different ways. In 1922, Lily Parr was a working-class girl from St Helens who had been on tour in Paris, climbed the Eiffel Tower, been recognised everywhere as an exceptional footballer, crossed the Atlantic Ocean, been out on the town in New York and met the American President in Washington. Lily was seventeen years old. Alice Mills was so struck by America, especially New England, that Preston never seemed the same. Within a year of coming home, Alice was starting a new life in Seekonk, Massachusetts, having married an American who had caught her eye when the team played in Pawtucket.

Florrie Redford's friendship with Carmen had grown closer than ever. After the tour, it was arranged Florrie would move to France to play for Fémina for the 1923 season, living with Carmen's family in Paris. Later, in 1930, Florrie emigrated to Canada, a move possibly influenced by her vivid memories from 1922. After the Second World War, Carmen herself went to live in Rochester NY and then New

York City. In 1954, she became an American citizen. Again, it is hard to believe Carmen's decision to begin a new life in America was not influenced by impressions forged during the 1922 tour.

Carmen's life was being changed in other ways by football. Until 1921, Carmen loved any and all sports. After the North America tour, however, football took over her life. The bond between Carmen and Preston became unbreakable. More than that, Carmen was moving towards her role as a warrior for equality, taking up the fight for survival of women's football as player, captain, club vice-president, and roving ambassador for the game. Still only twenty-two, Carmen had come a long way from the puppyish nineteen-year-old who had made it into Fémina's first XI in 1920.

Does this mean that the Dick, Kerr tour of 1922 was a major landmark on the road to equality? Not really. In the social landscape of the times, true equality was not yet achievable. Many spectators who came to watch them did so out of curiosity and novelty rather than a genuine appreciation of women's football. Some of the male players they faced, like many journalists who reported on the games, held patronising views about the 'weaker sex'. Even those people like Levi Wilcox who passionately supported the girls, perhaps even the girls themselves, did not think about equality in terms recognisable a century later.

Did the great adventure of 1922 move the dial, bringing equality a little closer? Indeed it did. The players knew they were confronting stereotypes, proving themselves, taking pride in being good at the game. Less consciously, they were growing in confidence and self-awareness, widening their horizons, feeling empowered by the collective identity. Inevitably, such a long tour involved moments of disappointment, self-doubt and homesickness; but also moments of fun, camaraderie and pride.

On 9 November, after that satisfying final week in Philadelphia, the team sailed out of New York harbour on board the White Star liner *Adriatic,* bound for Liverpool. With them sailed a multitude of memories and one especially proud shared possession, the leather football signed in their honour by President Warren G. Harding.

Chapter 5

Successes, Scandals and the Fight for Survival: The 1920s

At the beginning of this book, the Prologue considered the special place in history of the women's football match at Herne Hill, south London, in 1925, the first match of the ambitious tour of Britain by the French XI led by Carmen Pomiès. In particular, the Prologue dwelled on the worldwide interest in the match generated by images of the kiss between the two captains at the kick-off. Those images of the 1925 match that flashed across the world revealed keen interest in the 'novelty' of women playing football. It might seem (and was indeed intended to seem) as if women's football was new, exciting and in the best of health. But this was not really true. The 1925 tour, and the orchestrated fanfare of publicity to push it into public view, was actually a desperate attempt to recover lost ground.

By 1925, women's football was under siege in Britain, The Football Association 'ban' of December 1921 was stifling the financing and staging of fixtures in England. It was difficult to sustain the surging interest in the game that had been so apparent just after the First World War. Beyond the damage done by the FA ruling, there were structural weaknesses in governance and organisation. Fixtures depended too much on short-term arrangements. Financial management was often amateurish.

Even Dick, Kerr Ladies, fresh from their epic tour of the United States, struggled to maintain stability. The Dick, Kerr company was taken over by new owners, later known as English Electric, who did not support the women's football team. So after Dick, Kerr Ladies came home to Preston in November 1922, it was hard to keep up the momentum. They played only a handful of matches in 1923 and 1924. Many women's clubs in England, even successful ones like Plymouth and Stoke, withered away. Elsewhere in Europe, women's football was assaulted by a powerful social and political backlash. In Austria, for example, women's football made promising progress from 1923 but petered out by 1926.

The position of the women's game was more secure in France and was also beginning to grow in Belgium but, even in France, there were undercurrents of opposition to football as 'unwomanly' and 'unnatural'. In 1923, Gabriel Hanot, a fine footballer who had captained France before he retired from playing and became an influential journalist, stated firmly that 'football is not a game for girls'. Alice Milliat, who had done so much to promote the game, was beginning to waver. By 1925, Mme Milliat was voicing doubts that perhaps football was not entirely suitable for young women, and it might be time to focus on other sports, above all athletics. Despite the evident success of its league structure and independent federation, despite its extensive coverage in newspapers and magazines, the women's game in France faced a battle to ensure its long-term survival. Carmen Pomiès was up for the fight.

At the end of 1922, the true scale of the threats menacing the game in France was still hidden in the future. The 1922-23 and 1923-24 seasons provided some of the happiest, most fulfilling times of Carmen's football life. She was maturing as a player, Fémina began to win almost every trophy in sight and all this was achieved together with Carmen's best friend sharing the limelight as a central figure in this fight to promote the women's game. After returning to Preston from the North America tour, Carmen went home to France ready for the new season. Florrie Redford went with her, to live with the Pomiès family and to play for Fémina. For the next year and a half, Florrie became the shining star of women's football in France.

This was a significant change in Florrie's life. She had stayed in Paris before, in the run-up to Christmas 1920 and she already knew a lot of French players well from the many France-England games when she played against them. In December 1922, however, it was altogether different. This time, Florrie was not visiting France on tour; she was there for the foreseeable future as part and parcel of French football. Florrie was not only a 'guest star' with a reputation to defend, but she was also paid a retainer to act as a coach and mentor. In addition to her friendship with Carmen, and the excitement of playing football in new surroundings, Florrie's move was partly motivated by the fact there was not going to be much activity for Dick, Kerr Ladies that year.

Florrie made her debut for Fémina on 17 December, a remarkable day when Carmen scored the only goal of the game as Fémina defeated En Avant! in a game that kicked off at 10.00 to be followed at 14.00 by Florrie's first game for Fémina, a 4-1 victory over Ruche Sportive Féminine. Florrie seems to have then gone back to Preston for Christmas and New Year. Carmen was in the team that won 2-0 against En Avant! on 21 January and she scored five goals a week later, as Fémina beat AS Amicale 6-0, but Florrie was not on the team sheet for either game. By early March, Florrie was back, scoring a vital goal in a notorious grudge match against Olympique.

It was the beginning of a year of nonstop success for Florrie, who was soon widely celebrated in the sporting press as the best female player in France. Fémina did suffer a rare defeat against Les Sportives (match reports picked out Florrie and Carmen as two of the team's three best players) but winning was the norm. In April, Fémina won the Championnat de France by defeating Sportives de Reims 4-0 in the play-off final. Florrie scored the second, Carmen got the third and fourth.

Carmen's goals in this match reflected her changing role in the team. Until now, she had always been a defender or midfielder, even an emergency goalkeeper, but she was emerging as a dangerous attacking player. Of nineteen goals scored by the team that spring, Carmen scored seven. Perhaps playing and training alongside Florrie taught Carmen a lot about the art of finishing. Carmen was also becoming first choice

Successes, Scandals and the Fight for Survival: The 1920s

for teams representing France. After playing for the Probables against the Possibles in a trial match, she was selected for the France team to play Hey's Brewery of Bradford at the end of April.

This match was a great occasion for Hey's Brewery, due reward for their enterprise and ambition in coming to Paris to take on the best players in France. Eight thousand people (one of them Florrie) filled Stade Pershing to see the Bradford girls win 1-0. The only goal of the game was scored by Jennie Harris, one of Carmen's friends and teammates on the Dick, Kerr Ladies tour of the United States. Doubtless, Jennie enjoyed pointing out to Carmen that the French might have the superior league structure and governance but the English Way was still best when it came to winning.

Fun though it was to be riding a wave of success as the best player in France, playing for the championship-winning team, Florrie's time with Fémina involved her personally in a series of scandalous events that rocked French women's football in 1923, exposing some of the stresses and strains that might de-stabilise it. The first of these events was the 'scandal match' on 4 March 1923.

When Fémina played against L'Olympique du Pantin in the Championnat de Paris, Olympique were a rising force in France, captained by the formidable Violette Gouraud-Morris. Fémina were on top at first, with a goal from Florrie Redford. Just before half-time, with Femina leading 2-1, Olympique players, led by two of the four Laloz sisters, Geneviève and Thérèse, mobbed the referee to dispute a decision. Tempers frayed. At half-time, Gouraud-Morris gave a rousing speech to fire up her team. In the second half, another referee's decision further inflamed Olympique's sense of grievance. The row boiled over when the Laloz sisters were joined on the field by their brother, who proceeded to beat up the referee. Geneviève and Thérèse helped him do it. The match was abandoned amid a storm of recriminations.

The fallout from the attack on the referee was fiery and protracted. Thérèse and Geneviève were given lengthy suspensions. So was Violette. The row and its consequences went far beyond a scandal that inflamed football rivalries and caused a sensation in the press. In the short term, Olympique were so furious about the suspensions that they forfeited their next match with Fémina, claiming they 'could not field a team because of the suspensions of our best players'. In the longer term, it inflicted lasting collateral damage that tarnished reputations and weakened the foundations of women's football in France.

Ever since that first 'scandal match', a dark myth has hung over Violette Gouraud-Morris; that she was suspended for punching the referee. This myth fitted neatly with perceptions of Violette as an outrageous woman who dressed as a man, drove racing cars and frequently fought in the boxing ring against men, but it is simply not true. The Laloz sisters and their brother did the punching. Violette was punished because she was the captain. Her suspension was later reduced but the myth persisted.

The outcome of the 'scandal match' had a significant impact on Violette's image at a turning point in her life. It was in 1923 that Violette divorced her husband Cyprien; she was no longer Mme Gouraud-Morris. From this time, Violette Morris was even more openly than before the flamboyant personality who took female lovers and defied conventional stereotypes about the place of women in French society. In addition, a damaging rift developed between Violette and Alice Milliat, who took the full force of Violette's resentment against the punishment imposed on her.

One of many fascinations in the 'Affaire Olympique' is the way the life stories of Carmen and Violette were intertwined. Once, they had been rivals in athletics, with Carmen trying (usually in vain) to match her powerful rival in the javelin. Now, in 1923, they were on opposite sides in a different sense: Violette 'bringing the game into disrepute', while Carmen grew into the role of a champion defending it.

For Carmen, one way to carry on fighting for the women's game was to keep on winning. Fémina won the championships of Paris and of France and also the French cup, though that victory had a sour taste because Olympique refused to turn up for the final. Fémina played a low-key friendly match instead, against Les Sportives, and managed to lose 0-1. Another important way to promote and expand the game in France was through what Helge Faller has termed 'propaganda matches', in which players from established clubs took women's football to the French provinces.

Many 'propaganda matches' took place in April and May 1923, after the end of the regular season. Big clubs from the Paris region took the game to places in northern France such as Calais, Noyon and the medieval city of Provins, where Carmen and Florrie played for a Fémina selection against Les Cadettes. Nova Fémina of Toulouse played their 'propaganda matches' in faraway southern locations like Mulhouse on the Swiss border, Tarbes in Haute Pyrénées, Béziers and Carcassone. Occasionally, local teams might be involved but the usual format was for a 'travelling circus' of twenty-two or more players to demonstrate the skills and thrills of the game by exhibition matches.

After the summer break, there was a fresh round of 'propaganda matches' in advance of the 1923-24 season. In addition to matches in the Champagne region, special efforts were made to spread the game into Spain and Portugal. These ventures were successful in arousing interest and attracting spectators to attend the games. They also led to surprising controversy and scandals that closely involved Florrie and Carmen, with damaging consequences for French women's football.

At the beginning of September, Les Sportives de Paris arranged two matches to be played against Stoke Ladies in Barcelona. In the surging growth of women's football in Britain after the First World War, Stoke Ladies had emerged as one of the strongest teams, spearheaded by their demon striker, Daisy Bates, and the three Bridgett sisters, Eva, Ida and Lily. The driving force behind Stoke Ladies came from their father, Len Bridgett, who was a capable, energetic organiser. Len's younger brother, George Arthur, who had been a top striker for Sunderland in England's First Division until 1911, provided expert coaching and motivation.

Like all women's teams in England, Stoke Ladies were threatened by the adverse effects of the FA ruling of December 1921. Even so, Stoke persisted, hoping to rival Dick, Kerr Ladies as the premier team in England. That explains why, impressed by Dick, Kerr's tour of North America in autumn 1922, Len Bridgett took his team to Barcelona so they could test themselves against a leading French club; Les Sportives, led by their renowned captain Madeleine Bracquemond.

The event was organised by a local business, the *Cooperativa de Casas Baratas,* who donated a handsome trophy to be presented to the winning team over two back-to-back matches. Carmen did not play in these matches because Les Sportives was not her team, but she was there in Barcelona to keep Florrie company and act as go-between. The clear intention was to raise the profile of the women's game in Spain and to spread international goodwill but the first match caused sharp controversy.

> Les Sportives v Stoke Ladies, Industria Urgel-Villaroel, 8 September 1923.
>
> Stoke Ladies: E. Spooner, Ida Bridgett, Tilly Wagg, Daisy Bates, Theresa Cooper, Lizzie Carroll, Ada Derricott, Dolly Cooper, L. Bedford, Elsie Stanier, Eva Bridgett.
>
> Les Sportives: J. Smachteur, Solange Guille, S. Lacombe, T. Renaut, H. Rillac, G. Viotti, M. Bracquemond, B. Geuty, P. Puisais, G. Sprier, E. Journée.

Closer analysis of the team sheet for the first match helps to explain what caused all the fuss. Les Sportives complained bitterly about the presence in the Stoke team of their guest centre-forward, listed as 'L. Bedford'. The Paris players knew perfectly well that 'Bedford' was actually Florrie Redford of Preston, living in Paris, playing for Fémina, and probably the best player in France. The objections by

Les Sportives against 'Bedford', on the grounds that she was too good, proved to be wellfounded. Florrie scored three goals as Stoke won easily. It was agreed she should not play in the second match of the weekend. Stoke won again anyway, though only by 1-0.

Two weeks later, Florrie Redford and Stoke Ladies were battling each other again, this time in England, for a prestige match at Colne in Lancashire between Stoke and the reputedly 'unbeatable' Dick, Kerr Ladies. For Florrie, this was a chance to have a short holiday back home; but in any case, it was a game she dearly wanted to play in. Florrie had not been forgotten. The notes in the match programme said of her: 'Centre-forward: Can shoot with tremendous power and accuracy. Has scored more goals than any girl in football. Has returned specially from Paris to play in this match'.

Stoke won a famous victory 1-0 but, sadly, their rise to the top of the game in England did not last. Len Bridgett became distracted by his responsibilities in local government as town councillor. His brother George Arthur became deeply involved with the nearby men's professional team, Port Vale. Stoke Ladies simply faded away. Their sudden demise provided a harsh lesson on the fragility of women's football clubs, even when they were successful on the field of play. For Stoke, as for Dick, Kerr Ladies and Hey's Brewery, one-off matches and tours, however impressive at the time, could not make up for the lack of stable structures and governance.

Just over one week after the match in Colne, Carmen and Florrie were back together in France, taking part in another series of 'international propaganda matches', this time in Portugal. Alice Milliat took twenty-six of the best players in Paris to play four exhibition matches in one week, two in Lisbon, one in Coimbra and one in Porto. Carmen and Florrie played for Fémina against the 'équipe sélectionée de Paris' made up of players from eight different clubs. This intensive tour, promoted by *Sporting,* a leading sports newspaper in Lisbon, went well in terms of football, with all the matches being closely-fought, but was marred by explosive scandal off the field.

At an evening reception in Lisbon, hosted by *Sporting* magazine, there were sensational accusations of 'immoral behaviour' by many French players who had allegedly 'allowed or encouraged' sexual advances by Portuguese men. There is little or no hard evidence as to how far the 'immoral behaviour' might have progressed. Revealingly, there is no evidence of action being taken against the men involved, though some contemporary reports suggested the men had been guided by wild suppositions about the loose morals of French women in general, in contrast to the tightly-chaperoned girls in their own culture. But Alice Milliat was not on the warpath about Portuguese men. She felt angry that 'her' young women had let her down.

The cloud of disgrace already hanging over women's football in France after the *Affaire Olympique* got darker. In December, Alice Milliat and the FFSF ruled that twenty-four of the players on the tour should be suspended. Only two players escaped punishment, Carmen Pomiès and Florrie Redford. It is not quite certain why. Possibly, Carmen and Florrie were not present when the 'immoral behaviour' happened. Perhaps it was assumed they were 'not that kind of woman'. The more likely explanation is that Mme Milliat was reluctant to take action against her English guest star, who had an official position with the FFSF, or against Carmen who was Florrie's host.

Together with the earlier *Affaire Olympique,* the Portugal Scandal did lasting damage, as part of a slow process that gradually undermined Alice Milliat's support for women's football. Mme Milliat, so important as the founder and guiding hand of Fémina and the FFSF, was not only keen to avoid further embarrassments like Lisbon; she gradually distanced herself from women's football, now regarding the game as a distraction from her precious dream of full participation by women at the Olympic Games. To make matters worse, the furious hostility between Violette and the FFSF began to spread far beyond football. Later in the 1920s, the rift would explode into a *cause celebre* fought out in lawsuits and bitter recriminations.

The Portugal Scandal reflected the extent of the pernicious double standards in attitudes towards female footballers. This went deeper than just the ingrained sexism shown by the Portuguese men who believed it was 'normal' to treat French women as they did. It is striking that the fiercest criticism after the scandal was directed at the French women and girls. That night in Lisbon in October 1923 revealed how prevailing attitudes of the time set female footballers an impossible contradiction.

On the one hand, they were derided for being 'unwomanly', betraying their femininity by playing a physical sport that belonged to men. At the same time, they were portrayed as being altogether *too* feminine, as sexy temptresses in skimpy football attire who dangerously inflamed the passions of poor, helpless men. Such attitudes were often visible in the behaviour of raucous males who came to women's matches to jeer or to leer, in pompous denunciations of women's football in newspaper articles and letters to the editor, and in the way women footballers were ridiculed in cartoons that were supposedly funny but often heavy-handed, even cruel. Women footballers of the 1920s needed resilience, an independent mind and a thick skin.

Three cartoons of the time, one Dutch, one Austrian and one French, vividly illustrate the trend. The Dutch cartoon is unpleasantly crude, even pornographic. The Austrian cartoon, an unkind caricature of women's football in the *Illustrierte Österreichisches Sportsblatt* from August 1924, depicts a football match in which outsized, very domesticated women are busier catching the ball in their aprons rather than kicking it. The French cartoon portrays a formidable lady berating a man watching a women's match, binoculars in hand:

THE ADMIRER OF THE ROUND BALL
Woman: 'Now I understand Monsieur's interest in football! It's the women!

And you need stronger binoculars!'

Man: 'Erm, not at all. Erm, it's just my wanting to see the game better!'

True enough, not all men who watched women's football came to ogle fit young women, or to poke fun at them. Many men came for the novelty factor, with no hostile intent. Many professional players, ex-players and journalists were supportive and genuinely impressed by the standard of play. But sneering ridicule of 'unnatural' women was never far away.

For Carmen and Florrie and their Fémina teammates, the Portugal Scandal was put to one side as the 1923-24 season got going. By this time, women's football in France had an established structure that was way ahead of anywhere else. An elite group of leading clubs competed at the top level: Fémina, En Avant!, Olympique, Academia, Les Cadettes de Gascogne, Les Sportives Paris, Sportives de Reims. Newer teams such as Nova Fémina, and La Clodo, tried to catch up. There was an official transfer system and keen competition to sign up the best players.

Madeleine Bracquemond moved from En Avant! to Les Sportives; the four Laloz sisters moved first from En Avant! to Olympique and, a year later, from Olympique to join Clodo. Carmen Pomiès was recorded as transferring from Fémina to Dick, Kerr Ladies in May 1921 and back to Fémina again in December 1922. Many clubs ran additional 'farm teams'(one group photo shows all four Fémina teams together). The researches by Helge Faller have traced a total of 254 matches, counting 'propaganda games' and friendlies as well as league and cup fixtures, during the 1923-24 season.

Fémina soon asserted themselves as the team to watch by demolishing Ruche Sportive Feminine 8-0. Carmen scored four, Florrie scored three. Ruche was not a weak opponent; games against other clubs than Fémina were close affairs. Next, Carmen scored the winning goal against Muguettes de Charenton. Florrie scored in a 2-0 win over Les Cadettes, then all five goals as Sportives Reims were crushed 5-0, followed by two more in a win over Charenton. On the field that autumn, Fémina were just about unstoppable and it seemed all was well with women's football in France.

Successes, Scandals and the Fight for Survival: The 1920s

Even at this time, however, recognition and acceptance of the women's game remained elusive, as was shown by coverage of Fémina's win over Les Cadettes in the 18 November issue of *Le Petit Journal*. The match report was favourable enough and the magazine's front cover displayed a colourful, attention-grabbing artist's impression of the players in action but there was a sting in the small print. The accompanying text asked a dangerously loaded question about Le Football Féminin and came up with a rather lukewarm answer:

> Can fragile Womanhood adapt to the violent sports at which our youth excels? The answer to this often-asked question seems to be in the affirmative. We can appreciate this by inspecting two teams competing in the Championnat de Paris. The illustration shows a passage of play in head-to-head battle between F-S and Les CG.

Off the field, there were problems. In December, the disciplinary actions taken by Alice Milliat and the FFSF over the Portugal Scandal blighted Fémina's season. There was a lot of internal dissension and wrangling in committee rooms and this began to adversely affect the team. At the beginning of January, Fémina suffered a shock 0-1 defeat by Les Cadettes and were knocked out of the Cup. Relations between the two teams had always been friendly but Fémina were by far the superior team. Losing to Les Cadettes was an inexplicable humiliation.

Unwisely, Carmen went public with several letters, trying to explain the upset. One of her main arguments was that Fémina had been weakened by the absence of five key players (one of them was Florrie) but Les Cadettes pointed out they had had three of their own missing. Carmen was seen by many people as just a bad loser.

A week later, normal service was resumed when two goals from Florrie Redford in a 3-0 win over Les Cadettes ensured top place for Fémina in Groupe B of the Paris championship. This opened the way for Fémina to triumph once again in the overall Championnat de France. When the play-offs began in March, Florrie got two goals in winning the quarter-final and then scored three more in as Fémina beat Reims 4-0 in the semi-final. In the final, Fémina faced La Clodo, who had just won the Cup. Carmen scored the opening goal and Florrie got the fourth in a satisfying 4-2 victory.

Knowing the who, what, when and where of Fémina's championship-winning season is one thing. Knowing the emotional ups and downs of the players as the season unfolded is, obviously, much more elusive. But it seems safe to conclude that the months from September 1923 to May 1924 were some of the happiest times in the life of Carmen Pomiès. At twenty-three, Carmen was a mature, dominating presence in French football, already a certain selection for France. With Fémina, Carmen was at the heart of a high-quality team alongside close friends like Louise Ourry.

All footballers love winning, especially when it goes together with team spirit and togetherness. Perhaps above all, Carmen was playing alongside her special friend, Florrie Redford, almost universally admired as the best female footballer in France, and Carmen was proud and happy to be the reason why Florrie was in France at all.

For Florrie, it was like living in a new world. She had been to France before but that had been a very English experience as part of a touring team from Preston. In 1923, there was time between matches and training sessions for Florrie to live in Paris as if she belonged there. It was little short of life-changing. As a little girl, Florrie had lived in York, in a family of velvet-weavers. When her father moved to Preston to take a job at Dick, Kerr's engineering works, Florrie became a munitionette, a footballer, then a nurse in a mental hospital. Football took Florrie far beyond Lancashire, to France, to North America and back to France again, not to mention Barcelona and Portugal.

Living in the Rue de la Gaîté, close to the Boulevard Montparnasse, Florrie was immersed in a new language and a new culture, enjoying the uplifted self-esteem that went with being celebrated as the brightest star lighting up women's football in France. Getting to know Carmen's privileged, educated family, her cultured sisters and her singer-dancer brother, was all part of a memorable shared experience. Florrie had Carmen as best friend, translator and guide but she also had to find her own ways of adjusting to the special dynamics of a French-speaking dressing room and team culture. The photo of the Fémina team, with Florrie and Carmen wreathed in the smiles of league champions, tells its own story. But it was an end as much as a beginning. Soon afterwards, Florrie went home to England. Despite Carmen's development as a player, despite all Fémina's successes and the apparent stability of the game in France, women's football still faced ominous challenges.

This was true the game in England, where Stoke Ladies suddenly fell by the wayside and Dick, Kerr Ladies were playing far fewer matches than before the FA ban. The game in England badly needed a revival. In countries like Spain and Portugal, women's football faltered after promising beginnings. In Austria, the game seemed to be making progress from 1923 but met entrenched disapproval and ridicule. Hostility from male-dominated sports organisations, from the Church, from newspapers, was powerful and persistent. Women's football in Austria slowly ground to a halt in 1926.

The underlying fragility of women's football in France was starkly revealed when the 1924-25 season began. There was growing discontent with Alice Milliat, partly because of the fallout from the Portugal Affair, but also resentment of her perceived failure to respect the independence of the clubs. Alice Milliat's leadership of the FFSF was seen as high-handed and unfair, even by Fémina, the club she founded.

Problems had been brewing even in April, when Fémina won the title decider against La Clodo. The Fémina committee threatened to boycott the final in protest against FFSF; only after a tense meeting on 12 April did the club's advisory board decide to go ahead with the game. Tensions persisted through the summer. On 29 October, Fémina broke away from the FFSF. In November, after only two league matches, Fémina opted out of the Championnat de Paris. In December, Fémina joined forces with Les Cadettes to form an entirely new federation, the UFSFS, and to set up a new league, the Championnat de la Ligue Parisienne.

The turbulence undermined the stable organisational structures that had made women's football in France more secure than anywhere else. It caused upheaval within the clubs. For example, many players decided to leave Fémina for other teams. One of them was Simone Chapoteau, club captain since 1923 but who now moved away to join a recently-formed club, Nova Fémina. It was announced that Fémina's new captain would be Carmen Pomiès. In 1920, Carmen had been just a hopeful new recruit. Now she was battle-hardened and streetwise, well-versed in the politics of football and the threats to its existence.

In April 1925, Fémina easily won their new Ligue Parisienne, beating Les Cadettes 4-0 in the play-off final. The only others involved were smaller clubs and former 'farm teams', like Hirondelles, Montrouge, Basco and Côte d'Azur. Even in France, this was a divisive time for women's football, with an urgent need for revival and unity.

The situation was even more difficult in England, where Dick, Kerr Ladies struggled to maintain momentum. In *A League Of Their Own!*, Gail Newsham's loving account of the Dick, Kerr story, it is claimed that 'the team carried on playing throughout the 1920s'. Strictly speaking, this is true but the reality was that most seasons in the 1920s were short and only in the summer months. It was a far cry from the great days of 1921 when they played more than sixty matches in the calendar year.

Dick, Kerr's organising genius, Alfred Frankland, recognised the urgent need to re-energise the women's game. He promoted an ambitious new series of international matches by a French touring side. With his flair for presentation, Frankland had taken to labelling his Dick, Kerr girls as 'world champions', so the opening match of the tour would be a trial of strength between 'France' and 'England'.

Dick, Kerr Ladies, of course, represented England. 'France' was partly Fémina, stiffened by guest players from other Paris clubs, including Madeleine Bracquemond. Frankland planned to stage ten matches across England, Scotland and Northern Ireland, This was not just 'business as usual'. It was a major enterprise and something of a gamble, intended to re-awaken public interest in women's football and get back to the glory days of 1920-21.

Alfred Frankland had influential backers for the 1925 tour. Major Cecil Kent, who had lent his voice to protests against the FA ruling in 1921, had a central role, especially by involving the Shipwrecked Mariners Society as the charitable organisation that would be the focus of fundraising for good causes. With the help of the Shipwrecked Mariners Society secretary, Fred Howarth, Major Kent provided invaluable influence and administrative assistance in support of the tour.

Alfred Frankland was particularly keen to maximise the impact of the first game by his well-tried formula of saturation publicity through the press, local advertising and cinema newsreels. There was also a familiar emphasis on the fundraising for post-war charities that would be generated by the match. Another well-tried gambit, the celebrity kick-off, was to be by the famous singer and comedian, George Robey.

The venue was hardly worthy of the occasion. Once upon a time, Frankland had staged matches for crowds of 25,000 or more at venues like Goodison Park, home of Everton, Deepdale, home of Preston North End, and St James's Park, Newcastle. Due to the FA ban, those days were gone. The Herne Hill stadium, used mostly for athletics or greyhound racing, held no more than 10,000. There is no official record of the attendance at the France-England game; it was perhaps about 4,000.

Alfred Frankland did his utmost to cause a stir with the opening match at Herne Hill. Both teams were received by the Lord Mayor of London at Mansion House. They were also invited to tea at the Houses of Parliament as guests of the MP for Liverpool Fairfield, Major Sir Benn Jack Brunel Cohen KBE. Major Cohen was keen to support the disabled (he had lost both his legs at the Battle of Passchendaele in 1917) and was a founder of the British Legion. Like that other prominent citizen of Liverpool, Cecil Kent, Major Cohen wanted people to know about the huge sums of money women's football had raised for servicemen's charities since the war, and the part played by Dick, Kerr Ladies in making it happen.

The Liverpool connection was important, not only for the tea party but also for the detailed planning that had gone into the tour. Cecil Kent, who had spoken out in support of women's football at the time of the FA ruling in 1921, played a key role in assisting the 1925 tour. Like Sir Benn Jack Brunel Cohen, Cecil Kent was a founder of the British Legion and a great supporter of war charities. Kent was also a patron of the Shipwrecked Mariners Society, which was the main beneficiary of the tour. The Travelling Secretary of the society, Fred Haworth, provided vital help with the complex arrangements for matches, travel and accommodation. Backing from influential men like Cohen and Kent made significant contributions to the tour's success.

Carmen Pomiès was a key part of the campaign to revitalise women's football. Carmen personified the links between Paris and Preston. Her friendships with Florrie Redford and other Dick, Kerr girls had been close ever since the first French tour of England five years before. More than that, Carmen was already taking on the role of football ambassador, a role that was to become more and more important in the 1930s when Carmen was even more influential as organiser and team manager than as a player. It is clear, for example, that Carmen was observing and learning from the presentational skills deployed by Alfred Frankland. The kiss between the captains before the kick-off that put Florrie and Carmen in the limelight for a

Successes, Scandals and the Fight for Survival: The 1920s

moment in history meant more than was evident to most of those who witnessed it at the time.

It was impossible to sustain the intensity of the publicity lavished on the opening match at Herne Hill, but that was only the first of ten matches planned for the tour; all of them promoted vigorously by local advertising. In one sense, this publicity did indeed succeed in attracting sizable crowds and raising awareness of women's football, at least for a time. But it was covering up underlying problems, especially the lack of structures such as regular leagues or annual competitions. Even so, the launch of the 1925 tour made a strong statement. Dick, Kerr/England won that eventful opening match 4-3, though the result mattered less than the occasion. The teams then journeyed north and the French team received a grand welcome when they arrived once again at Preston's Bull and Royal Hotel.

The games in the North were competitive. DKL won 3-2 at Padiham near Burnley and 4-1 at Mellor near Blackburn, before a 2-2 draw at Fallowfield, Manchester. The French XI finally won a match, 2-1 at Hyde. The show then moved on to the West of Scotland for a close, exciting game at Rugby Park, Kilmarnock, watched by 2,000 spectators and raising £2,000 in aid of the Shipwrecked Mariners Fund, followed next day by a game at Dumfries.

The match at Kilmarnock was significant because it took place at the stadium of the local men's league team, Kilmarnock FC. Clubs in Scotland, it seemed, were willing to allow women's teams to use their grounds, cheerfully ignoring the ban imposed by the English Football Association in 1921. The match at Dumfries was notable because Carmen played as goalkeeper, just as she had done on the North America tour in 1922. The pace of the 1925 tour did not slacken; next up was a sea crossing to Ireland, to play matches in Belfast and Dublin.

The visit to Ireland was a significant venture at an important time. The Partition of Ireland, bringing peace after the Irish War of Independence and bitter civil war, had been finalised only three years before. It was hoped the French tour would aid the growth of women's football in both the Protestant North and the Catholic South and spread international goodwill. The outcomes were mixed. The match in Belfast was a notable success. It was played at a major stadium, was well attended and put on an exciting game that was in the balance until the last few minutes when Dick, Kerr Ladies got their second goal. But the Dublin game never took place, banned at the last moment after pressure from above. The decision of the authorities in the Irish Free State to force cancellation of the match arranged for Dublin reflected the latent hostility to women's football that was entrenched in socially conservative Catholic societies. Similar trends had blocked the women's game in Spain and Argentina.

These two outcomes reflected both the groundswell of latent support for women's football and how vulnerable it was when prevented from playing at top-level venues with good pitches and space for large crowds. The match in Belfast was proudly advertised as French Ladies v Dick, Kerr's Famous XI, to take place at Belfast's most important stadium, Windsor Park. Those interested in attending were urged to take advantage of special excursion tickets to Belfast from stations all over Northern Ireland. In contrast, Belfast newspapers announced gloomily the cancellation of the scheduled game in Dublin and bemoaned the formidable barriers holding back equality for women in the Catholic South.

BAN ON LADY FOOTBALLERS
French XI Cannot Play in Dublin

The censoring of posters, films, jazz, dancing, silk stockings and bobbed hair are some of the activities of the Free State Purity League. The latest development is a ban on lady footballers, consequently the French Ladies Football Team, who delighted Belfast football enthusiasts with a brilliant exhibition of Ladies' soccer, cannot play in Dublin, as all playing grounds are forbidden them. The Southern Church holds pronounced views on the subject of ladies' attire, and also have the opinion that football is not a woman's game.

The impact of the venture in the North was positive. The 1925 tour was followed by a surge of interest in women's football in Belfast, spearheaded by an authentic star footballer and charismatic local personality, Mary Ann Seaton, universally known as 'Big Molly'. Carmen and her French teammates were going to see a lot of 'Big Molly' in the future, on their tours in 1932 and 1936.

The 1925 tour ended with two final matches, at Chorley, near Preston, and back again to London for a farewell match at Herne Hill. In each of these games, Dick, Kerr Ladies scored six goals. Unsurprisingly, the French squad was by then very tired and thinking of home. In the nine matches played, 'France' had won one, drawn two and lost six. Carmen had been at the heart of everything about this tour, as captain, leader, organiser and interpreter, not to mention emergency goalkeeper in Dumfries and scorer of half of the goals by her team.

In many ways, the French tour had achieved success. Advertising had been thorough and effective. Links with local dignitaries had been cordial. Most games were well attended in spite of the obstructionist effects of the FA ban on the use of officially-recognised grounds. The tradition of French teams on tour in Britain was given renewed impetus; there were to be many more such tours in the 1930s.

A postcard from 1925 exemplifies Alfred Frankland's flair for showmanship, not to say exaggeration. Its boastful caption read:

THE FAMOUS DICK KERR INTERNATIONAL LADIES AFC:

WORLD CHAMPIONS 1917-1925

RAISED OVER £10 000 FOR EX-SERVICEMEN, HOSPITALS AND POOR CHILDREN

WINNERS OF 7 SILVER CUPS AND 3 SETS OF GOLD MEDALS.

But the reality was quieter. The fame of Frankland's beloved team was transient. The 1925 tour was not a launchpad for a new surge of women's football. Obstructionism against women playing football remained powerful and pervasive. The structural problems relating to organisation, finance and suitable venues for staging matches were still present. From 1926, for Dick, Kerr Ladies and a relative handful of women's teams in Britain, the game was managing little more than survival as a summer sport.

For Carmen, the game was still very much alive. League football in Paris was still going, with Fémina its perennially dominant team. 1926 was when Carmen broke through into the France national team to play her first official full internationals against Belgium. These were important contests. By the mid-1920s, Brussels, especially its top club Atalante, was catching up with Paris and Preston as one of the powerhouses of women's football. The first 'real' internationals between France and Belgium had been inaugurated in 1924.

At that time Fémina and other leading clubs were in dispute with the FFSF. Carmen, like several other leading contenders for selection, was left on the sidelines. In April 1926, however, Carmen was an obvious choice for her national team. She was outstanding in trial matches, for the Probables against the Possibles, and played midfield in a 1-0 win over Belgium in Brussels-Molenbeek. From then on, Carmen played in almost every France-Belgium match until they came to an end in 1937.

1926 was a good year for Carmen. In May, she and Fémina won the French Cup again, 1-0 after extra time against Clodo. In June, Fémina won the league title for the third time in four seasons, defeating Les Cadettes in the final. 1927 was a good year, too. Carmen played again for France against Belgium in Paris. This time Belgium won 2-1, with both goals scored by Jenny Toitgans. (Carmen got revenge for the 1927 defeat. A year later, again in Paris, France won by 6-0. Carmen scored three).

Like Carmen, Jenny was an athlete as well as a footballer. She competed in the discus at the 1928 Olympics in Amsterdam.

Carmen and Jenny became friends. They played against each other many times. Jenny would later take part in the Belgian tour of England in 1934, with Carmen playing a key role as go-between ensuring smooth relations with Alfred Frankland and Preston football.

In January 1928, Carmen was elected as one of three vice-presidents at Fémina. It was a sign of her leadership qualities on and off the football pitch. In her third international, a 4-2 win over Belgium in Brussels-Schaerbeek, Carmen captained her country for the first time. Fémina kept on winning, clinching a sixth Championnat de France with a 4-1 win over Dunlop. But this relentless tide of success for Fémina and for Carmen herself could not hide the fact that women's football in France still faced instability and uncertainty. In 1927 and 1928 the simmering conflict between Alice Milliat and Violette Morris was once again in the headlines. The dispute was not directly about football but, nonetheless, it cast a dark shadow over the game.

Violette Morris carried controversy with her wherever she went. Violette was already a distinctive, larger-than-life personality even before she was at the heart of the *Affaire Olympique,* the great 'scandal match' of 1923 that led to a feud with her former mentor, Alice Milliat. The feud crossed over into athletics, which was Mme Milliat's chief concern, because even in her thirties Violette was still one of the best javelin throwers anywhere. The trouble was that Violette, especially since her divorce in 1923, pursued an increasingly flamboyant lesbian lifestyle. The sporting authorities regarded her as a dangerous embarrassment.

In 1927, Alice Milliat pushed the sports federation into revoking Violette's registration as an athlete. This effectively banned Violette from taking part in the 1928 Olympics, to be held in Amsterdam. The next Olympics was scheduled for Los Angeles in 1932, so Amsterdam would be to all intents and purposes Violette's last chance. Violette fought back. There were angry public statements, newspaper articles, a long-running lawsuit, that lasted into 1929. It did not do Violette any good and, because she was still one of the best female footballers in France, the affair harmed the standing of the women's game. Alice Milliat's commitment to football weakened even more.

In 1929, another of Carmen's famous football contemporaries was placed in the limelight by a short silent movie, *La Femme et le Sport* (Woman and Sport) which presented Madeleine Bracquemond as a star in any and all sports: gymnastics, hurdles, javelin, football, rugby, single sculls, tennis, golf, fencing, ice skating, horse riding, riding a motorcycle, driving a racing car and piloting an aeroplane. The film makes a striking impression because Madeleine was indeed a fine-looking woman and a gifted athlete. Then again, it is sometimes unintentionally hilarious. In golf, 'Mado' makes an impressive swing but completely misses the ball; in single sculls the energy of her rowing is impressive but the boat goes every which way but straight.

As for female equality, the messages put across by the film are very contradictory. Yes, the film portrays a flattering image of a sporting wonder woman, but it begins with Madeleine in the Bois de Boulogne, stylishly dressed, accompanied by a little dog. It ends with her even more elegantly attired in twinset and pearls, showing off her skills in needle-point. It is clear from *La Femme et le Sport* that in 1929 the advance of women toward equality through sport still had a long way to go.

As the 1920s came to an end, women's football in France, and even more so elsewhere, was facing once again a long hard fight against powerful social and political currents that would become stronger during the 1930s. It was also clear that Carmen Pomiès, midfielder, goalscorer, goalkeeper, captain, vice-president, friend to most of the best female players in Europe, would be on the front line of the fight.

Chapter 6

Keeping the Flame Alive: The 1930s

'Carmen Pomiès was the glue holding together women's football in Europe in the interwar years'.

(Steve Bolton, 2020)

A photograph from 1936, showing Carmen Pomiès with the Lord Mayor of Belfast at a reception for the French women's football team, symbolises her role as a roving ambassador for women's football in the 1930s. It's a role Carmen took on many times, cementing football alliances from Paris to Preston, from Brussels to Belfast. No longer was Carmen a promising young player, or 'just' an influential captain; she was a leader, an organiser and influencer.

By the early 1930s, the women's game badly needed such a champion. There was still, all across Europe, a deep pool of potential enthusiasm. Lots of young women and girls were keen to play. It was not difficult to attract an audience. But the forces of opposition and ridicule seemed stronger than ever. Too often, flurries of interest and involvement petered out because of organisational failings, or were crushed by hostile forces of social conservatism.

In the summer of 1928, for example, a 'football event' in Oslo, capital city of Norway, sparked a lot of attention and publicity. Crown Prince Olaf carried out the celebrity kick-off. Star quality was added by the presence of Norway's most famous sporting icon, the ice-skating world champion Sonja Henie. Sadly, there was no systematic follow-up to exploit the public attention aroused by the tournament.

In 1930, Lotte Specht, a young butcher's daughter in Frankfurt-am-Main, launched a lively campaign in local newspapers to promote an organised league for women's football. Lotte attracted plenty of enthusiastic recruits but she also provoked a furious backlash from local conservatives, above all her own father. Lotte was forced to give up her football dreams. She became a travelling cabaret singer-dancer instead.

Even in France, where women's football had provided a model of success in the 1920s, there were difficult challenges ahead. Already, there had been internal disputes between leading clubs about league structures and governance. The game had been hurt by the storms of adverse publicity hanging over Violette Morris. Then came the Wall Street Crash and the slow, cumulative effects of the Great Depression.

The depression strengthened social and political forces of anti-feminism, reinforcing ideas about the role of women as mothers or mothers-to-be, about jobs 'belonging' to men who were the breadwinners. Married women found it harder to obtain a job, or keep it if they already had one. An existing social agenda that attacked women in sport as 'unwomanly' gained new momentum.

In this context, the French football tour of Britain in the summer of 1932 assumed special significance, both for the tourists and for the home countries. Like the 1925 tour, it was a conscious effort to fight back, to rekindle the enthusiasm and uplift that had pushed the women's game forward in the early 1920s. Carmen was ready for the responsibility, determined to keep the fight for women's football alive.

1930 began well for Carmen. In April she played her fifth full international in Antwerp, a comfortable 4-0 victory over Belgium. In May Fémina won yet another Championnat de France, Carmen's seventh league title, though winning it was a close-run thing. Fémina were lucky to get a 1-1 draw in their play-off match against CASG de Marseille. In the replay, Fémina were losing 1-2 in the second half but then rallied to win 4-2. Carmen scored one of the goals in the late comeback.

There was still turbulence at the top in French women's football, with wrangling between and within the leading clubs. In January 1931, Carmen suddenly resigned as vice-president of Fémina. After long debate in the club committee, it was decided Carmen would be re-appointed at the next annual general meeting. The episode revealed how important Carmen was to the fortunes of football in France, but also showed the continuing tensions and uncertainties that were destabilising it. On the pitch, it was business as usual in 1931. Carmen captained France against Belgium in March, playing centre-forward and scoring one of the goals in a 4-0 win at Douai. Four weeks later, she led Fémina to an eighth national league title, beating Les Cadettes 1-0 in the final at Montbéliard.

This was also a significant period in Carmen's life away from football. In the summer of 1930, she was in Czechoslovakia for the third Women's World Games. Alice Milliat and the FSFI (Fédération Sportive Féminine Internationale) had always hoped that women's athletics would achieve full recognition at the Olympics but, despite her persistent campaigning, female participation had been negligible in the 1924 Paris Olympics and only five women's events had been grudgingly included at the Amsterdam Games in 1928. This meant that Milliat and the FSFI had to put special emphasis on the Women's World Games.

The World Games had begun in Paris in 1922, then proudly proclaimed as the Women's Olympiad, but pressure from the male-dominated IOC (International Olympic Committee) forced a change of name. So, in Gothenburg in 1926, Prague in 1930 and London in 1934, the title had to be Women's World Games. Carmen was there in 1922, heavily involved in the Paris Games. She was probably there in Gothenburg in 1926. We know from what she later told the Rochester *Democrat & Chronicle* in 1947, that she was at the Stadion Letna in Prague along with 200 athletes from seventeen countries for the third World Games in September 1930.

By this time, Carmen was approaching thirty years of age. Her days competing for medals in the javelin were far in the past; she was involved perhaps as helping out with training, or just as cheerleader for the competitors. Her presence in Prague reflects her boundless enthusiasm for sport and also her commitment to the cause of equality.

Whatever their differences over the administration of women's football, Carmen and Mme Milliat were on the same page when it came to fighting for acceptance of women in sport.

Carmen's trip to Prague also offers a reminder of her fortunate freedom to travel and to follow her interests wherever they took her. It was the same for her siblings. Hélène was busy as a writer and would-be intellectual, a committed member of the left-wing Association of Revolutionary Writers, though she was hardly earning a fortune in the process. Little is known of Yvonne except that she was a talented pianist, though not at a level where she could pay her own way. The exception was Georges Pomiès, who was on his way to fame and fortune.

Georges had had some early success as a *chanteur* in the clubs and nightspots of Montparnasse but, from about 1925, he made a bigger impact as an expressive modern dancer. In 1928, Georges's career really took off when the film director Jean Renoir, a rising star of French cinema, chose Georges as one of the three lead actors for his silent movie *Tire au Flanc* (The Sad Sack). Suddenly, the Pomiès sisters had a famous film-star brother to be proud of. In 1930 they could go to the cinema to see him star as 'Alfred the Knight' in *La Joie d'une Heure* (Hour of Happiness). It was followed in 1931 by another film, *Anatole.*

Georges was even more famous for his artistry in modern dance in an era when exotic 'interpretive' dancers were all the rage. In Weimar, Berlin, Anita Berber attracted admiration and notoriety for her daring and often scandalous dance routines. In Paris, the great name was the Black American dancer Josephine Baker, famed for her skimpy and suggestive 'banana' costume. Many modern dancers of the 1920s were, consciously or otherwise, following in the footsteps of the legendary Isadora Duncan, who had pioneered a new style of elaborate and artistic dance choreography in the years before the First World War.

Georges Pomiès had a direct connection with Isadora Duncan, because his long-term dance partner and girlfriend was Lisa

Duncan. Georges and Lisa made a striking pair. Georges was the rising star, considered exceptional for his technical mastery and innovative style. Five years older than Georges, Lisa was already internationally renowned as one of the 'Isadorables', the six young women including Anna Denzler and Margot Jehle who had become the adopted daughters and dance disciples of Isadora Duncan. (It is interesting to speculate how the twenty-first century attitudes of the MeToo movement might have judged the morality, or not, of Isadora Duncan's motives for adopting six young women to be 'clones' of her own artistic persona).

After Isadora Duncan died in 1927, the 'Isadorables' broke up and Lisa formed her partnership with Georges. Born in Dresden, (her birth name was Liesl Milker) Lisa provided the glamour and the famous name, while George provided the cutting-edge imaginative choreography as they acquired a growing reputation in France and around Europe. What heights of fame Georges Pomiès might have gone on to reach if he had not died tragically young in October 1933 can only be guessed at.

The double act between Georges and Lisa put them at the forefront of the cultural scene in Paris. His film career introduced Georges to new friends and contacts in French cinema who invited him into a select inner circle of actors, writers, directors, agents and journalists. Evidently, the Pomiès sisters were introduced to this world, too. We know from their contributions to a 1939 book about Georges that Hélène and Lisa became friends. We also know that Carmen later worked as secretary to one of the great leading ladies of French cinema, Renée Saint-Cyr; it's tempting to believe this might have been related to links first made through Georges.

By 1932, therefore, a halo of success and fulfilment was hanging over the talented Pomiès family. Georges was moving up in the world of arts and culture, poised to enter the age of talking pictures in a new film *Chotard & Cie* (Chotard & Company), directed by Jean Renoir. In his spare time, Georges had aspirations to be a poet and intellectual; it was in 1932 that Hélène got him to join the Association of Revolutionary Writers. And Carmen, captain of France, was ready for new football adventures.

For Carmen, 1932 began as most years did. She captained France again in Brussels, playing midfield in a tight match that ended in a goalless draw. In April, Fémina won the league championship yet again, for the ninth time. Fémina cruised to a 4-0 victory over Dunlop at Valenciennes, with Carmen scoring the fourth goal. But black clouds were already looming over the women's game in France, with infighting in committee rooms between representatives of the leading clubs. One year later, this would culminate in a serious crisis that menaced the survival of women's league football in France.

Another important factor was the introduction of professionalism into men's football. This was orchestrated by Gabriel Hanot and Georges Gambardella, who pushed through a vote for professionalism in July 1930, but its actual system only came into operation for the 1932-33 season. Although this did not have a direct impact on women's football, it strengthened underlying assumptions about football as a game exclusively reserved for men. In the words of Laurence Prudhomme-Poncet in her *Histoire du Football Féminin au XXth Siècle*, 'the official professionalisation of the game in France in 1932 deepened the divide between men's and women's football, which would grow wider as the years passed'.

At the end of July, Carmen set off from Paris for a new tour of England and Northern Ireland. The French team was mostly from Fémina but with a few guest players. The tour was a significant venture because since 1925 there had been no tour of a similar scale and ambition. Just as in England, women's football in France needed renewed energy and momentum. Alfred Frankland knew this. In the winter of 1930, he had received encouraging enquiries from Czechoslovakia about the possibility of taking Preston Ladies to play there. Frankland proposed staging exhibition matches, with a French team to provide the opposition, but the organisational and financial difficulties proved too great and the project did not get off the ground.

It has been claimed there was a French tour to England in the summer of 1931 but this is something of a myth. What actually happened was that the recently-married Madeleine Bracquemond was in England on holiday with her husband, Eugene Jeannot. To honour her return to Preston, Madeleine captained a 'French XI' made up of a few visiting French players and local girls. So the 1932 tour, arranged as usual by the indefatigable Alfred Frankland, was a significant effort to get back to the good old days of the early 1920s. It was a less expensive tour than 1925, yet still an important one. Four matches were to be played against DKL/Preston, two in northern England and two across the Irish Sea, in Belfast and Bangor.

Coming back to play against Dick, Kerr Ladies re-connected Carmen with friends old and new. The familiar faces included Lily Parr and Lizzy Ashcroft. The new blood included Margaret Thornborough, who was not only a key player on the pitch but was later to become Alfred Frankland's assistant manager and a close friend and colleague to Carmen. There was also the traditional Girls Day Out at Blackpool with its wide beach and outdoor swimming pool. Not for the first time, the weather was cool and windy, overcoats required.

One familiar face was missing. Perhaps influenced by her happy experiences on the North America tour eight years before, or perhaps just because of a job opportunity, Florrie Redford had emigrated to Canada in 1930 to pursue her nursing career and begin a new life. For Carmen, Preston without Florrie was something new. Much of her football life had been shaped by playing with and against Florrie and the special bonds of friendship between them. The two would not meet again until 1945. Although they kept in contact through letters and mutual friends, never again would they be the dazzling duo who had shone so brightly in the golden years of women's football from 1920 to 1925.

Both matches in England, as so often happened when French teams played against DKL/Preston, ended in home wins, by 2-0 at Abbeydale Park in Sheffield and 7-2 at Moor Park, Preston, where both Lily Parr and Margaret Thornborough were among the goalscorers. The Preston match was part of a really important occasion. For three days, the whole of Moor Park was taken over by the Lancashire Agricultural Show. Moor Park also had a neat connection with past history. The very first game played by Dick, Kerr Ladies in 1917 had been staged to raise funds for the original Moor Park VAD hospital and thus to help Britain's war effort

There were 202 stands at the 1932 Show, for 150 different classes of animals, but the football match against the French XI was the highlight of the final day, when 18,641 people passed through the turnstiles. People were queuing to get in over an hour before the show opened. Many had travelled far to be there, including busloads from Yorkshire. A crowd estimated between 10,000 and 12,000 watched the football.

Alfred Frankland's showmanship was still alive and well. As the French women ran out before the match, kitted out in blue jerseys, red stockings and black berets, they were welcomed by the Life Guards Brass Band playing the Marseillaise. After two days of relentless rain, the pitch was a quagmire even though heavily sanded and the conditions undoubtedly favoured the home team. Carmen scored one of the French goals, though the result was perhaps less important than the sense of occasion. The success of the 1932 game at Moor Park match made it a model for future showground matches, at Salford in 1933 and at Bolton and Garstang in 1934.

The matches in Northern Ireland were both eventful and important. When the French touring team had played there in 1925, the games were, as was often the case with Dick, Kerr Ladies, exhibition matches by a 'travelling circus' imported from outside the local experience. Since then, however, women's football in Northern Ireland had developed a life of its own, led by an authentic local heroine, Mary Ann Seaton.

'Big Molly' as she was universally known, played a huge part in the rise of women's football in Belfast. Many of the teams were supported by local factories such as the Ropeworks and the Linen Mills, where Molly worked. In 1927, the best women's team in Scotland, Rutherglen, led by their own iconic player Sadie Smith, came to play matches in Belfast, one of them labelled 'Scotland' v 'Ireland'. Rutherglen came again in 1928, playing four matches at Larne, Ballymena, Derry and Belfast. In 1931, teams from Northern Ireland and Scotland played each other in the Isle of Man.

'Big Molly' was indeed big, almost five feet eleven inches tall. If not quite the six-footer of popular legend, Molly was blessed with exceptional physical strength. She played once or twice against men's teams, reputedly leaving a trail of bruised bodies and bruised egos in her wake. The power and aggression of the strongest female players often grew in the popular memory. It has been claimed that Lily Parr was also a six-footer, but this was a myth. Lily was actually five feet eight inches tall, about the same height as Lizzy Ashcroft and Carmen Pomiès. Molly Seaton's presence was guaranteed to double the attendance at any match; the poster for a trial match to select the national team in 1931 announced in bold letters: 'Molly Seaton is a Certain Starter'.

So when the ship bringing the French team from Heysham on the Lancashire coast docked in Belfast early in the morning, there was strong public interest laced with local pride. The games in Belfast and Bangor were significant milestones in the development of the game in Northern Ireland. Carmen was well aware of the symbolic value of these games. She was not merely captain of the touring team but also team manager. Over the years, Carmen had learned much from Alfred Frankland and his clever tricks to attract publicity; Mr Frankland was there in Belfast to give his support. So, too, were some of the DKL girls including Lizzy Ashcroft. The French team was given a reception by the Mayor at City Hall. By happy coincidence, it was possible to add a ceremonial flourish to the occasion, courtesy of the French Navy.

A squadron of four French warships was in Belfast at the time, part of a joint naval exercise. The French players were taken on a tour of the harbour and the French flagship *L'Oise*. The crews of the French ships were given leave to attend the match, while Lieutenant Bertrand Geli of *L'Oise* was in the centre circle with the two captains, Molly and Carmen, for the celebrity kick-off.

The sense of a special football occasion was enhanced by a huge crowd of 15,000 spectators. Famous names in men's football officiated: Mick Hamill as referee, Joe Bambrick and Fred Roberts as linesmen. The game was fiercely contested, with the reputedly glamorous and 'exotic' Frenchwomen proving as physical as the home team. The French XI won a close encounter by 4-3, with both Carmen and Molly among the scorers. But there were casualties. Carmen was injured and missed the second half, an Irish player, Miss Rice, was carried off on a stretcher, and Molly Seaton spent the night at the Royal Victoria Hospital.

Newspapers from Belfast and the mainland were suitably impressed. One report expressed amazement that Solange Manca, the French vice-captain, was not a single girl, as it was automatically assumed all female footballers were, but married, with a child at home, and did not have her husband on the tour to 'look after her'.

Neither Carmen nor Molly was fit to play at Bangor the next day. It was a less dramatic game than in Belfast but a notable day for the Irish team who won 1-0. Miss Collins, the Irish goalkeeper was declared 'woman of the match'. The report in the *Ballymena Observer* noted that the French players were more skilled but that 'both sides looked at home on a football pitch'.

At a civic reception in Bangor, there were gracious little speeches by both Alfred Frankland and the 'impressively multi-lingual' Carmen Pomiès. There was also a sightseeing tour of the Ards peninsula, followed by tea at the Regent Palace Hotel. This was all carefully choreographed, part of a diplomatic mission flying the flag for women's football. New friendships were made, with declarations that the French tour had made the women's game in Northern Ireland stronger and must be followed up by more such tours in the future. Many of these promises would come true but difficult days lay ahead, for the game and for Carmen personally.

1933 began well enough before spiralling down into an *annus horribilis*. Fémina won most of their early-season matches. In April, Carmen played for France once again, as captain, in a 3-1 victory over Belgium in Roubaix. But then the long-standing tensions between the leading clubs and simmering disputes within the FFSF came to a head. At the end of May, the FFSF suddenly announced it was abandoning women's football altogether. The climax of the 1933 season, with the play-off finals for the Parisian championship and the Championnat de France, was abruptly cancelled. What Helge Faller has called 'the long golden era' of French women's football was sliding into muddled, bad-tempered decline.

This crisis made the Preston Connection more important than ever. In August, Carmen led a new French tour of northern England, playing six matches across Lancashire and Yorkshire in just over a week: at Preston, Salford, Hull, York, Buxton and Harrogate. The game at York was against Terry's Athletic Club (Terry's was and still is famous as a producer of chocolate). Fémina won comfortably 5-1. All the other matches were against DKL/Preston and all ended in defeat.

In the game at Hull, Carmen was injured and forced to miss the second half. One year before, Carmen had been injured in the tempestuous game in Belfast and could not play the next match. In sport, of course, injuries can and do happen to anyone at any time but these mishaps were perhaps milestones in Carmen's life in football. Now thirty-two, she was no longer invincible or invulnerable. The injuries were part of her transition from player to leader and organiser. On the pitch, Carmen was one of the most significant players in women's football in the interwar years; off the field, she was to be perhaps even more important.

Although less ambitious than previous ventures in 1920, 1925 and 1932, the 1933 tour was a success, especially in providing continuity to the links between Paris and Preston. Then, as soon as Carmen was back home again, she was involved in the fightback to rescue the women's game in France. Fémina and other leading clubs broke away from previous affiliations and founded a new football federation, the FFFF. Complicated plans were put in place for a new-look league competition for the 1933-34 season. Such plans, however, could not disguise the fact that women's football in France was fighting to survive.

In the autumn of 1933, the stress and anxiety of the struggle to keep the flame of women's football alive was completely overshadowed by personal tragedy. On 7 October, Carmen's beloved younger brother Georges died, aged thirty-one, at a sanatorium in Dreux, a historic town fifty miles west of Paris.

Georges was at the height of his fame in 1933, both as a dancer and as a film actor. A magazine review of Georges performing in partnership with Lisa Duncan on tour in Belgium in March gives an insight into Georges the 'master of modern dance technology'. The reviewer was evidently a purist about modernity, being mightily impressed by Georges but much less so with Lisa's romantic, old-fashioned style, considered too much like that of her adoptive mother Isadora. (Regardless of the hostile views of the critic, Lea Daan, audiences thought Lisa was wonderful):

> What we were allowed to admire as a real modern dance technology was done by Pomiès. This gifted artist's dances are masculine, stylish and expressive, with rhythm and movement sensitively matched to the music. We can mention 'Tennis', performed without music but wonderfully conveying the moves familiar to those who play the game, and 'Sonata' where the interpretation was virile and temperamental.
>
> [Lea Daan, *Georges Pomiès & Lisa Duncan*]

In June, the Pomiès sisters could go to the cinema in Paris to see Georges's latest film. Not long before, they had been able to bask in the reflected glory of his leading role in *Chotard & Cie,* directed by the great Jean Renoir and starring the much-loved comic actor, Fernand Charpin, with Jeanne Boitel - and Georges Pomiès. Now his latest film was out, *Ciboulette* (Chives), a comedy-musical set in the markets of Les Halles in the 1860s. But Georges was dangerously ill with gastroparesis or perhaps stomach cancer. Within a few months, Georges was dead.

Although the loss of Georges was a cruel shock for his three sisters, it was not a bolt from the blue; Georges had fallen ill in April 1933 and spent weeks in and out of hospital. What we know about it comes mostly from Hélène, who edited a book in tribute to his memory. *Georges Pomiès: Danser C'est Vivre* (To Dance is to Live) was published in 1939, with recollections of Georges from thirteen people who knew him, including Lisa Duncan and Hélène herself. To read Hélène's account is to realise how important Georges was to her, and how protective of him she felt. The book reveals how Georges suffered from ill-health in childhood, how he was sensitive and funny as well as talented, and that he died of 'complications after surgical interventions'.

Hélène's chapter on Georges is suffused with the grief and loss felt by his sisters. Remarkably, it is also the only known documentary record of Hélène, Yvonne and Carmen being together in the same time and place, though there must have been hundreds of others. Fourteen years later, in an interview for the *Democrat & Chronicle* newspaper in Rochester NY, Carmen's words about Georges show equally her pride in his talents and how much she still missed him.

Life had to go on. By Christmas, the inaugural FFFF league championship was under way. In April 1934, Carmen played for France against Belgium in Paris but, for once, was not on the winning side; Belgium won 2-0. Later that month, Fémina became champions yet again (their tenth consecutive league title) after beating Dunlop 2-1 in the final. But all was not well with women's football in France.

In the twenty-first century, in the age of Trump, Brexit, MeToo and 'cancel culture', the term culture wars is thrown around the worlds of journalism and social media in the apparent belief that culture wars are a recent phenomenon. But culture wars have run through history. The Reformation, the English Civil War, the French Revolution were all, amongst other things, culture wars. So was the rise of right-wing political movements in France in the 1930s. Deep divisions between Left and Right were part and parcel of the French Third Republic from its beginnings. Powerful interests in French society had never accepted the agenda of republican democracy and there was an ever-present political, religious and social backlash, mostly from the Right. This was the France of the 1930s. Women's football was in the firing line.

With the onset of the Great Depression, the anti-feminist backlash was becoming louder and more visceral, emboldened by the rise of right-wing ideologies elsewhere in Europe. Ultimately, after military defeat in 1940, German occupation and the installation of the Pétainist Vichy regime, the backlash would take over France completely. Vichy's racist, socially conservative, anti-feminist slogan was 'Travail, Famille, Patrie' ('Work, Family, Nation').

On 6 February 1934, France's culture war erupted into violence. In January 2021, the great journalist-historian Neal Ascherson sent a letter to the editor of the *Guardian* seeking parallels in France's past to the storming of the Capitol in Washington:

> That day in Paris in 1934, rightwing crowds, fuelled by antisemitic fantasies and fascist myths, tried to storm the Assemblée Nationale and overthrow parliamentary democracy. They were beaten off (16 people died), but they remembered that day as a moment of patriotic sacrifice, and the boast that "I was there on 6 February" inspired the ultra-right collaborators in the murderous Milice, who hunted down resisters and Jews during the Nazi occupation a few years later.

Neal Ascherson's letter was coloured by the wisdom of hindsight. Unlike Washington DC in January 2021, the right-wing mobs milling around the Place de la Concorde in February 1934 did not actually get inside the Assembly. Nobody was killed. The rioters came from disparate movements old and new. Many were followers of Charles Maurras and *Action Française,* whose motives were Catholic, monarchist and anti-Semitic, harking back to the days of the anti-Dreyfusards thirty years before. Others had newer pro-Fascist sympathies. There was no coup d'état but the government was panicked into resigning. The foundations of republican democracy were weakened. None of this had any direct connection to women's football but anti-feminism was a strong current in the backlash from the Right in 1934 and afterwards. Associations campaigning for votes for women steadily lost support. Fighting back against these hostile forces required courage, persistence and resilience.

For Carmen, there was always the summer tour of Britain to keep up the fight. In August 1934, however, it was a Belgian team, not a French one, that crossed the Channel. Carmen was central to this tour as a link between Brussels and Preston, helping the flow of correspondence to and from Alfred Frankland and acting as translator for the entire tour. In August, the Belgian team took the Hook of Holland & Antwerp Continental boat train to Harwich and London. At Liverpool Street station, a Preston reception committee, Alfred Frankland and his trusty lieutenants Lizzy Ashcroft and Margaret Thornborough, was there to meet them. Carmen was there, too, central to the whole enterprise as interpreter and go-between.

With typical bravado, Frankland had been promoting his Dick, Kerr/Preston Ladies team as 'world champions'. Advance publicity made much of the fact that the Belgian tour party was virtually the Belgium national team that had just won a famous victory over France (and Carmen) in Paris. So their tour was to be a trial of strength to decide which team could call itself 'world champions'.

It was a hectic tour, with matches almost every day. Most were in northern England, close to DKL/Preston's home territory: Halifax in Yorkshire, Bolton, Morecambe and Accrington in Lancashire, New Brighton and Widnes on Merseyside. In between, there was a lengthy journey to South Wales to play a game at Tredegar near Newport. This game attracted huge public interest, watched by a crowd of 15,000.

Because Carmen was on hand, and also her friends Andrée Gauckler and Marie-Louise Derriot, the opportunity was seized to arrange a special friendly match. The three French visitors combined with Dick, Kerr Ladies reserve players to form a 'French XI' at the agricultural show in Garstang, a small market town just north of Preston. Carmen scored three times but ended up on the losing side, four goals against seven, in what seems to have been a light-hearted game played more for fun than competitive pride.

As for proving who was the best team in the world, DKL/Preston won most of the matches but the Belgians secured a prestigious victory at Bolton, winning 2-1 in torrential rain that turned the pitch into a mudbath. Alfred Frankland claimed it was the first defeat his team had suffered in more than 300 games since losing to the French at Stamford Bridge in 1920, but perhaps this says more about his flair for hyperbole than strict statistical accuracy. Overall, the tour was declared a great success. Plans were made for a reciprocal tour to Belgium. These plans did not materialise, though the Belgians would tour England again in 1939.

Carmen may also have been in London in 1934, to attend the Women's World Games, at White City stadium, though not as a competitor. Athletics was another aspect of women's sport that was going backwards. By this time, it was already clear there would be no place for women athletes at the 'Nazi Olympics' in Berlin in 1936. The fifth Women's World Games, scheduled for Vienna in 1938 would never happen either.

For Carmen, being at the heart of the Belgian tour and re-connecting with her football comrades in Preston was a happy interlude in a year of tribulations. Back home in France, the women's game was still going through turbulent times. When the new season began in December, fewer teams than ever were involved. To make matters worse, Fémina became embroiled in an ugly dispute with their main rivals, Dunlop, which effectively ruined the entire 1934-35 season.

The cause of controversy, as so often, was Violette Morris. By 1934, Violette's public persona was more scandalous than ever. Even at forty-one, she decided to make a comeback in football and joined Dunlop. Fémina protested furiously. The federation ruled that Violette was eligible to play. Fémina refused to back down and announced that the club would default in all games against Dunlop in the coming season.

The turmoil at home made the Paris-Preston connection more important than ever for the survival of the game. In April 1935, DKL/Preston set off for France for their first tour there since 1920. They were sent on their way by the Mayor of Preston, who gave each player a sprig of white heather for good luck. This did not have the hoped-for effect. The main match, in Paris, was a decisive French victory by 5-2. Perhaps the absence of Lily Parr helps to explain this rare defeat, though the DKL team included stalwart friends of Carmen such as Lizzy Ashcroft and Margaret Thornborough.

In August, the French girls were back in England again for their annual summer visit. Carmen captained 'Team France' in seven matches against DKL/Preston during the two-week tour: at West Ham (London), Coventry, Pontypool (South Wales), Chester, Liverpool, Leyland and Barrow-in-Furness. The French team managed one win and one draw in between five defeats. It was a less crowded schedule than the Belgian tour the year before. It seems also that Carmen stayed behind in Preston afterwards. She even found herself playing cricket.

The focus on cricket during the 1935 tour was a new departure. For example, the match at Coventry on 6 August was advertised as part of a 'double-header', a Grand Holiday Attraction in which the football followed on from a cricket match, with Marks and Spencers Ladies of Coventry taking on the combined English and French Ladies. We do not know how many French Ladies apart from Carmen took part. Later, back in Preston, Carmen was part of a cricket team captained by Margaret Thornborough against a selection from the Preston women's cricket league. As she was in most sports, Lily Parr was one of the best players.

The cricket matches were reminders that these close footballing friends were multi-talented sportswomen. Between 1935 and 1937, in fact, Lily Parr spent far less time on football than she did playing cricket and hockey. In cricket, Lily finished high in the league batting averages, while local newspapers were full of reports about Lily's amazing strength and skill with hockey stick in hand. As for Carmen, it was further proof, if any were needed, that she was up for any game you might care to think of.

That summer was one of Carmen's happiest times in England. Snapshots of Carmen's life 'off-duty' from football show her playing crown green bowls with Margaret Thornborough, walking in the park side-by-side with Lizzy Ashcroft, or simply messing about in the park with her friends. One photograph shows a giggling pyramid of five of them, including Lizzy, Margaret, Lily and Andrée Gauckler: it's a bit of a shock to realise that the pyramid consisted not of teenagers but mature women in their thirties. Carmen did not feature in the photograph but that may well have been because she was the one holding the camera.

Such snapshots reinforce the impression that Carmen felt as much at ease in Preston as she did in France. The friendships in Carmen's life we know about were almost all linked to sport. She had been playing against, playing with and living among the Preston girls for much of the preceding fifteen years. 'Posh girl from Paris' Carmen may have been but there was something about her pals from Lancashire that had a special appeal. How far this was due to personalities or how far Carmen's visits to northern England were an escape from things in France she felt uncomfortable about is hard to judge. But Preston was indeed 'home' for Carmen.

In April 1936, Carmen played her last full international for France, a 3-1 victory over Belgium in Paris. Carmen scored all three goals. But the women's game in France was shrinking. The 1935-36 league season was low-key with fewer clubs involved. The main football events of the year were two tours in Britain, first to South and South West England in June and then in August, back to northern England and another visit to Belfast.

The first tour was propagandistic, taking the game to new venues and new audiences. The French XI played, as usual against DKL/Preston, at Southsea Common near Portsmouth, at Ryde on the Isle of Wight and then at Bristol, Kettering and Southampton. In a sixth match, at Yeovil in Somerset, a combined Anglo-French team won 3-0 against Yeovil Ladies.

In the August tour, the French took on DKL/Preston at Ripley in Derbyshire, and in Lancashire towns not far from Preston: Blackpool, Bacup and Nelson. Then Carmen and her team crossed the Irish Sea once more to play against the Northern Ireland national team. The French got a warm and friendly reception in Belfast, with a civic reception, lots of coverage in the press and lavish hospitality. As in 1932, the two captains were Carmen and 'Big Molly' Seaton. Both were still dominant players and team leaders, but they were now battle-scarred veterans. This was the last time they would challenge each other on the football pitch.

The walls of history were closing in on women's football in France. In January 1937, Carmen played her last-ever championship match for Fémina. She scored the winning goal but it was a hollow triumph. The league season collapsed into chaos, with financial problems and many cancelled matches. Carmen kept on fighting. In August she led another tour of England not, for once, as player and captain but as team manager, in charge of a weak, inexperienced team with only a few league players alongside many high-school girls. They played nine matches in the Midlands and the North but lost all of them, most by big scores. The 'best' result was a 2-4 defeat in South Wales, at Pontypridd, the worst was by thirteen goals to nil.

These were hard times for women's football in France. In her *History of French Women's Football in the Twentieth Century*, Laurence Prudhomme-Poncet chooses 1937 as the end date for the story of the game from its beginnings in 1917. One striking phrase in the book pronounces: 'It was in 1933 that women's football in France condemned itself to die'. The political divisions and culture wars in France that were the backdrop to this slow death of women's football were deeper than ever.

From the summer of 1936, France was governed by the *Front Populaire* (Popular Front), a left-wing coalition headed by Leon Blum. The Popular Front included communists and radical socialists and a few liberal democrats. Its followers included pacifists, like Blum himself, and social reformers. There was a furious right-wing backlash against Blum's government, from Catholic social conservatives, monarchists and a growing number of Frenchmen who displayed fascist sympathies for the social policies of Mussolini's Italy.

Looking back, many similarities can be discerned between the French Right in the 1930s and the anti-Dreyfusards at the turn of the twentieth century. Looking forward, it is easy to recognise social and political forces that would underpin the collaborationist Vichy regime established under Marshal Pétain and Pierre Laval in 1940. Looking sideways at the political situation in Europe meant, above all, the Spanish Civil War. Blum's Popular Front was heavily influenced by pacifism and by fear of Fascism. There was fellow-feeling for the Spanish republic and its fight for survival against the military revolt launched by Francisco Franco in July 1936 but also fear of the backing Francoism was receiving from Fascist Italy and Nazi Germany and fear that Spain's war might spill over into France.

In these dangerous times, there were many more important things going on than the struggle to keep women's football alive, and there were many reasons beyond culture wars why the game in France was subsiding, but the hostile social and political context was indeed a major factor.

Carmen was less overtly political than her sister, Hélène, but the evidence suggests that Carmen leaned towards the Popular Front. Three of the ministers in Leon Blum's government were women, in a country that did not allow them to vote until 1946. The fight for equality in France would not be won by supporting the enemies of the Popular Front. As for Hélène, there was little doubt about her political stance. Early in 1937, Hélène's name appeared proudly on the title page of *Nouvelles Espagnoles* (Stories from Spain), a book sympathetic to Spanish culture edited by a left-wing French-Spanish intellectual Jean Cassou and translated from Spanish into French by Hélène. The preface was by Henri Barbusse, a Communist philosopher.

The situation in Spain got steadily worse during 1937. In April, worldwide shock and condemnation were aroused when Guernica, a city in the Basque region of northern Spain, was destroyed by German bombers. with horrific civilian deaths. In June, the city of Bilbao was overrun by Francoist forces. In August, while Carmen was guiding her young footballers through their tour of England, the Papacy recognised Franco's rebel regime as the legitimate government of Spain. Public opinion in France was bitterly divided between fear of Fascism and fear of Communism.

As the Spanish republic slid towards final defeat, Britain and France stuck to a policy of non-intervention, even though Fascist Italy and Nazi Germany poured troops and resources into Spain to support the Francoists, while the Soviet Union sent troops to defend the Republic. France was uncertain how to deal with the rise of militarism in Germany and fears that Hitler would use force to overturn the post-war peace. Divisions in France intensified, not only between Left and Right but also within the Left. It was amidst this tense political and international situation at the end of 1937 and early in 1938 that the full extent of the crisis facing women's football in France became stark. There was no league football in the 1937-38 season, only ad-hoc friendly matches. Then scandal returned to haunt the game. Violette Morris was charged with murder.

By late 1937, Violette was achieving new peaks of notoriety. Already widely known for her vast size, her mannish dress, her boxing matches, her racing cars and her well-publicised lesbian affairs, Violette was now openly espousing pro-Fascist political sympathies. There were even accusations she was a German spy, though there is no evidence for this. Then, at Christmas 1937, Violette shot dead Joseph Le Cam, who had come to *La Mouette,* the houseboat where she lived, brandishing a knife and accusing Violette of 'stealing' his girlfriend. After an angry confrontation, Violette pulled out a pistol and fired four shots. Le Cam died later in hospital.

The Violette Morris murder case caused a public sensation, with lurid press coverage, Violette went on trial in March 1938 but was acquitted on the grounds of self-defence. Carmen knew Violette better than most. Carmen had competed against her for medals in the javelin, shared bruising encounters on football pitches, not least in the 'scandal match' against Olympique in 1923, and witnessed at first hand the never-ending rows about Violette in the federations running women's athletics and football. Carmen had good reasons to respect Violette, as a feminist, an athlete, a fine footballer and an authentic war-heroine at the Battle of Verdun in 1916. Carmen also had reasons to resent Violette as the source of the stream of scandals and embarrassments that inflicted serious collateral damage on French women's football. Violette's scandalous behaviour was not the main cause of the problems facing women's football in 1938, but she was certainly no help, either.

1938 was the year France hosted the FIFA World Cup. Few people in France had paid much attention when France, captained by Alex Villaplane, competed in the inaugural World Cup, in Uruguay in 1930. By the time of the next tournament, hosted by and won by Italy in 1934 the World Cup was becoming a significant event, and French football had gone professional. When France hosted the 1938 World Cup, it aroused great public attention. France fielded a strong team with credible hopes of winning the trophy. The climax for France was a cataclysmic quarter-final in Paris, won by Italy, who went on to win the final. The defeat in Paris led to French protests about murky Italian tactics and supposed political pressure on the referee. While all eyes were on the men's team, women's football in France was dying quietly, unnoticed.

The tide was running against women's football elsewhere in Europe, too. In Italy, there had been a surge of enthusiasm for the game, led by Brunilde Amodeo. Brunilde (her name is reliable evidence her parents were opera-lovers) and her sister led the way in playing and organising football for girls in Milan. Despite, or perhaps because of, the eager support for football from women and girls, Achille Starace, Mussolini's National Fascist Party Secretary, denounced football as 'unwomanly, endangering the reproductive power of women's bodies'. For Fascist ideologists, some sports were good for women and girls but football was strictly for men.

In Austria, too, a promising revival of women's football in the 1930s was cut short, blown away by adverse social and political winds. From 1934, the game in Austria, which had flourished briefly in the early 1920s, was revived under the leadership of Edith Klinger, whose energy, determination and organising abilities helped to establish a thriving network of football clubs centred on Vienna.

Edith's role was not as a player but as a referee. She gained her qualifications from the ÖFB (Austrian Football Federation) and began officiating at matches, men's as well as women's, until the ÖFB realised the implications. There was a rush of enthusiasm for *Damenfussball*, helped along by Vienna's most influential sports journalist, Willi Schmieger. An excellent 2020 book, *Eine Klasse für Sich* (A Class of Their Own) by Helge Faller & Matthias Marschik, paints a vivid picture of how well the women's game in Austria was developing. The women's game spread from Austria, to Czechoslovakia, Hungary, Yugoslavia and Poland. There were plans to set up a Mitropa Cup for women's football in Central Europe.

But Edith Klinger and her football friends were living in the wrong times. They faced a tidal wave of hostility from the ÖFB, from social conservatives, from the Church and from a rising right-wing patriotic movement, the *Fatherland Front*. Already under heavy pressure, the women's game was finally killed off in April 1938 when the *Anschluss* brought about the annexation of Austria into Hitler's Third Reich.

What happened to *Damenfussball* in Austria and Central Europe and to Brunilde Amodeo and her fellow football enthusiasts in Italy reflected depressing truths about the destiny of women's football in the interwar years. The game did not die out because of any shortage of women and girls who loved to play. Lots of girls in Milan wanted to join Brunilde in football games and wear football shirts that showed their affinity with Internazionale. Lots of women in Vienna, Zagreb or Brno wanted to join clubs like Operett, HSK or Vindobona.

Women's football was stifled and suppressed by enemy action - from male-dominated football federations like the English FA and the ÖFB, driven by the condescending and complacent attitudes of privileged, blinkered older men, and from rooted stereotypes of women as submissive and dutiful wives and mothers, relentlessly reinforced by the churches. In the 1930s, newer strands of reaction were taking hold: Fascism in Italy, the Fatherland Front in Austria, '*Kinder, Küche, Kirche*' ('Children, Kitchen, Church') in Nazi Germany, *Action Française* and its street-fighters, the Camelots du Roi, in France. All mobilised older anti-feminist ideas for their intimidating propaganda. Finally, these ideologies went beyond culture wars into a new world war that, along with much else, halted women's football completely for a generation.

Carmen was not yet ready to give up the fight. In August 1938, she was back in the old routine, leading a new French tour of England, happy to be with her football friends, happy to share the camaraderie with her French teammates. She did not realise it was for the last time. The 1938 tour was typically intensive, with nine matches at venues old and new. Carmen played as strongly as always in the first few matches but had to miss the games at Cheltenham and Fleetwood because of injuries. She was back on the field for the final matches

Right: Bateau mouche passing the Tour Eiffel and Globe Céleste, *Exposition Universelle*, Paris 1900. (BNF Gallica)

Below: The Fémina team, February 1920 Carmen sits to the left of goalkeeper Louise Ourry. (BNF Gallica)

Left: Violette Gouraud-Morris, captain of Fémina, 1920. (Archiv Helge Faller)

Below: Carmen with players of the French XI training at Moor Park, Preston, 1920. (Courtesy Steve Bolton)

Line up in order of size. The French XI on tour, 1921 (Carmen is second from left). (Archiv Helge Faller)

Celebrity kick-off. Plymouth Ladies v 'France', Home Park 1921. (Getty images)

12 Pages

12 Pages

Le Petit Journal

HEBDOMADAIRE
61, rue Lafayette, Paris

illustré

PRIX : 0 fr. 30
18 Novembre 1923

Le Football Féminin

La fragilité féminine s'accommode-t-elle des sports violents auxquels excellent nos jeunes gens ? La question, souvent posée, paraît résolue par l'affirmative. On peut s'en rendre compte en suivant les différents matches qui doivent qualifier deux équipes de sportives pour le Championnat de Paris en football. Voici une phase de la lutte qui met aux prises Fémina-Sport et les Cadettes de Garrogne.

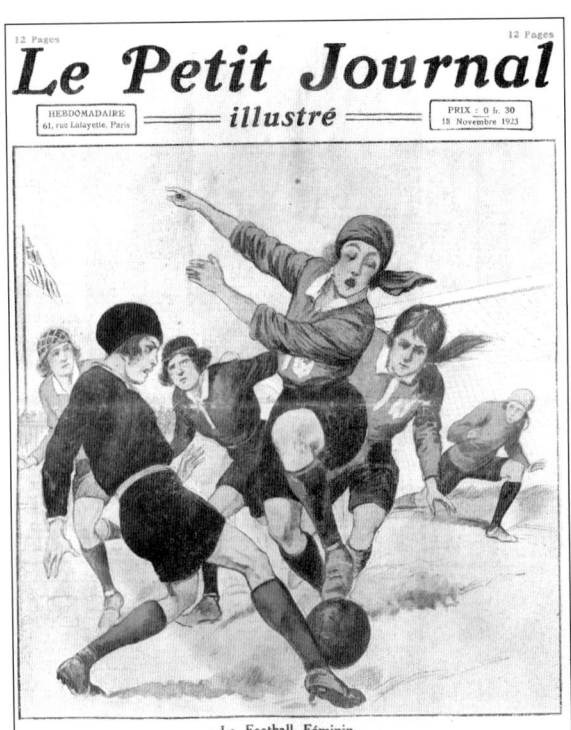

Left: Le Football Féminin
Le Petit Journal illustré, November 1923. (Archiv Helge Faller)

Below: Satire, Misogyny or Pornography?
Cartoon in a Rotterdam newspaper, 1911. (Archiv Helge Faller)

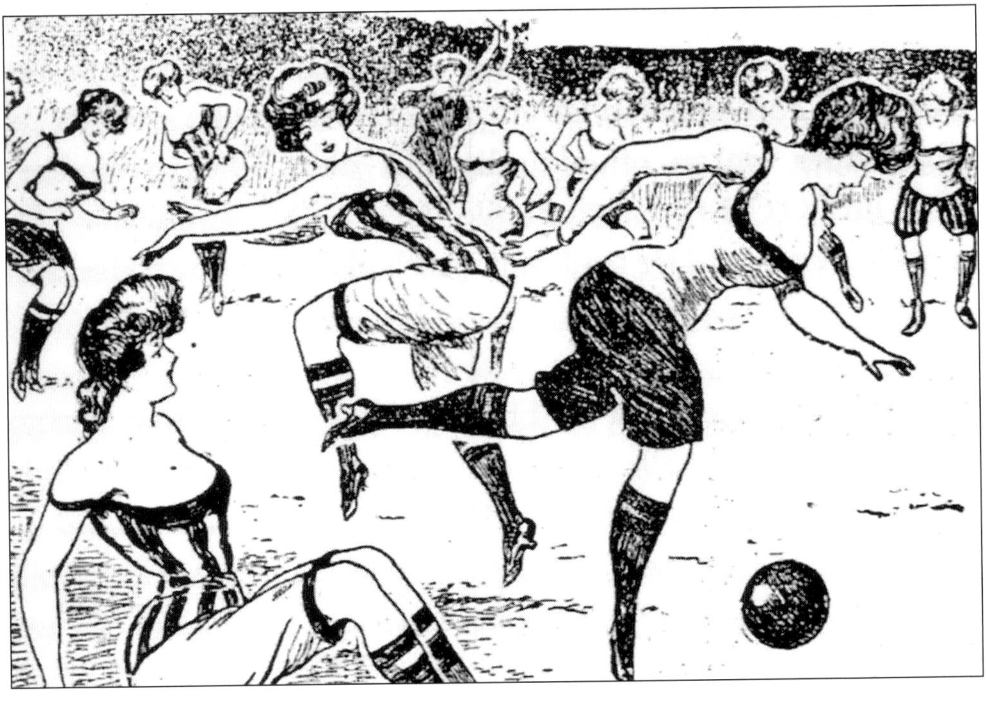

It's Arrived! (We Did It!) Austrian cartoon ridiculing women's football, 1924. (Archiv Helge Faller)

Dynamic midfielder. Carmen in action for Fémina, 1923. (Archiv Helge Faller)

Left: Best player in France? Florrie Redford in action for Fémina, 1923. (Archiv Helge Faller)

Below: Scandal in Lisbon. Reception for the French women footballers, hosted by Sporting magazine. (Archiv Helge Faller)

Dazzling Duo. Florrie and Carmen (front row centre) celebrate winning the championship, 1924. (Archiv Helge Faller)

Moment of history. Carmen and Florrie at the kick-off, Herne Hill, 1925. (Getty images)

A German postcard of 1925 celebrates *Damenfussball*. (Ullstein Bild/Getty images)

Ambassador. Carmen, Lizzy and friends on board *L'Oise*, Belfast 1932. (The Lizzy Ashcroft Collection, courtesy Steve Bolton)

A rare defeat. France 0 Belgium 2, Paris, April 1934. (AFP via Getty images)

Ambassador. Carmen welcomes the Belgians, Liverpool Street, 1934. (Getty images)

Medal commemorating 'England' v 'France', Garstang 1934. (The Lizzy Ashcroft Collection, courtesy Steve Bolton)

Above left: Carmen's second home; walking in the park with Lizzy, Preston, 1935. (The Lizzy Ashcroft Collection, courtesy Steve Bolton)

Above right: Carmen hoists Jeanne Bratiaud during training at Blackpool, 1938. (Getty images)

The Fearless One. Carmen on the high diving board at Blackpool, 1938. (Getty images)

Original press caption: Mlle Carmen Pomiès, captain of the French football team, prepares to dive from the high board into the pool at Blackpool, watched by Marjorie Thomas of the English team. The team of lady footballers is renewing an old rivalry with Preston Ladies. The final match of the tour will be played on Wednesday at Macclesfield. The French girls are keeping fit at Blackpool, training on the beach and in the pool.

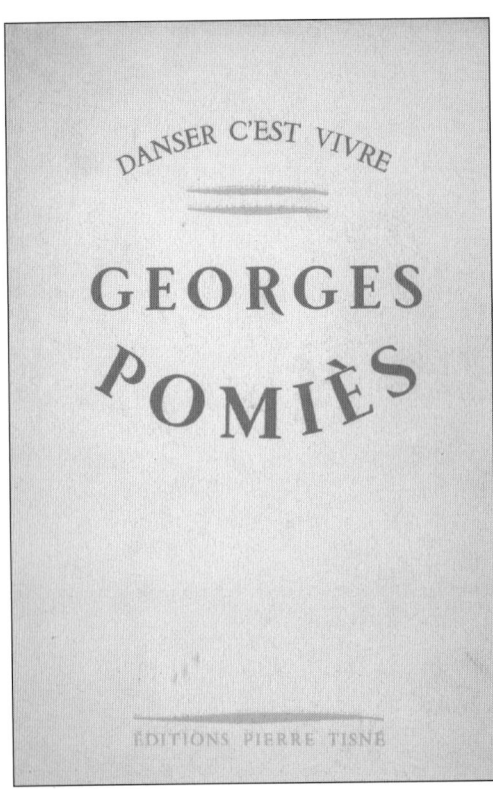

Remembering a talented brother. Georges Pomies: Danser c'est Vivre. This 1939 tribute to Georges was edited by his sister Helene.

Family snapshot of Georges at home (From *Danser c'est Vivre*)

Right: Resistance, Paris 1944, 'Nicole Minet' (real name Simone Segouin). Carmen was there with her rifle, too. (NARA)

Below: Vive de Gaulle! Liberation of Paris, August 1944. (Getty images)

Left: *Blood on the Mountain*, 1947.

Below: Rochester NY and the High Falls c1950. (Getty images)

Carmen Pomies Seeded No. 1 For GVC Invitation Net Test

Carmen Pomies of the Tennis Club of Rochester was seeded at the top of the draw for the Genesee Valley Club women's invitation tennis tournament, in which a field of 29 will compete.

Mrs. Jean Mayzak Huhn and Mrs. John Jung, both of the Tennis Club, were seeded second and third, and Mrs. Don Woods of the host club rounded out the ranking quartet for the tournament.

Play will open tomorrow and continue through the finals next Sunday. Miss Pomies, Mrs. Huhn and Mrs. Jung drew first-round byes, while Mrs. Woods drew Miss Jean Maben, another host club member, as her initial round foe.

First-round matches in the lower bracket will be played tomorrow, in the upper bracket Tuesday.

First-round pairings:

Tomorrow: 6:30 p. m., Mrs. Hiram Sibley, GVC, vs. Miss Anita Kushner, Maplewood Y; 9:30 p. m., Mrs. Edward Macomber, CCR, vs. Miss Elizabeth Day, Med. School; 10 a. m., Mrs. Alexander Beach, CCR, vs. Mrs. John Miller, GVC; 7:30 p. m., Mrs. Butler Cox, GVC, vs. Miss Jane Van Husen, TCR; 2 p. m., Mrs. John Egan, TCR, vs. Mrs. Merritt Cleveland, GVC; 8:30 p. m., Mrs. Douglas Coupe, GVC, vs. Mrs. Frances Blum, TCR.

Tuesday: 7:30 p. m., Mrs. John Dunn, GVC, vs. Miss Pat Preisler, Med. School; 9:30 p. m., Mrs. W. McQuilken, GVC, vs. Miss Catherine Burnham, UR; 10:30 a. m., Mrs. Eleanor Sanford, TCR, vs. Mrs. William Roby, GVC; 2:30 p. m., Mrs. Roy Hock, TCR, vs. Miss Marney Drescher, GVC; 10:30 p. m., Mrs. Allen Macomber, CCR, vs. Miss Jean Fox, GVC; 6:30 p. m., Mrs. Donald Woods, GVC, vs. Miss Jean Maben, GVC; 8:30 p. m., Miss Mary Scott, TCR, vs. Mrs. Martin Donahue, GVC.

CARMEN POMIES
... *heads seeded list*

Right: Tennis star. From the *Democrat & Chronicle*, Rochester NY, April 1948. (Courtesy of newspapers.com)

Below: *SS Liberté* docks at New York, 1950. Carmen sailed home on *Liberté* in 1954. (Getty images)

A place in history. Memorial to Dick, Kerr Ladies, Deepdale, Preston. (Courtesy Dave Wilson, Lancashire Photography)

The Climb to Equality.
The women footballers who played high on Mount Kilimanjaro, 2017. (Courtesy Petra Landers)

at Workington and Macclesfield but was not fully fit. The obligatory Girls Day Out at Blackpool was as much fun as ever. One press photograph shows Carmen in full gymnastic mode on Blackpool Sands, holding her friend and teammate Jeannine Bratiaud high with her powerful legs.

During the tour, Carmen also got news of her old friend Florrie Redford, who was planning to come home from Canada to visit friends and family. When Florrie did get back to Preston that autumn, she played for the team again, at Whitehaven, but now, aged forty and out of practice, Florrie was no longer the 'Alex James of women's football'. Florrie and Carmen would always be friends but never again could they be the dazzling duo who had terrorised opponents in the glory days of the early 1920s.

In 1939, Carmen's year began well in family terms, with the publication of a handsome book, *Georges Pomiès: Danser C'est Vivre* (To Dance is to Live), edited by Hélène, with many fine photographs and thirteen chapters by those who had known Georges best, such as Paul Franck, who ran the theatre club l'Olympia and was the man who first persuaded Georges his true talent was as a dancer, not a singer. The most personal contributions came from Lisa Duncan, Georges's long-term dance partner and girlfriend, and from Hélène herself.

Carmen played no direct part in *Danser C'est Vivre*, but was close at hand to observe its impact. It was a big step forward in Hélène's career as a writer and a time for family and friends to come together to share grief and memories with those who had known Georges best, including those from the worlds of theatre and cinema. It was around this time that Carmen became secretary to the film star Renée Saint-Cyr.

For French women's football, the future was bleak in 1939. The league system had finally collapsed. In March, Carmen wrote a petition pleading for action to save the football side of the club from going under. It was read out at a committee meeting of Fémina Sports. The committee rejected the petition and offered a demonstration of handball instead. Carmen organised and played in a few friendly matches for Montrouge, formerly one of the 'farm-clubs' associated with Fémina, but that was it.

There was no French tour of England in 1939, nor for years to come. It was the Belgians who toured England that last summer before the war. Unlike the 1934 tour, Carmen was not involved. All the well-worn traditions were observed; one snapshot shows the Belgian team doing intensive physical training on the beach at Blackpool. But the tour ended in deep anxiety about the approaching war. Alfred Frankland got a telegram from the War Office asking for assurances that the Belgians would get away in time for a safe journey home.

In Paris, as everywhere in Europe that August, Carmen, Hélène and Yvonne knew war was coming; what they read in the papers and saw in cinema newsreels told them so. What the consequences of this war might be nobody could know. In 1939, it was still possible to believe that France was one of the strongest military powers in the world. Nobody could envisage the rapidity of the Fall of France in 1940, or the global conflict now known as the Second World War that would take shape in 1941. But war was coming.

A striking press photograph of July 1938 shows Carmen Pomiès poised on the high diving board at Blackpool's outdoor swimming pool. It is the Girls Day Out for the French football team and their friends from Preston; a tradition that had been in place ever since nineteen-year-old Carmen Pomiès first came to Blackpool on the inaugural tour in 1920. The caption accompanying the photograph explained the context:

> Mlle. Carmen Pomiès, captain of the French football team, prepares to dive from the high board into the pool at Blackpool, watched by Marjorie Thomas of the English team. The team of French lady footballers are renewing an old rivalry with Preston Ladies. The final match of the tour will be played on Wednesday at Macclesfield. The French girls are keeping fit at Blackpool, training on the beach and in the pool.

In a few weeks time, the woman on the diving board will reach her thirty-eighth birthday but she is still an impressive physical specimen, athletic, fit, totally fearless. She is comfortable in her own body, totally at ease in familiar surroundings and in the happy banter with her young football friend, Marjorie. Carmen does not yet know it, but she is here in Blackpool for the last time. There will be one more such Girls Day Out next year, for the Belgian touring team, but Carmen will not be there.

Perhaps it's just as well Carmen cannot see into the future to know what will be happening at the end of the summer of 1939. Then, like everyone in France, she will be glumly observing the clouds of war darkening the skies over France and Europe: the slow-motion diplomatic train-wreck of the Anglo-French Military Mission to Moscow hoping for a last-minute alliance with the Soviet Union, the shock when the Nazi-Soviet Pact was signed instead, the grim realisation this would mean the invasion of Poland and that France and Britain would soon be at war against Nazi Germany.

In July 1938, the woman on the high diving board cannot know any of this, nor how awful the consequences will be, bringing defeat and occupation to France and death and destruction everywhere. The unique French-English football friendship forged in 1920 will be just one of the countless casualties, great and small, of that terrible war, along with the end of women's football in the interwar years. A long, exciting episode in the life of Carmen Pomiès is ending. She will not come back to Preston until 1945.

Chapter 7

Carmen's War

From 1920 until 1939, the life of Carmen Pomiès was intertwined with Preston and her close friendships with the football community of Dick, Kerr Ladies. After the summer of 1939, these links were broken by war. The separation was made brutally complete by the rapid German conquest of France in May-June 1940 and the establishment of a new pro-Fascist French government with its capital in the provincial city of Vichy. Football was pushed to the sidelines as Carmen's life was shaped by war. France was liberated in August 1944 but Britain's war continued until May 1945. So Carmen's visit to Preston in October 1945 was a long-delayed, very emotional moment.

Carmen's friends were delighted to see her and were proud to tell the world she was a heroine of the French Resistance. But the realities of Carmen's War are shrouded in uncertainty. Most of the evidence comes from second-hand reports based on what Carmen said. The first of these reports is a letter Carmen sent to Preston in 1941. The second is a letter she wrote to Alfred Frankland after the liberation of Paris in 1944, that was reported in the *Daily Mail.* The third comes from a report in the local newspaper. celebrating her return to Preston in October 1945.

In 1946, not long after her visit to Preston, Carmen left France for the United States, starting a new life in the city of Rochester, NY. It's possible that Carmen had already made this momentous decision before she came to Preston, that her visit was to say both hello and goodbye. Carmen would live happily in Rochester for more than four years before moving on to live and work in New York City. During her time in Rochester, Carmen was featured in two lengthy articles in the local newspaper; both devoted much space to Carmen's role in the French resistance.

Without the evidence of these second-hand accounts, little would be known about Carmen's War. There are no surviving letters to or from Carmen or people close to her, nor does Carmen's name appear in books and documents about the resistance. Carmen's sister Hélène witnessed the resistance in the Alps and wrote a book about it, *Du Sang sur la Montagne* (Blood on the Mountain) published in 1947, but the book is composed of literary short stories, not factual autobiography. It tells little about what Hélène was doing and nothing at all about Carmen and Yvonne. So the story of Carmen's War is essentially the story as told by Carmen herself, or at least as others understood what Carmen told them. Can we believe this story? Well, yes and no.

There is no reason to suppose Carmen had any intent to deceive. But for her, as for anyone who lived under German occupation and French dictatorship from 1940 to 1944, telling the whole truth was all but impossible. For anyone who went through it, occupation was a corrosive, corrupting experience, forcing people into myriad evasions of unpleasant truths, staying silent in case of informers, making daily compromises in order to survive. Whatever Carmen told people in Preston, or later on in Rochester, it could never be the whole truth.

Nor would the whole truth have been recognised by Anglo-Saxon listeners, either. People in Britain, even more than people in America, knew a lot about the war - they had just lived through it and it dominated almost every conversation - but their sense of the history of the war they knew was very unbalanced. Carmen's friends in Preston had vivid memories of a war in the West: Dunkirk, the Blitz, rationing, the Battle of the Atlantic, the Dam Busters, D-Day, American GIs in pubs and dance halls, street parties to celebrate VE Day. These memories did not include defeat or occupation.

Nobody should ever belittle the loss and sacrifice, the trauma and tragedy that the war inflicted on many of its citizens, but Britain escaped its worst evils. There was no starvation, nor death camps, nor terror of the secret police, or fear of the army of informers who aided them. The Blitz caused terrible damage to cities like London, Coventry and Liverpool but in 1940-41 the technology of mass destruction by aerial bombing was in the early stages of development. From 1943, cities like Hamburg, Tokyo and Dresden were devastated by firestorms more horrific than most people in Britain could imagine (and, if they could, there was a temptation to regard it as righteous punishment of Germany and Japan for starting the war in the first place).

Few people in Britain understood the brutality and mass destruction of the war on the Eastern Front. There was little understanding that the lives lost in the Soviet Union amounted to more than twenty million, or that 170 towns and cities were obliterated along with 70,000 villages. Few realised that, as the war ended, thirty million refugees and displaced persons were in holding camps or trudging across Europe trying to find their old home or a new one; or that another thirty million were homeless.

From a British perspective, the morality of the war was a simple equation. The war had been won. Good had triumphed over evil. In the United States, of course, the issues were even more clear-cut. Americans bore no blame for helping to cause the war. Apart from Pearl Harbour, Americans had not come under direct attack and never had reason to fear occupation, let alone understand what it was actually like. Americans had not known shortages or rationing, in fact, their war was accompanied by a sustained consumer boom that raised living standards higher than in the 1930s. For people in Rochester, or for people in Preston, it was all but impossible to grasp the ways in which living under occupation made it hard to separate good from evil.

To those who knew her or read about her, Carmen's story was simple and uplifting. She had been 'in the resistance', a heroine fighting for what was good. Against her were evil German occupiers and certain French men and women who collaborated with evil. In between were huge numbers of 'innocent bystanders'. Carmen knew and understood this way of thinking. She also knew from hard experience how different it had been in real life. This meant that, sometimes, Carmen was reticent and selective in the memories she related. Even more, it meant that her listeners and readers were ready to believe what they wanted to believe about 'the Resistance'.

For Americans, and for cinemagoers in Britain also, it was comforting to think almost exclusively about the Germans as the enemy, about the SS and the Gestapo, with 'the Resistance' bravely standing against and ultimately defeating the ruthless Nazis. The Vichy regime, and the extent of compliance and collaboration by French men and women, was only dimly perceived. The classic 1942 film *Casablanca* has helped to keep this myth alive for eighty years. Rick (Humphrey Bogart) is the American bar owner who tries to stay neutral but is drawn into helping 'the Resistance'. Victor Laszlo (Paul Henreid) is not only husband to the gorgeous Ilsa (Ingrid Bergman) but also the charismatic leader of a vast, united underground movement in which like-minded people all over Europe worked together for a common cause.

Such a movement never existed, nor could anything so interconnected ever exist, because within weeks it would have been penetrated and snuffed out by the forces of repression underpinning the occupation. The idea of 'the Resistance' did, however, have a powerful grip on the public imagination in Britain and America. It shaped how they wanted to think about Carmen Pomiès as 'heroine of the resistance'.

Carmen's War began slowly, with the *Drôle de Guerre* (Phoney War). From September 1939 to May 1940, France was at war but not fighting a war, simply waiting for Hitler's next move. When the real war came, France was swiftly overrun. France surrendered and the Third Republic was overthrown. A new authoritarian regime was established, headed by the aged war hero of 1916-18, Marshal Pétain, and the devious political manipulator, Pierre Laval. Most of northern France became the Occupied Zone under direct German rule. To the south was the Free Zone, a semi-independent France ruled from Vichy, a spa and resort town in central France. This arrangement lasted until November 1942 when the Germans extended direct rule over the whole of France.

In 1940, the options for French men and women were stark. They could cooperate with their new rulers, keep quiet and try to stay out of trouble, flee abroad to join the Free French forces led by General de Gaulle, or join one of the localised groups that engaged in smaller or larger acts of resistance. None of these options was easy.

These complexities were not in the minds of readers of the *Lancashire Evening Post* when it welcomed Carmen's return to Preston in October 1945:

> When the London train steamed into Preston this afternoon, it brought back to the town Mdlle Carmen Pomies, who was last here when she captained the French women's football team against Dick, Kerr Ladies and England in international matches before the war. After five years of almost complete cessation of sport in France, Mdlle Pomies has returned with the approval of the French Minister of Sport and Education to explore the means of organizing women's international events between France and England.

The *Post* reporter reminded readers of Carmen's long-standing connections with Preston:

> Mdlle Pomies has happy memories of Preston. She was met at the station by Mr A. Frankland, former manager, and Miss M. Thornborough, assistant manager of the old Dick, Kerr team. She is staying in Preston with

Miss F. Redford, who was 'the Alex James of women's football' after the last war.

The article reflects familiar themes in Carmen's story. Her long-standing role in promoting sport for women was reflected in the fact that her visit to Preston was with the approval of the French Ministry of Sport and Education. Her attachment to Dick, Kerr Ladies over the preceding twenty-five years was reflected in the welcome from Alfred Frankland and Margaret Thornborough and the reunion with Florrie Redford. There is also a new admiration of Carmen as a heroine of the resistance.

When it came to describing her life under occupation, Carmen was, to some extent at least, giving readers the sort of mind-pictures they wanted to see and hear: 'Ah, our sport suffered terribly with the Germans. Football, it was stopped completely for women. But we kept on playing, even though it had to be in secret'. When the reporter suggested this must have been a tricky business, Carmen:

> crinkled her nose and laughed. 'Ah, but those Germans, they were slow. We played on a men's ground when they weren't looking. But they would have thrown us in goal if they caught us'. Since the war, Mdlle Pomies has reunited members of the Cercle Athletique de Montrouge, the Paris club which tried to keep sport alive during the war. Hockey was played and it's likely the first women's international events will be hockey matches. Tennis, too, was played. 'German girls used to come to Montrouge to play hockey and tennis' said Mdlle Pomies. 'It was a favourite trick to steal their clothes, leaving the frauleins to wander around in an undressed state!

There is nothing dishonest about these recollections but they hardly get beneath the surface. They show Carmen's determination to keep football alive and low-level pranks against dull-witted Germans, not organised resistance. Other sources tell us more about Carmen's dangerous activities with the French underground.

The article of October 1945 was not the only occasion that the *Lancashire Evening Post* highlighted Carmen's links with Preston. Late in 1941, the *Post* told its readers of a letter it had received from Carmen. *'BRAVO ENGLAND!' SAYS FRENCH WOMAN IN SPAIN* was the headline, followed by some reminders of the great days of Dick, Kerr Ladies, the money they raised for charity, and their famous tour of America.

The *Post* then turned to the letter from Spain, to explain that 'Mdlle Pomies is in Spain and times have changed sadly for her. She wonders what we think of her countrymen. Writing in a neat hand in English, she says:

> I have been downhearted when thinking that from now on you might hate us for good. But be sure that 85 per cent of the French people are with you, hope for you and fight for you in spirit. Only those who profit out of friendship with the hated are on the other side. We French are with you, admiring England to the utmost, wishing for the day we shall meet again.

Under the heading Listen in Joy, the *Post* describes Carmen's letter as a poignant cry from the heart of a Frenchwoman who loves England and the English people:

> My best minutes in these awful days are to listen to the BBC, and every time after I feel much better. We are very, very unhappy. But this does not count. We are all hungry. But this does not count. All our eyes are turned on you. All our hearts beat for you. And nothing in the world will stop that. I know the English people, brave to the utmost,

and determined up to death. Bravo! You are giving the world the best lesson. I am proud to have always praised England and for such a reason was my dear father three months in goal. Some day, we will all meet together again to celebrate out liberty, owed to the English courage that will save the whole world.

The tone of Carmen's 1941 letter is a long way from the superficial jollity of her comments reported by the same newspaper in 1945. What she wrote in 1941 sounds like the Carmen we know from her football days, defiant, loyal and a born fighter. It plainly comes from the heart, with its passionate French patriotism, hatred for the German occupiers and the Vichy regime, and admiration for England. But Carmen's estimation of French opinion is wildly optimistic and there is some rather desperate wishful thinking about how ultimate victory will be achieved one day.

When the letter was posted, German forces were closing in on Moscow. America had not yet joined the war. Victory was so far away as to be practically invisible. In this grim context, questions arise: about Carmen's role in the resistance, about why she was in Spain in 1941 and what she was doing there; or even if she was in Spain at all.

It was not impossible for Carmen to have been in Spain. Her family, especially her sister Hélène, had close connections with Spain. After the Spanish Civil War, the Francoist regime kept Spain neutral in the Second World War but still sided with Germany and Italy. Passing from France into neutral Spain was very difficult but, with the right connections, it could be done. On the other hand, a letter postmarked in Spain does not prove the letter was sent in person from Spain. Carmen was living and working in Paris, in the Occupied Zone. Letters were subject to censorship, with potentially dangerous consequences. It would make sense if someone else had posted the explosively anti-German letter on Carmen's behalf. We just do not know.

The question of Carmen's whereabouts in 1941 is made more mysterious by one piece of evidence that is very difficult to make sense of. In the records of Border Crossings from Canada into the United States, the name of Carmen Pomiès is listed for 4/7/1941. Why on earth Carmen might have entered the United States from Canada on the Fourth of July 1941 is, to say the least, puzzling.

There is no trail of evidence to show any crossings of the Atlantic by Carmen in 1941, something theoretically possible but highly unusual. It is even more of a puzzle to find any reasons Carmen might have had to do so, or how it might be connected to her presence in Spain later in 1941. Perhaps she really was in North America in the summer of 1941. Perhaps the Carmen Pomiès who crossed the border in July was a different Carmen altogether. Perhaps our Carmen really was in Spain later that year. Perhaps her route to and from America was through Spain. These are all questions without answers. So, what evidence *do* we have about Carmen in 1940 and 1941?

In May 1947, about a year after Carmen had arrived in Rochester NY to live and work there, readers of Rochester's *Democrat & Chronicle* newspaper were able to learn a lot about Carmen in a feature article titled *Pour le Sport* by Henry V. Clune. Memories of the war were still fresh and Henry Clune was full of admiration for 'Miss Pomies' and her role in wartime resistance:

> She lived in Paris through the long cruel years of the German occupation, and served through this time as a member of the French underground. She had to be careful, since her father, who was an almost open loyalist, was three times arrested and slapped in jail for months at a time. This kept the finger of suspicion on Miss Pomies. The Germans watched her like a hawk. 'But I managed to get a lot done for the cause', she said with a smile. 'The Germans were often thick – what do you Americans say, blockheads?'

Thus far, Henry Clune's message is very similar to the *Lancashire Evening Post* in 1945. Women's football came into the picture again as Henry Clune informed his readers how the game was banned but Carmen and others were able to organise matches in secret, helped by the fact that the Germans were 'blockheads'.

But the article also paints a vivid picture of Carmen's radicalisation through the persecution of her father. Even more valuable were the references to Renée Saint-Cyr and what was happening to French cinema during the occupation:

> Before and during the war, her regular job was secretary to the lovely Renée Saint-Cyr, France's Number Two movie actress. Mlle Saint-Cyr was, like Miss Pomies, an ardent loyalist, active in the Resistance. But she was compelled by the German command in Paris to continue her movie career and the films she made were for German entertainment. But what Renée Saint-Cyr did in the dark of night, Miss Pomies said, made a notable contribution to the resistance.

Three years later, as she was bidding farewell to Rochester to move to New York City, the *Democrat & Chronicle* put her in the local limelight again, in a feature article for women readers. It presented a glowing image of Carmen the resistance fighter:

> ABOUT WOMEN
> From Underground to UN Skyscraper
> By Pat Fallon
>
> Carmen Pomies knew the underground well. Fooling the Germans was a dangerous game and the stakes were high. The Germans thought she was on their side but she wasn't. Carmen was in liaison with the German High Command Office which checked the documents of

all persons leaving Occupied France for the Free Vichy sector. She won the total confidence of the Germans she dealt with, and was able to route a person towards freedom simply on her recommendation.

'I don't know exactly how many people we managed to get across the border', Carmen said, 'but it wasn't just the numbers. The individuals we handled were often the ones most sought by the Germans. One slip by us would have meant torture and death for all of us in our underground group.'

These sources are invaluable but also in some ways problematic. The evidence comes from Carmen's viewpoint and often in her own words. The American journalists appear to have misunderstood some of what they heard from Carmen and to have only a limited grasp of the context of life under occupation in Vichy France. It is also true that Carmen's flattering picture of Renée Saint-Cyr is less than objective. She was not at all 'compelled' to carry on her movie career, she desperately wanted it. Nor is there much evidence of Renée Saint-Cyr having been an 'ardent loyalist' active in the resistance. Many people in France thought film stars like her 'went along with the Germans' to keep up their luxurious lifestyles.

Yet, even though Carmen may have been letting her employer (and herself?) off lightly, these articles from the *Democrat & Chronicle*, taken together, sketch an outline picture of what Carmen was up to in the first years of the occupation. From an early stage, she was angry about the treatment of her father, and perhaps angry his business had been disrupted in the process. Henry Clune tells us Carmen was secretary to 'the lovely Renée Saint-Cyr, France's Number Two film actress' (Number One was Danielle Darrieux) and Carmen was closely involved in French cinema.

Renée Saint-Cyr was already an established star long before the war and was indeed, along with Danielle Darrieux, one of the top two French screen goddesses. 'Renée Saint-Cyr' was her stage name. She was born Marie Louise Eugenie Vittore in 1904, at Beausoleil in Monaco, on the Côte d'Azur. She was to have a long life; when she died near Paris in 2004, it was a few months short of her 100th birthday.

Renée Saint-Cyr was accustomed to wealth and privilege by birth, marriage and career. Her father was a hotel owner, her mother was an opera singer. Aged twenty-one, Renée married Charles Leopold Lautner, a wealthy jeweller from Vienna. (Their son, Georges Lautner, became a famous screenwriter and film director after the war), Even before her marriage, Renée was already getting film roles. In the 1930s films like *The Two Orphans* (1933) and *The Last Millionaire* directed by René Clair in 1934, made her a star in France, Germany, England and Italy.

Renée Saint-Cyr starred in three big movies in 1940: *Red Roses*, made in Italy and directed by Vittorio De Sica, *Night to Remember*, and *Chemin de L'Honneur* (The Way of Honour). After the Fall of France, the Germans were happy to see French cinema continue much as before. The films were popular, attracting huge audiences, and the Germans liked to keep up cosy illusions of normality in France. Stars like Renée Saint-Cyr and Danielle Darrieux were important assets.

The French film industry had to tread a fine line in Vichy France, trying to keep its own identity while conforming to the new political ideology. In 1941, the Nazi Minister of Propaganda, Josef Goebbels, set up a new film production company, Continental Films. Goebbels was too clever to make German control obvious. He allowed French filmmakers to make French films, though without Jewish actors, writers or directors, of course, and not on 'decadent' themes. Many were 'safe' historical dramas. They filled a need. Audiences rose much higher than before the war. Setting up the new system took months, during which French film production virtually closed down.

Renée Saint-Cyr made no films in 1941 but starred in many big films in 1942 and 1943, notably *La Symphonie Fantastique*, a lavish 'biopic' of the nineteenth-century composer Hector Berlioz, *Madame et le Mort* (Woman of Death) and *Maria Martine*, for which she won a Best Actress award. In 1944, film production stalled again as the war turned against Germany. It is easy to see why Carmen Pomiès became an influential secretary for a French film star. Carmen was unlikely to be overawed by working for such a high-profile actress. Carmen was four years older and, after all, her brother Georges had been a film star too.

It also becomes easier to see how Carmen might have been, as Pat Fallon put it, 'in liaison with the German High Command Office'. Working directly for the German military command seems improbable but working with Continental Films would be enough to explain why Carmen had access to documents permitting persons to move out of the Occupied Zone; and thus extremely valuable to her 'underground group'. The story of Continental Films might even solve the mystery of Carmen being out of France in 1941, in Spain or even in North America, because that was when film production was suspended and her employer was temporarily inactive.

Yet, even this plausible scenario shows what a double-headed monster resistance could be. On the one hand, Carmen acted as a brave foot-soldier in the underground, doing something both valuable and risky by smuggling out safe-conduct passes. At the same time, to be able to make her honourable contribution to the cause, Carmen had to work closely with the German bureaucracy – in other words, to collaborate – and, while her courageous acts of resistance had to be hidden secrets, cooperation with the Germans had to be very public. Life under occupation could never be simple or safe, for film stars or for secretaries.

An excellent film released in 2002, *Laissez-Passer* (Safe Conduct), directed by Bertrand Tavernier, provides fascinating insights into French cinema during the occupation. The film shows the vital importance of the documents Carmen was stealing to help the underground. It has a lovely running joke about the costume dramas and historical epics that were produced in such numbers because their themes were so 'safe'. The joke was that such period films invariably featured banquets with tables groaning under glorious mountains of food. The film crews who looked after the sets were all starving but they all knew the tempting food piled high on the tables was made of papier-maché and painted cardboard.

Tavernier's film also captures the sense of oppression in occupied France, as much from the French dictatorship as from the German occupiers. France did not just lose the battle in 1940. Defeat had led to political revolution and a pro-Fascist French government with Marshal Pétain as its figurehead. The Vichy regime did not just collaborate with the Germans. It imposed a right-wing political agenda under the slogan, *Work, Family, Nation*, that was nationalist, racist and socially reactionary. People got accustomed to a climate of fear, intimidated by propaganda, censorship and the danger of being arrested for saying the wrong words in the wrong place.

Living with the occupation day by day was ugly and perilous. It was impossible to keep a clear line between collaboration and resistance, or to remain neutral. To have a job, or a ration card, to drink in a bar, to listen to the radio, involved some degree of compromise with the regime. Most Americans (most British people, too) had only a limited grasp of the compromises and complexities of living under occupation. They were happy to believe in the united front and simple courage of the 'French underground' rather than consider how fractured the resistance movements in France really were.

By November 1942, however, the Vichy regime was creaking as the fortunes of war changed. After American armies invaded North Africa, Germany felt compelled to tighten control over France. German forces invaded the Free Zone and established direct military rule, though the police stayed under French authority. In one sense, this made resistance harder. In another sense, the way the war was trending against Germany encouraged more and more French people to believe resistance might succeed. In 1943, with the Allied invasion of Italy and then the fall of Mussolini, more and more people joined resistance groups. As the numbers went up, so the Allies gave more support by dropping supplies from the air.

In 1950, Pat Fallons's article in the *Democrat & Chronicle* contained tantalising evidence of Carmen Pomiès being involved in this kind of activity. The specifics are hazy, with nothing to indicate exactly when the events took place, though the context suggests it was in the later stages of the war, probably in 1943 or early 1944:

> Carmen's part in the French underground was in a Paris maternity hospital and her 'patients' were less often bundles from Heaven than bundles from Britain - propaganda dropped from airplanes. These bundles, until they could be distributed, were usually hidden in hospital beds with actual patients, or camouflaged beneath the blankets. The Germans paid little attention to the hospital. Once a British plane flew too low, crashed, and burst into flames. Carmen and another nurse were the first to reach the burning plane. They pulled out the one surviving flyer and took him and his secret cargo to safety.

This makes a terrific story that would be worthy of the screenplay for a film. Small wonder those who knew Carmen in Preston or Rochester were full of admiration for her as a 'heroine of the resistance'.

On the other hand, these events lack context and corroboration. For one thing, it is difficult to fix exactly when they happened. Also, some of the evidence is problematic. Carmen was a remarkable woman but it's hard to see how she had had time to qualify as a nurse, though hospitals also need secretaries. There are the usual doubts about how well Pat Fallon understood (or wanted to understand) the nuances of life under occupation. Once again, gullible Germans are being easily outwitted by clever and resourceful agents of the underground.

So the complicated, oppressive realities, that the Gestapo and the SD were ruthlessly efficient, working with the French police and a network of informers, remain hidden from view in the story of Carmen and the burning plane. True, there were many such night flights to France by SOE, (the Special Operations Executive) and other agencies but the French people who received them were often caught, tortured and killed. In 1943, the average life expectancy for agents sending secret radio broadcasts from occupied France was six or seven weeks. There is even a question of how completely Carmen's own words can be trusted. Were her recollections perhaps embellished to maximise the sense of drama?

Regardless of such questions, despite all the internal rivalries and betrayals within, the resistance groups were steadily gaining strength in 1943 and 1944. In the beginning, most acts of resistance were localised and opportunistic, but from 1943, resistance was on a much larger scale. From exile in Britain, General de Gaulle was directing the military command of Free French forces, ready to take part in the liberation of Europe, planned for 1943 but then delayed until 1944. Partisan groups loyal to the French Communist Party emerged. In remote mountainous regions such as the Dordogne and the Alps, partisan fighters, the *Maquisards,* increased in size and ambition. By 1944, these disparate elements of resistance were being brought together as the FFI, the Free French Forces of the Interior.

The diverse strands of resistance were united in hatred of the Germans and the Vichy regime, but not much else. They had very different visions of France's future after the war. Some were loyal to the French Communist Party. Others were Catholic ultra-conservatives. Many of those loyal to Charles de Gaulle were nationalist and anti-Communist. Ranged against all of them were right-wing groups loyal to the Vichy regime. In the south, the *Milice Française,* led by Paul Touvier, collaborated closely with the Vichy police and the Germans. The Gestapo organised the *Brigade Nort Africaine,* an anti-resistance militia formed mostly of men with criminal records, to carry out violent acts of repression against resistance groups and 'saboteurs'.

There was a football connection to the North African Brigade. One of its leaders, Alex Villaplane, had been a fine footballer of the 1920s and captain of France at the 1930 World Cup in Uruguay. In the 1930s, however, Villaplane lost his enthusiasm for the game and became fixated on horse racing and gambling. He drifted into petty crime that brought him several spells in prison. The Gestapo released him so that he could recruit other criminals for service in the dirty war against enemies of the regime.

By 1944, France was facing political upheaval, perhaps even a civil war like the one already unfolding in Italy. Tensions were high as the expected Allied invasion came nearer. The forces of resistance in France were on high alert, waiting for their moment to contribute to the liberation. After the D-Day landings in Normandy on 6 June, the partisans were impatient for action.

One key front in this expanding partisan war was the Vercors, the high plateau in the Alps above Grenoble. Carmen's sister Hélène was there to witness events in the Vercors; she wrote a book about it, *Du Sang sur la Montagne* (Blood on the Mountain) published in 1947. Carmen's experiences of the war were almost all in or near Paris but the bylines of her chapters show Hélène was mostly at Meylan, near Grenoble.

Du Sang sur la Montagne is not a personal memoir or chronological history and provides few precise details in chapters that are literary short stories rather than narratives. The first, *Rosette,* traces the radicalisation of a woman after she sees the dead body of a girl killed in reprisals. How far this might be based on Hélène's own experience it's not possible to judge. The stories are, however, stylishly written, evocative and atmospheric, revealing an intimate knowledge of the high mountain villages like Saint-Nizier-de-Moucherotte where the Vercors partisans had their supposedly impregnable stronghold.

But the Vercors plateau was not impregnable and what Hélène witnessed there in July-August 1944 was one of the great tragedies of the resistance. The partisan army in the Vercors was large, confident and well-equipped with arms and supplies dropped by British and American aircraft. Expectancy reached fever pitch after the Normandy landings in June. The partisans believed the Germans were on the run, that this was their moment. Above all, they wanted to be Frenchmen liberating France, not just wait for freedom to be granted to them by the Allies.

The leaders of the rising declared the independence of the 'Free Republic of Vercors'. In late July, 4,000 *Maquisards* launched a major military offensive. But the mountains of the Vercors Massif did not protect them and the Germans were not yet finished. After some early successes, the *Maquisards* came up against nearly 10,000 enemy troops, many of them Romanian, who were well-armed and battle-hardened. The rising failed, with terrible casualties. 700 partisans were killed in battle. Two hundred civilians died in reprisals. They died heroically but their sacrifice was wasted.

Ten days after the rising in the Vercors was crushed, American forces invaded southern France to open up a new front. Ten days after that, Paris was liberated. Carmen was there in Paris in those hectic weeks leading up to the Liberation, out on the streets carrying a rifle. It was a story Pat Fallon was delighted to tell in 1950:

> The days that preceded the liberation of Paris in August 1944 were the most exciting of Miss Pomies's life. As the Allied armies pressed close to the western gates of the city, the frantic occupiers were as jittery as doped-up mobsters, careering through the streets in all sorts of military vehicles, shooting at anything that moved. Miss Pomies escaped death or serious injury when a German truck bristling with machine guns swept a street where she was walking. She darted into a doorway just as a bullet went over her shoulder and killed a woman nearby. Since she was a certified member of the underground, and

an active, fit young woman, Miss Pomies was given a rifle, and was for a time in what might be loosely described as the 'Home Guard' during the final siege of Paris. 'I never had any occasion to shoot the gun,' she said. 'But I could have done if there had been the need'.

In any list of joyous memories for the French people, few can compete with the liberation of Paris. Four years and seventy-two days after the shameful day the Germans arrived in the city in June 1940, French forces led by General de Gaulle led the Allied military parade through the Arc de Triomphe. It sparked scenes of uninhibited happiness that lasted for days. Carmen's letter to Alfred Frankland in 1944 described the 'delirious joy' of the moment and her pride that 'I took my place on the barricades and fought my part'.

Liberation Day was also highly political, carefully staged to present Charles de Gaulle as the soul of the French nation, the charismatic leader who could proudly claim to have kept alive 'free France' since 1940 and that now 'France has been liberated by the French'. This was, of course, a convenient myth. The reality was that France had indeed lost the battle in 1940 and that liberation was due to the vast military machine of the United States and the Grand Alliance.

Most French people understood this. Paris in 1944 was utterly pro-American. But France badly needed a unifying national myth to cover over deep divisions in French society. A key part of the liberation myth was that huge numbers of men and women had been in the resistance all along. A lot of French people knew better; they poured scorn on the *'résistants de quarante-quatre'* (the resisters of '44), those opportunists who joined the struggle only at the last minute, when they knew victory was close and it was safe to do so.

For the time being, such thoughts could be pushed aside in the glow of the moment. Carmen and the many other female fighters such as the legendary 'Nicole Minet' (real name Simone Segouin), who carried their guns through the days leading to the Liberation knew they were living through an epic moment of history. They gained a sense of equality and fulfilment that would burn in their memories forever.

The liberation had not come easily. It took weeks of frustration before Allied armies broke out from the Normandy beachheads and drove east toward Paris. The days before liberation were tense as resistance groups harassed German forces. There was fear of violent reprisals, perhaps even the deliberate destruction of Paris, before the Germans finally pulled out. In the event, the worst fears did not come true.

There was no farewell orgy of repression by the Germans, though thirty-five résistants died in the skirmishing before 25 August. Paris was not razed to the ground like Warsaw had been, though Adolf Hitler did indeed issue an order to destroy the city. The German commandant, General Dietrich von Choltitz disobeyed Hitler's order. This gained Choltitz a favoured place in history, even though he had been complicit in war crimes on the Eastern Front. For a few days at least, there was time for relief and rejoicing.

However joyful, the Liberation could not unite or heal the nation just like that. In Paris and all over France, there was a pent-up thirst for revenge against collaborators. In the shadows, instant 'summary justice' was carried out. Many known collaborators were shot out of hand without waiting for any legal process. There was much talk of *épuration* – purification of the nation by revenge against the guilty ones.

There was *épuration legale,* such as the trial for treason of the leaders of the Vichy regime, Marshal Pétain, the presidential figurehead, and Pierre Laval, the political mastermind who pulled the strings. Laval was executed. Pétain was also sentenced to death but this was commuted, partly because he was ninety-one years old and partly because of his heroic military record in the 1914-1918 war. *Epuration legale* was not only for the great and famous, it swept up people from many levels of society. One was the disgraced hero of French football, Alex Villaplane. For his crimes as leader of the *Brigade Nord Africaine,* the many beatings and murders in collaboration with the Gestapo, Villaplane had earned the nickname 'Mohammed of the SS'. At Christmas 1944, he was executed by firing squad at Fort de Montrouge.

There was also *épuration sauvage,* (unofficial 'wild purification') including a rush of vengeful humiliations of women deemed guilty of *collaboration horizontale.* Women denounced for sleeping with the enemy had to endure having their heads shaved in public, jeered at by onlookers, with angry women to the fore. Less publicly, there were many assassinations carried out as uncontrolled acts of private revenge. One such act of revenge ended the life of another famous ex-footballer, whose life had been closely interwoven with that of Carmen Pomiès.

In April 1944, not long before the Allies landed in Normandy, Violette Morris became an early victim of *épuration sauvage.* Violette's footballing days were far in the past by 1944, but she was never out of the public eye for long. Violette's notoriety, for her outrageous lesbian lifestyle and for being tried for murder, was inflamed by the fact that during the occupation, she became a collaborator, helping the Germans with cars from her garage business and by being an informer. Violette was also accused (falsely) of having been a super-spy passing state secrets to the Germans before 1940 and as the 'Hyena of the Gestapo' who supposedly participated in sadistic torture of suspects during interrogation. On 16 April, as Vichy France braced itself for the invasion, Violette died in a hail of bullets when her Citrôen car was ambushed by the Maquis on an empty road in Normandy. The Bailleul family, two adults and their two children, died with her.

It is, of course, impossible to know how Carmen reacted to the news of the death of Violette Morris, but the question is worth asking. This was a woman who had been Carmen's fierce rival in athletics competitions and had played against her many times on the football pitch. They had also played together for France. Carmen knew all about Violette's exceptional bravery on the Western Front during the

First World War. Perhaps Carmen rejoiced at the elimination of a collaborator; perhaps she had ambivalent feelings about the Violette she had known in the 1920s, or about the two children who died alongside her. Taking sides in a civil war is rarely simple or clean.

How Carmen reacted to life in Paris after the liberation is uncertain. Her own personal position was somewhat ambivalent. Carmen had indeed made valuable contributions to the resistance. On the other hand, Carmen had also worked for Renée Saint-Cyr, a film star who had lived an enviable life of luxury during what was for most French people a time of suffering and loss. Renee Saint-Cyr eventually resumed her career as a star of French cinema but the shadow of Vichy hung over her. What Carmen later told the Rochester *Democrat & Chronicle* about Renée Saint-Cyr's ardent support for the resistance 'in the dark of night' had a tone of defensiveness and over-statement. It is evident how sensitive the subject was for Carmen.

Superficially, France made a good recovery from the nightmares of defeat and occupation. The dominant leadership of General de Gaulle fostered the illusion that France was still one of the great powers. Political stability seemed assured; France did not slide into civil war the way Italy did in 1944-45. Relations between French and the Allied armies who liberated them were excellent. One example of this was Carmen's friendship with Ardean Miller.

Miller worked for the Eastman-Kodak company in Rochester NY. In 1942, he enlisted for war service as a US army photographer. In 1944, Carmen helped him while he was in Paris, presumably as a translator. They would become firm friends after Carmen moved to Rochester in 1946. After Paris, Ardean Miller followed the American forces as they drove east towards Berlin. He was present at the liberation of KZ Buchenwald. The photographs he took there are still famous seventy-five years later for their haunting images and for the exceptionally high technical quality of the colour photography.

Americans like Ardean Miller could return home with uncomplicated feelings of having been part of a 'good war', a struggle between democracy and dictatorship in which good triumphed over evil. In France, however, the war had divided even further a nation already deeply divided before the war began. The poisonous legacies of the Vichy years would linger in the collective memory for two generations after 1945.

Even to talk about the past, never mind heal its wounds was too much for most French men and women, so they avoided doing so. Cling to the resistance myth. Blame all the war crimes on evil Germans like Klaus Barbie, the SS chief known as the 'Butcher of Lyons'. Bury the memory of all the betrayals of French by French. Forget how decent French people had looked the other way when the Jews of France were rounded up, held in the squalid camp at the cycling stadium in Drancy and then deported to the camps in the East.

This was what Henry Rousso called the Vichy Syndrome. It permeated through almost everything in French life - books, films, education, conversations at dinner tables, keeping the painful past away from the light. Rousso's book, *La Syndrome de Vichy,* first published in 1994, was a big step forward in the slow process of coming to terms with the past. In 1969, the release of a masterly two-part documentary film directed by Marcel Öphuls, *Le Chagrin et la Pitié* (The Sorrow and the Pity), should have broken through the Vichy Syndrome but France was not yet ready in 1969 (the premiere of *The Sorrow and the Pity* was in Germany, not in France). Marcel Öphuls had to wait until 1981 for his film to be shown on French television.

Even in 2002, after the release of *Laissez-Passer*, Bertrand Tavernier's warm-hearted tribute to French cinema in the Vichy years, the ghosts of the past would not let go. Tavernier's film highlighted two fictionalised heroes based on real life, the director Jean Devaivre and the scriptwriter Jean Aurenche. But Devaivre, still alive and kicking at eighty-nine, furiously attacked Tavernier for 'deceiving, robbing and betraying his friendship'. The row hit the headlines and led to a lawsuit. A legal ruling forced Tavernier to change the film's credits. The Vichy Syndrome was still alive.

Another notable feature of the resistance myth was its treatment of the women who had played such important roles in the resistance. Once France had been liberated the memory of what these women had contributed was marginalised. In the words of the historian Robert Gildea, the political leadership of France after 1944 was 'very nationalist, very military and very male'. How France remembered the resistance was likewise nationalist, military and masculine. This trend was not only French. After the war, the many Italian women who had played a vital role in the partisan war against Mussolini's Fascist regime were marginalised in exactly the same way.

What Carmen and Hélène Pomiès thought about all this is a good question. Carmen's political outlook, and how close she was to her older sister, are difficult to judge. Yes, they were both on the side of resistance. Yes, they were both admirers of Charles de Gaulle (despite her left-wing views, Hélène dedicated *Du Sang sur le Montagne* to De Gaulle). Yes, they were both delighted that in 1946, at long last, women in France were granted the right to vote, though twenty-eight years later than women in Britain. But how far the sisters agreed about the future we do not know. Carmen had been pro-American since the age of eighteen; Hélène's sympathies leaned more to the Left.

Like most French people, the Pomiès sisters watched anxiously as De Gaulle and the Allies piloted France through the turbulent final months of the war. France was soon restored as a 'great power'. When the war in Europe ended in May 1945, France became one of the four occupying powers of defeated Germany. As the United Nations took shape, France became one of the five nations on the Security Council. President de Gaulle assumed huge, symbolic international prestige.

Recovering from the dislocation of the war and the Vichy years was a challenge, for the Pomiès family and for the nation. It is very likely that the business that had made Charles Pomiès wealthy was badly affected by the war, disrupting the comfortable bourgeois existence that the family had known until 1940. As for France, political institutions had to be rebuilt at a time of instability and economic crisis. Moderates and conservatives were agreed about the urgent need to block the rise of the PCF (French Communist Party) they disagreed about almost everything else.

The centrist political parties wanted to restore something very similar to the old Third Republic, with a strong parliamentary system and a presidency that was largely ceremonial. Charles de Gaulle, the man who had wielded vast authority ever since even before the liberation, the man many people thought was the living symbol of the nation, wanted a new politics headed by a powerful executive president. Nobody could doubt who that powerful president would be.

The political wrangling over the new constitution rumbled on from late 1945 for almost a year. In October 1946, the constitution of the Fourth Republic was finalised; it was to be headed by a weak presidency. Charles de Gaulle suddenly announced he was retiring from public life and went off into a self-imposed political wilderness. It would be twelve years before he returned to public life. But Carmen Pomiès was not there to witness the dramatic events in France in October 1946. Long before then, in April 1946, Carmen had arrived in Rochester NY, to begin a new life in America.

Chapter 8

Carmen in America

```
                              No. 7320827
Name......POMIES, Carmen Charlotte Marianne......
residing at....45 W. 76th St. New York..........
Sept. 29, 1900               May 17, 1954
Date of birth..........     Date of order of admission..........
Date certificate issued ... May 17, 1954 ..................by t}
...U. S. District........Court at. New York City, New York
Petition No.....621231.......
Alien Registration No...6274111...
           Carmen Charlotte Marianne Pomiè
                    (Complete and true signature of holder)
```

Certificate of US Citizenship issued to Carmen Pomiès, May 1954

In April 1946, Carmen Pomiès arrived in New York to begin a new life in America. We do not know exactly when and why Carmen made this big decision. Perhaps she already knew in October 1945, when she visited Preston to see old friends and stay one last time in Florrie Redford's home. Whether Carmen was running away from France or running towards America is an open question. Probably, like almost all emigrants, she was guided by both 'push' and 'pull' factors.

Carmen's life was at a crossroads in 1945. 'Push' factors weighed heavily in her decision to begin a new life across the Atlantic. Life in France was much less secure than before the war; and, at the age of forty-five, Carmen had to face the fact her time in football was over. Economically, it seems likely her father's business had taken a battering because of the war and that Carmen needed work at a time of post-war economic chaos. Politically, there was great instability and uncertainty. Emotionally, the back-biting and divisiveness in France, the accusations of collaboration or profiteering, and the conflicted memories of war and resistance, were hard to live with.

By contrast, the United States offered a fresh start. Looking across the Atlantic from war-torn Europe it was easy to be influenced by many powerful 'pull' factors. Americans were upbeat, looking to the future. They had not known occupation, nor war on their own doorstep. The US economy was booming. American soldiers liberating Europe had spread feelings of optimism wherever they went. Carmen had been enthusiastically pro-American in 1918, and she harboured happy memories of America from her football tour in the autumn of 1922. It was perhaps not by coincidence that Carmen chose Rochester in Upper New York State; not far from where she had crossed the border from Canada on that 1922 tour.

Then, too, Carmen already had connections to Rochester. Henri Gaudriot ran the Teale Motor company there and his wife had been one of Carmen's friends growing up in Paris. The Gaudriots were offering Carmen a job, using her secretarial skills. More than that, during the liberation of Paris, Carmen had acquired a new American friend from Rochester. Ardean Miller worked for Eastman-Kodak, already famous for developing new techniques of colour photography, with its headquarters in Rochester. In 1942, soon after America entered the war, Miller had enlisted as a US Army photographer. Carmen befriended Ardean Miller in 1944 during the liberation of Paris and helped him with his work, as a translator and guide.

After Paris, Miller followed the Allied armies east. Before he left he may have planted seeds in Carmen's mind that made Rochester an enticing future destination. The friendship between Carmen and Ardean Miller proved lasting. After arriving in Rochester in 1946, Carmen became a close friend of Mrs Miller and was a frequent visitor to 576 Beach Avenue on the shore of Lake Ontario.

These connections help to explain why citizens of Rochester already knew quite a lot about Carmen even before she arrived in the city. An

Associated Press report of 19 April, picked up by the local *Democrat & Chronicle,* newspaper, excitedly informed citizens of Rochester about the arrival of a new resident. The AP story, under the heading *FIRST FRENCH LINE SHIP DOCKS SINCE WAR BEGAN,* reported:

> New York, April 19 (AP). The first steamship operated by the French Line to dock here since Pearl Harbor arrived today with 256 passengers after a fifteen-day trip from Le Havre. The vessel was the 13,000-ton *Desrirade.* Among the passengers were Mlle Carmen Pomies, a French athlete, and J.B. Verlot, who will head the United States office of the French National Railroads.

Newspaper readers in Rochester learned more about Carmen from an article titled *FRANCE RESIDENT EN ROUTE TO THE CITY,* which informed them:

> The first French Line steamship to dock at New York since Pearl Harbor arrived yesterday with 256 passengers. Among them was a French woman athlete and former member of the French underground who will be coming to Rochester. The French woman, Mlle Carmen Pomies, who worked with other patriots during the German occupation, will be the guest of Mr and Mrs Henry Gaudriot at 964 Winston Road North according to an Associated Press dispatch. Mademoiselle Pomies was captain of a women's hockey and tennis team which toured England before the war. She came to the United States once before, with a women's soccer team.

Much of this striking, though not precisely accurate portrait of Carmen was no doubt derived from her friends and hosts the Gaudriots as well as from the AP report. The picture can be further fleshed out by evidence from official documents recording her arrival, especially the Resident Alien's Border Crossing Identification Card, which shows Carnen's Alien Registration number was 6274111; that she was born Sept 29 1900 in Paris, France; Sex female, Marital Status single, Occupation secretary. The card offers a laconic personal description: Read, Yes, Write, Yes, Nationality, France, Height, 5ft 6 in, Weight, 140 lb, Complexion, Medium, Hair, Brown, Eyes, Gray, Visible Distinctive Marks or Peculiarities, None. The card also shows Carmen's Quota Visa number, 663. Issued in Paris, France Feb 13 1946.

When Carmen arrived in New York harbour in April 1946, she was revisiting exciting memories. On the Dick, Kerr Ladies football tour, when she was twenty-two, Carmen had travelled through Upper New York State on her way south from Canada. The team had stayed in New York City and crisscrossed the eastern seaboard to play matches in towns and cities from Washington to New England to Philadelphia before sailing out of New York past the Statue of Liberty on a White Star liner bound for Liverpool. Coming through New York to Rochester was a happy new beginning.

Rochester was then and still is today a prosperous city, always near the top of lists of the most desirable places to live in the United States. Buffalo, eighty miles to the south-west, is a bigger city with heavy industry and vital transport links, but Rochester is a key centre for modern businesses, such as Eastman-Kodak, Western Union and Xerox. In higher education, the University of Rochester and the Rochester Institute of Technology have glowing reputations for science and innovation.

Carmen often told friends and acquaintances in Rochester how much she loved the city, not only for its comfortable, affluent lifestyle after the hard times in France during and after the war, but also for its beautiful setting. South of Rochester, the Genesee River winds through a green wilderness of steep forested hills. At the heart of the city is the dramatic High Falls where the river becomes a wide wall of water tumbling down northwards on its way to Lake Ontario. Curving along the shore of the lake, with its beaches, sailboats and limitless vistas across the water toward Canada, is Beach Avenue with its fine houses under the trees. Carmen was a frequent visitor to Number 576, home of her friends the Millers.

At first, Carmen's address was 964 Winton Road North, home of the Gaudriots, who had given her a job in the Teale motor company and done much else to smooth her arrival in Rochester. Later, Carmen set up home on her own, at 176 Akron Avenue. Among the many green spaces in the city was the Tennis Club of Rochester, where it did not take long for Carmen to make an impact. Football was in the past now (it's interesting that her visit to Preston in 1945 was to promote women's sport through hockey and tennis, not football) but sport was still as important as ever to Carmen. The natural flair, the athleticism and the competitive spirit still burned brightly. It was not long before Carmen achieved local celebrity status as a serial winner of tennis trophies.

So Carmen seems to have very swiftly assimilated to her new life in America. This was made clear in May 1947 when the *Democrat & Chronicle* published an article about her by Henry W. Clune. Evidence from that article relating to Carmen and the French resistance has already appeared in Chapter Seven, under the heading *Pour le Sport*. Henry Clune had much to say about Rochester's impressive new resident.

> Miss Carmen Pomies has done almost everything in sports apart from box six rounds against Philadelphia Jack O'Brien. She is French and only a year out of her native Paris. She is of medium height, stocky, with dark wavy hair attractively parted on the side. She resembles English women tennis players you see at the Wightman Cup. As a matter of fact, she has been a tournament player in France. Tennis is just one of the games she has played in her long career in sports. 'I have been a jack of all trades in sports, never the master of any one,' she explained, 'I liked them all. They say French women are effete and frivolous but they are more interested in sports than American women. Here, you have a few specialized

champions, but the rest of the girls hardly play games at all. Their lives are softer. They have too much of everything.'

Miss Pomies now lives in Rochester, which she says is like heaven after the privations and suffering of Europe. She is secretary to Henry Gaudriot, head of the Teale Motor Company, whose wife and Miss Pomies were girlhood friends in Paris. Miss Pomies's father was a businessman, a manufacturer of dentures. It was his purpose to have his daughter study dentistry, hoping this would make her valuable to his business. She tried to follow his desires, like a good daughter. But she soon abandoned her studies to be a teacher at a girls school in Preston, England. There her love of sports found fulfilment and she joined an English women's soccer team. Instead of returning to her English school, Miss Pomies returned to her Paris home. Twice after that she engaged in international athletic competitions, winning the javelin in Prague and London. She played soccer, water polo, basketball, tennis, went ski jumping in Switzerland and rode in mountain bicycle races.

Henry Clune seems rather unsure of the finer details in Carmen's football career and her connections with Preston. Later in his article, his colourful account of Carmen's 1922 football tour with Dick, Kerr Ladies gets somewhat jumbled. There may have been other little misunderstandings, too, but *Pour le Sport* paints an authentic, highly informative picture of Carmen's life and personality:

While she was doing all these sports, her younger brother was making a sensational reputation as an interpretive dancer. He was gaining international recognition when he died suddenly of a mystery illness, aged only 30. Miss Pomies is chic, feminine and Frenchy. She speaks excellent English. She is highly educated. She studied

Spanish in Spain and talks the language fluently, and French, of course, but the outrages perpetrated by the German oppressors during the war caused her to abandon learning the language.

After a vivid account of Carmen shouldering her rifle on the streets of Paris in the frantic days leading up to the Liberation [see Chapter Seven] Henry Clune looked more closely at Carmen's first year in Rochester. One interesting detail is that the Harley School attempted to persuade Carmen to take on a role supervising sports at the school but she declined, saying that being a 'professor' would not suit her, because it might detract from her own enjoyment of sport. Another relates to Carmen's connection to Ardean Miller and his wife. Finally, there is evidence of how happy Carmen was in Rochester:

Shortly after the Liberation, Miss Pomies met Ardean R. Miller. He is now a distinguished photographer of this city, who was then an army photographer. Miss Pomies was able to help him. Since her arrival in Rochester last year, she and Mrs Miller have become good friends. When she first met Ardean Miller, she had scarcely heard of Rochester. Now, she is devoted to Rochester and she intends to become an American citizen. I love everything about Rochester,' she said. 'People here complain about the rain. But I love the rain. It makes everything so green. I love walking in the rain. You people who have lived here so long do not realise how wonderful it is. You have warm houses when it's cold; you have quantities and quantities of wonderful food. You have lovely scenery and shops that have everything. I pinch myself sometimes, to be sure I'm not living in a dream'.

Without the *Democrat & Chronicle,* especially Henry W. Clune's vivid, warm-hearted pen picture of 1947, little would be known of

Carmen's life in Rochester; and Carmen continued to make regular appearances in the paper for her triumphs on the tennis courts of Rochester and the Genesee Valley, whether in singles, ladies doubles, or mixed doubles. In 1950, another glowing feature about Carmen appeared in the *Democrat & Chronicle*. In the *About Women* section, with the title *From Underground to UN Skyscraper,* Pat Fallon's chatty article focused mostly on Carmen's role in the French resistance. It was also a fond farewell. After four years in Rochester, Carmen was moving on to New York City to work as a translator at the United Nations.

Some people in Rochester already knew Carmen was leaving. A snippet of news in July 1950, headed *Off the Handle,* announced:

> A testimonial party for Carmen Pomies, Tennis Club of Rochester feminine star, was held at the clubhouse last Friday, Bastille Day. Carmen, who holds a deep spot in her heart for her home city on the Seine, leaves Rochester later this summer to take over new duties with the United Nations in New York City.

Pat Fallon's article, as its title suggests, was primarily about Carmen as heroine of the French resistance but also included admiring and affectionate references to a woman whose four years in the city made her well known to citizens of Rochester:

> Carmen Pomies, who once knew the French underground well, left last Sunday for UN offices in the slim, reaching skyscraper overlooking New York City's East River. Scores of people will miss her; for her friends here are legion, especially members of Rochester Tennis Club. There, on nights and weekends, she has been a familiar figure on the courts, her bright hair bobbing from the bounds of a hair ribbon as she darted about, returning smashing serves with the strength and skill of a professional.

The sports-minded knew and admired her, looking to her record as a women's tennis champion of the city both in '47 and '50. They also recalled she was once candidate for the French Olympic ski team, an exceptional field hockey player and no mean ice skater. Further, she had toured the States before World War Two as a member of the French Women's soccer team, and gained high respect from sportswriters for lady athletes in la belle France. She engaged in a different sport during the war – namely, fooling the Germans.

Then, after lively anecdotes of Carmen and the resistance, Pat Fallon concluded her piece by asking Carmen about the future of the United Nations. Would it succeed in furthering world peace? 'We had better,' she said with a smile.

As with all the evidence we have about her four years there, Carmen seems to have felt happy and fulfilled in Rochester. It also seems she had changed her hairstyle; Henry Clune's 'dark wavy hair attractively parted at the side' and Pat Fallon's 'bright hair bobbing from the bounds of a hair ribbon' seem a bit different from the shock of frizzy dark hair seen in so many team photos during Carmen's time in football. But in other ways their evidence reveals the familiar Carmen, still active and athletic, even in her late forties, still confident and fearless, still good at making friendships.

The *Democrat & Chronicle* articles have inaccuracies and exaggerations, such as Pat Fallon's mistaken reference to the 'French Women's soccer team' of 1922, and a recurring tendency to overstate Carmen's contribution to the resistance. They betray the eagerness of postwar Americans to hear what they wanted to hear about their 'gallant French allies'. Yet the positive descriptions of Carmen in Rochester, and the newspaper snapshots of a tennis player, relaxed and confident as she smiles in the glow of victory, suggest a woman at peace with her surroundings and with herself.

Still, there are many unanswered questions. Did Carmen remain in close touch with her sisters and her parents in France? Were there letters to and from Florrie Redford, or her other football friends in Preston, such as Margaret Thornborough and Lizzy Ashcroft? How fulfilled did Carmen feel about her working life and career prospects? And why did Carmen decide to move on to New York City?

Answers to these questions are in short supply. We know Carmen sailed home to France in October 1948, aboard the French liner *De Grasse,* making the return voyage to New York eighteen days later. According to the ship's passenger list, Carmen's home address was 176 Akron Avenue, Rochester; her occupation was listed as 'stenographer'. (In 1950, according to US City Directories, her address was 1050 East Avenue, occupation 'office secretary'). The trip to France was probably on her own, to see family and friends, though it's possible that Carmen may have travelled together with the Gaudriots, her French bosses at the Teale Motor Company.

France in 1948 was politically more stable than had been the case when she left two-and-a-half years before, but the economic situation was still difficult. French living standards were far behind America, where the war years had produced an abundant consumer boom. In France, the long postwar economic boom known as the '*Trente Glorieuses*' had barely begun. Like most of Western Europe, France depended heavily on American aid through the Marshall Plan.

So, while Carmen talked happily of Rochester, where 'people have everything', her friends and family could tell her about the awful winter of 1947 or the housing crisis in Paris. Perhaps conversations included international affairs and France's war in Indochina. Perhaps there was news of Renée Saint-Cyr's latest film, or time to talk with Hélène about the reception of *Du Sang sur la Montagne*, published in 1947.

Most migrants experience some degree of homesickness when back in familiar surroundings, but it seems unlikely Carmen had any regrets in 1948 about her new American identity. She had already told people of her intentions to become a US citizen, and she may already have been thinking about New York. In 1946, there had been persuasive reasons why Carmen chose to start her new life in Rochester but perhaps that was never her idea of a final destination. Carmen was a girl from the big city and she had always had an adventurous eye for travel and new experiences. Perhaps she had applied for the position at the United Nations a long time before it actually materialised. Perhaps she had been aiming for New York all along.

At all events, the move to New York City was a significant moment in Carmen's life. It is also a landmark for what we know and do not know about her life. For all the gaps in her story, there is a trail of evidence substantial enough to provide a more or less continuous narrative of Carmen's first fifty years. After that, however, her trail becomes more and more cloudy and elusive, almost as if Carmen were a ship sailing away into the mist. Within a few years of arriving in New York, that mist would become almost impenetrable.

Unlike her time at the forefront of women's football between the wars, there are few photographs of Carmen in America. So the faded snapshots of her in the pages of the *Democrat & Chronicle* fill an important gap. Almost all of them show a relaxed and confident woman smiling in the glow of victory on the tennis courts of Rochester and the Genesee Valley region.

In the mid-twentieth century, New York City had an almost mythical image in the minds of Europeans. France, along with the rest of continental Europe, had gone through years of war, occupation and grim hardships. Britain had avoided the horrors of occupation but was a grey land of bomb damage, rationing and 'austerity'. In contrast, the United States was the land of abundance. For Americans war did not mean suffering and hardship. It was a time of national well-being: bright lights, full employment, rising living standards. This abundance was symbolised by New York, the city of skyscrapers, glamour and optimism.

Carmen had first got to know New York in 1922, on the Dick, Kerr Ladies football tour. She travelled to New York again in 1946, on her way to her new life in Rochester. When she moved to New York to work as an interpreter at the United Nations, Carmen was on familiar ground, no longer just a visitor but a permanent resident, intending to become an American citizen. She finally achieved this in May 1954. Carmen carried on living in New York at least until 1960 but surprisingly little evidence has been found about her time there.

Carmen began working at the United Nations at an important time when there were high hopes the UN might succeed where the League of Nations had failed. The idea of the United Nations had taken shape from 1941 with a series of declarations and summit conferences leading up to the San Francisco Conference of April 1945. A year later the first session of the UN General Assembly took place. The imposing new headquarters building in New York seemed like a symbol of a new, better world order, guided by American values. By 1950, the Cold War had begun, dividing Germany and Europe. China was under Communist rule after the revolution of 1949. Despite these developments, high hopes for the UN persisted. Many thought the new Secretary-General, Dag Hammarskjöld, appointed in April 1953, might achieve great things.

By then, Carmen's time with the UN was coming to an end. The records show she stopped working there in May 1953. At that time, the City Directories listed Carmen's home address as 45 West 76th Street, located in an elegant part of the Upper West Side, close to Central Park, an area which now has protected status as the 'Central Park West historic district'. West 76th was just round the corner from the Natural History Museum in Theodore Roosevelt Park. It was, and is, a very desirable address.

Soon after leaving her position with the UN, Carmen sailed home to France; and she stayed there for a long time, eleven months, before returning to New York in April 1954. In May, Carmen received official confirmation she was a US citizen. That is pretty much all the hard evidence about Carmen's first years in New York. It presents several intriguing questions:

What job(s) did Carmen have to pay her way after leaving the UN? Who were her friends and contacts in New York? How was she able to have such an elegant, expensive address as West 76th Street? Why did Carmen go back to France in 1953? What made her stay in France for so long? Were there any complications affecting Carmen's application to become an American citizen?

Although little specific detail is known about Carmen at this time, there is vivid and abundant evidence about the city she was living in; what was happening there, what was being seen at the cinema or on television; what people were talking about at dinner parties, whether it was about politics, sport or world events. In the world of entertainment, the talk of the town before the 1951 Oscars was of Bette Davis and Anne Baxter in *All About Eve,* with a bit part for then little-known Marilyn Monroe. Carmen may well have gone to see Gene Kelly and Leslie Caron dancing to the music of George Gershwin in *An American in Paris.* The hit film of 1953 was the Pacific War epic, *From Here to Eternity.* Whatever Carmen was doing, we can guess what she and her friends may have been talking about.

This was not only the age of popular culture and consumerism. It was also the age of the Cold War: the Marshall Plan in 1947, the Berlin Airlift of 1948-49, the Communist Revolution in China, the Soviet Atomic Bomb, and the Korean War, which began in 1950. This was not just an American war. It was fought under a multinational United Nations Command backed by twenty-two nations. Throughout Carmen's time at the UN, the Korean War was in the news; the dramatic decision by President Truman to sack General Douglas MacArthur in April 1951 dominated the headlines for weeks on end.

The Korean War also intensified an already-existing Cold War paranoia. America was gripped by McCarthyism and the 'War Against Communism'. Although the Cold War was already beginning even before the Second World War had ended, it took time for a new full-blown 'Red Scare' to take hold of America. The Revolution in China in 1949 was a turning point. The public face of this Red Scare was an obscure senator from Wisconsin, Joseph McCarthy. The public arena which McCarthy came to dominate was HUAC (House Un-American Activities Committee).

McCarthyism induced sustained political and public hysteria in the United States. There was special emphasis on 'rooting out Communist sympathisers' at the State Department, putting diplomats and 'internationalists' under suspicion, such as the prosecution of a diplomatic expert on China, Alger Hiss in 1950. 'Atom spies' Julius and Ethel Rosenberg were executed in 1953. 'Liberals' in cinema and television were targeted. Many actors, writers and directors were grilled by HUAC and blacklisted.

It is possible that the McCarthyite tide washed close to Carmen. She was a foreign national. She worked at the United Nations, next to diplomats and 'internationalists'. The process of obtaining US citizenship required her to complete an Alien Registration Card. If the FBI ever did a background check on Carmen, it might have revealed she had a left-wing sister who had collaborated with Communist writers in the books she edited and translated before the war. The backstory to the end of Carmen's work at the UN until May 1953 may even help to explain why she spent eleven months in France from that point. Did Carmen choose to finish working at the UN? Did she have a new career to begin, or was she having to wait a long time for bureaucratic wheels to finish turning before her citizenship application could be approved?

Carmen duly went through all the necessary bureaucratic hoops to become a US citizen: Alien Registration Form no 6274111, Petition for Naturalisation no 621237, finally her Certificate of Citizenship, stamped on 17 May 1954.

But that was at a time when Carmen had only just returned to New York from her extended visit home to Paris. Precisely why Carmen went home in May 1953 is uncertain. We know how - with SS *Veendam* of Holland-America Line bound for Rotterdam via Southampton and Boulogne, which is presumably where Carmen left the ship. But we do not know why, nor the reasons why she stayed in France so long. Whatever her reasons, Carmen had time enough to reconnect with family, friends and acquaintances.

If still alive, her father would have been in his eighties and her mother in her late seventies. Perhaps Carmen's return home was linked to their ill-health, or death. Perhaps both Hélène and Yvonne were there; it was five years since Carmen had last been 'home'. Perhaps Carmen socialised with René Saint-Cyr, back at her peak of popularity in 1953 with two historical costume dramas, *Le Chevalier du Nuit* (Knight of the Night) and *Le Prince de la Maison Rouge* (Prince of the Red House), adapted from an Alexandre Dumas story with Renée Saint-Cyr as Queen Marie Antoinette. The most talked-about French film was a sweaty-palms thriller directed by Henri Clouzot, *The Wages of Fear*, about desperate men driving trucks loaded with unstable nitro-glycerine across the mountains of Central America.

As for Paris and France, huge changes had taken place since Carmen had been there in 1948. This was now a time of renewed prosperity and elegance under the Fourth Republic, the time of the *Trente Glorieuses*, of living standards going up and up and Paris back to its glamorous best. But it was also a time of political instability and anxiety. Throughout Carmen's time in France, the news about the war in Indochina got worse and worse; French colonial rule over Vietnam was hanging by a thread. As Carmen set out on her voyage back to New York in April 1954, French forces in Indochina were on the brink of humiliating defeat at Dien Bien Phu.

Carmen's many voyages across the Atlantic make an important thread of her life story. She made at least ten crossings, possibly more. In 1922, she sailed to Quebec and Montreal by Canadian Pacific and from New York home to Liverpool with White Star Line. In 1946, her journey with *SS Desirade* took fifteen days to reach New York before she travelled on to Rochester. Then she made return sailings in October 1948, and again in 1953-54. Carmen's many ocean voyages belonged to an age long gone; since the 1970s regular traffic between Europe and America has been a few hours in the sky, not several days at sea. Nowadays there are cruise ships, but nothing to compare with the buzz and glamour of the ocean liners Carmen knew so well.

Of all Carmen's ships, the most prestigious was *SS Liberté,* the flagship of French Line, which carried her from France to New York in April 1954. Only a small part of the history of *Liberté* was French. The ship began life in 1929 as *SS Europa,* built at Hamburg for Nord Deutscher Lloyd Line. In 1931, *Europa* won the Blue Riband for the fastest westward crossing. In 1945, *Europa* was captured by the Americans, briefly used to take US troops home from Europe and then handed over to France to be reborn as *Liberté.*

In 1954, *Liberté* even had a starring role in *Sabrina*, a hit romantic comedy directed by Billy Wilder, starring Audrey Hepburn and Humphrey Bogart. *Liberté* takes centre stage in the final scenes of the film as Hepburn and Bogart sail off towards France and a happy ending. It was no accident *Liberté* featured so prominently in *Sabrina*. *Liberté* was the ship the director, Billy Wilder, always chose for himself. It is also true that many passengers, including African-Americans, preferred to sail with French Line rather than Britain's Cunard Line, because the French ships were regarded as less class-ridden and 'snobbish'. Of course, nobody can say if Carmen saw *Sabrina* at the cinema after arriving home but, given the connection to *Liberté* and the storyline about an American girl in Paris, it seems more likely she did than she didn't.

A few weeks after *Liberté* brought her back to New York, Carmen received confirmation of her US citizenship. She stayed in New York for the next two years, though it is not clear where she was working or who her friends were. But then some sudden crisis seems to have occurred. In October 1956, Carmen returned to France again, not this time by sea but flying New York-Paris with Air France. Why?

Chapter 9

Knowns and Unknowns: The Road to Champcueil

In February 2002, the US Defense Secretary, Donald Rumsfeld, mused in public about the difficulties of knowing exactly what was going on in the world. Just more than a year later, at government briefings on the hunt for weapons of mass destruction following the invasion of Iraq, Rumsfeld's ideas circulated widely and became the target of much derision from journalists and commentators. Rumsfeld's words that his critics deemed 'bizarre' and 'ridiculous' ran as follows:

> Reports that say that something hasn't happened are always interesting to me, because as we know, there are known knowns; there are things we know we know. We also know there are known unknowns; that is to say we know there are some things we do not know. But there are also unknown unknowns - the ones we don't know we don't know.

Donald Rumsfeld was indeed a controversial, provocative politician who frequently came under attack from critics of the Bush Administration and the war in Iraq. There were many instances where Rumsfeld richly deserved the insults thrown at him. But what he said on this occasion was neither 'bizarre' nor 'ridiculous' but a statement of profound wisdom, about history, science or the evaluation of intelligence. Ever since 1955, this principle has been known to security professionals as the Johari Window.

Finding out about what happened to Carmen Pomiès during her years in New York from 1956 is not as important for world affairs as the hunt for Saddam Hussein's supposed arsenal of nuclear and biological weapons was in 2003 but it is almost as difficult. There is a handful of 'known knowns' – scattered pieces of specific evidence to prove where Carmen was and what she was doing – and many 'known unknowns' which at least enable the right questions to be asked in trying to fill gaps in the story of Carmen's life. Beyond that lurk veritable black holes of 'unknown unknowns'.

The last of the 'known knowns' of Carmen in America dates from 1960, when she sailed from France to New York on *SS Flandre*. For the last twenty-two years of her life, from arrival in New York in October 1960 until she died on 29 September 1982, at Champceuil, Essonne, a few miles south of Paris, no hard evidence has yet come to light to show what Carmen was doing, or even which country she was living in. After the age of sixty, Carmen may have experienced any number of new travels and new friendships but, unless fresh evidence is unearthed, they will remain 'unknown unknowns', hidden in the mists of time.

Historians know their responsibility to stick to the factual evidence and eschew speculation. In the case of Carmen Pomiès, however, the slender evidence means that any attempt to trace the course of her life after 1960 (and even much of her time in New York and France from 1953) must depend almost entirely on speculation and guesswork in order to place Carmen in the context of her life and times. Questions are more plentiful than answers. Were Carmen's last years mostly in America? Or mostly back in France? We do not know. Here are the known knowns:

May 1953:
Termination of Carmen's work at the United Nations Address listed in City Directories at 45 West 76th Street, New York, NY 19/05 Sailed New York-Boulogne with *SS Veendam*, Holland-America Line

April 1954:
21/04 Arrival in New York from Le Havre by French Line *SS Liberté*

May 1954:
17/05 Certificate of US Citizenship 7320 827 (Supporting documents: Petition for Naturalization 621237; Alien Registration Form 62741111)

August 1956:
16/08 Flight New York-Paris by Air France 709/0815 (Carmen Pomiès named as US citizen on the passenger list)

November 1958:
08/10 Marriage in Paris between Yvonne Clementine Louise Pomiès and Roger Joseph, Henri de Morot de Grésigny

October 1960:
22/10 Voyage from Le Havre-New York by *SS Flandre,* French Line. Address listed in City Directories at 277 East 56th Street Manhattan NY

May 1963:
25/05, Death of Hélène Pomiès at Versailles

February 1977:
09/02 Death of Yvonne at Geneva in Switzerland

September 1982:
29/09 Death of Carmen Pomiès recorded at Champcueil, Essonne Social Security Death Index, SSN 132-22-6211 (issued New York pre-1951) terminated. Postal address listed as PO Box 912, US Consulate, Paris

The starting point has to be that apparently sudden decision to fly home to France in 1956. On 16 August, at New York International airport, Carmen Pomiès boarded an Air France Lockheed Super Constellation airliner. AF 079 left New York at 08.15, for an eleven-hour flight via refuelling stops at Gander in Newfoundland and Shannon in the West of Ireland, before arrival at Paris-Orly.

This flight placed Carmen in exclusive company. Commercial air travel between Europe and America was new, rare and extremely expensive. Air France had inaugurated its 'direct' schedule linking New York and Paris only in 1950. In those days, almost everyone flew first class, with tickets costing the modern equivalent of thousands of dollars, more than most Americans could afford. In subsequent years, the advent of jet airliners capable of carrying more passengers per flight brought costs down, but the introduction of jets was slowed down by a series of disasters involving the Comet, Britain's groundbreaking jet airliner, in 1953 and 1954.

So Carmen was doing something that was expensive, dangerous and out of the ordinary, for people in general and for herself in particular, when she boarded flight 079 for Paris. All Carmen's transatlantic crossings over a period of more than thirty years had been by sea. This raises an obvious question about her flight in 1956 – why? As with many episodes in Carmen's life, it is yet another 'known unknown'. But the apparently sudden decision to fly home suggests urgency. Was there a family emergency calling Carmen back to France? Was it prompted by a personal crisis such as loss of her job, or the breakdown of a relationship?

Speculation about a family crisis leads first to the possibility one of Carmen's parents had died. Much-travelled as she was, Carmen seems to have kept close family ties. After settling in America, she had sailed 'home' to France in 1948 and again in 1953. When she flew home in 1956, her father Charles, if still alive, would have been well into his eighties; her mother, Adéle, a few years younger. It is plausible that bereavement, perhaps the death of the last surviving parent, was the cause of Carmen's return to Paris.

It is also possible there was a family crisis involving her sisters, though little is known about Hélène and Yvonne after the war. (One of

Knowns and Unknowns: The Road to Champcueil

the more remarkable gaps in what we know is that the last time we can be certain all three sisters were all together at the same time was after Georges died in 1933). Then again, it cannot be discounted that something happened in New York that triggered Carmen's sudden departure, that she was rushing away from her American life rather than rushing home to France, but that line of enquiry leads only to more unknown unknowns.

The question why Carmen flew home in 1956 is made more intriguing by the mystery of what happened next. There is no proof Carmen went back to the United States until October 1960, when she sailed from Le Havre with *SS Flandre*. That would mean Carmen stayed in France for more than four years, and did so very soon after she had obtained her long-awaited US citizenship. If so, considering the course of Carmen's life since the end of the war, it would be difficult to explain.

It is, of course, entirely possible that Carmen did not stay in France for four years. Perhaps she flew back to New York in 1956 or 1957 to resume her life there (at that time it would have been highly unusual to buy a one-way ticket with Air France or any airline). Perhaps the voyage with *SS Flandre* in October 1960 was merely returning home to New York from a short visit to France in 1960. This leads to a guessing game full of 'unknown unknowns' - France or America?

Supposing that it was indeed a four-year stay in France, its causes may have been either in New York or in Paris. Perhaps Carmen was retreating from something bad in her career or her personal life in America. Perhaps the death of the last surviving parent led to complications to do with the will, or legal issues concerning the sale of her father's assets. This might well have been the end of the Pomiès home at 4 Rue de la Gaîté; when Hélène died in 1963, it was at Versailles, not Montparnasse.

There are other, even more speculative possibilities. Perhaps one of her parents, or Hélène, or Yvonne, or even Carmen herself, needed intensive long-term medical care. Such suppositions may seem nebulous but they are in a sense necessary to have any sense of Carmen's French or American identity after 1956. Was she being pulled back towards her French self? Or was she in Paris as a visitor, impatient to get back to her newer roots in New York?

It is noteworthy that, in November 1958, Carmen's middle sister, Yvonne, got married, at the age of sixty. Yvonne's husband, six years younger than herself, came from an aristocratic family whose titles went back to 1650, the time of Louis XIV, the Boy King. Was Carmen there for the wedding? It seems more likely than not. If so, was Carmen already in France beforehand, or did she make a special return from New York to be there? Beyond that lurk other unknowns. Had Yvonne been prevented from marrying sooner, perhaps because she was the main carer for her mother, Adéle? Was the wedding a way out of a dislocating family upheaval? The truth may be simpler and more prosaic, and is anyway out of reach. We just don't know. On the other hand, Yvonne's wedding may be one small clue hinting that Carmen did perhaps stay in France for four years from 1956.

If so, Carmen lived through an eventful time. The long war in Indochina had ended, for France at least, in 1954, but this did not end France's post-colonial nightmares. A civil war in North Africa, between the FLN (National Liberation Front) fighting for Algerian independence and French settlers supported by the Army wanting to preserve *Algérie Franaise*, re-opened deep divisions that shook the foundations of the Fourth Republic. By 1958, there was unrest on the streets. At the height of this May crisis, Charles de Gaulle ended his twelve years of self-imposed political exile. He was received as a saviour in Algiers, and by many people in France; though there were also angry demonstrations against the 'strong presidency' the Gaullists were demanding. De Gaulle won. By October he was President of the Fifth Republic.

For Carmen and Hélène even more than most French people, it would have been difficult to hold a neutral position about the return of President de Gaulle. In 1944, they had both been enthusiastic admirers of General de Gaulle and had greeted him as 'saviour of the soul of France'. Judging what they thought about Gaullism and the

Fifth Republic in 1958 is much less clear-cut. If Carmen was indeed in Paris in May 1960, she would have had a close-up view of the political storm caused by the U2 Crisis and last-minute cancellation of the summit meeting in Paris between President Eisenhower and the Soviet leader Nikita Khrushchev. Instead of the Paris summit leading to a new era of 'peaceful coexistence', the Cold War hardened.

If, on the other hand, Carmen was in America for most of those four years, the background noise would have been very different. In the United States, these were the years of rampant consumerism, watching *I Love Lucy* on television, following the drama of Fidel Castro's Cuban revolution. One known known about Carmen is that she arrived in New York in October 1960, just in time to vote in the presidential election in November. It's tempting to wonder whether she did so, and if her vote went to Richard Nixon or John F. Kennedy.

After her return to New York in 1960, finding Carmen becomes even more of a mystery. It is known her address at that time was 277 East 56th in the East Side of Manhattan. It is known that Hélène died near Paris in May 1963. It is certain that Carmen made at least one journey back to France but entirely uncertain as to when she did so. Finally, it is known Carmen died in 1982, at Champcueil. Trying to work out where Carmen was and what she may have been doing in the last quarter of her life feels less like a task for a historian and much more like an archaeologist who has only a few scattered artefacts and bits of broken pottery to work with.

In tracking the arc of Carmen's last years, whether in America or in France, some events stand out as constants, for example, one event in the world news of 1961 that we may safely assume caught Carmen's attention. On the night of 17-18 September, on a mission to mediate peace in the Congo Crisis, Dag Hammarskjöld, Secretary-General of the United Nations, was killed in a plane crash. Carmen had been working at the UN when Hammarskjold was appointed in April 1953. Wherever Carmen was in September 1961, the tragic death of Dag Hammarskjöld will have left a mark. In the following years, many memorable events will have made similarly strong impressions upon Carmen in the 1960s, wherever she was living: the Cuban Missile Crisis, Martin Luther King's 'I have a dream' speech, the assassinations of President Kennedy in 1963 and Dr King in 1968, protests against the Vietnam War, the Prague Spring, the youth revolutions of 1968, the sudden shock of President de Gaulle's decision to give up power in France in April 1969, Neil Armstrong walking on the Moon.

These were the years after Carmen passed the age of sixty and they are years of impenetrable mystery about what happened to her. They were also years during which Carmen was passing beyond her natural span of energy and employability. By 1970 she was approaching her seventieth birthday, facing retirement and old age. Even more than in the mystery years of 1956-60, it is hard to know where Carmen was living. After coming back 'home' to New York in 1960, did she live in America for most of the rest of her life? If so, what about her work, friendships and social life? Why is it so hard to pick up any trail of evidence beyond her social security number? How long before she died did Carmen return to France? Or had her ocean crossing in 1960 been no more than a brief visit to say goodbye to New York and the people she knew there, before a final chapter of her life in France?

Behind these unanswered questions lurk other questions about old age and infirmity. In the first three-quarters of her life, Carmen was a vibrant personality, a gifted athlete, a high-energy woman with high-level social skills, extraordinarily good at making friends and connections. But old age and ill health can make people turn in on themselves, leading a smaller, lonelier life as family, friends and contemporaries become fewer and fewer, leading to a life more in the memory than in the present.

One remarkable aspect of the Pomiès family is the absence of any new generation. Georges died young in 1933. There is no sign of marriage or children for Hélène, nor Carmen herself. Little or nothing is known about Yvonne apart from her marriage, at the age of sixty, to Roger de Morot de Grésigny. It seems the multi-talented Pomiès family line simply died out with Carmen. Whenever Carmen returned to France for the last time, it remains unknown whether she still had a circle of family, friends and neighbours to keep her company.

When did Carmen outlive her travel bug? Did she write and receive letters? Were Carmen's last years scarred by dementia, like her old friend in Preston, Margaret Thornborough? More questions without answers.

The 1970s, even more than the 1960s, are blank pages in Carmen's story. For someone who made such an impact on the world for the first sixty years of her life, this is frustratingly difficult to explain. Perhaps her life just closed in because of age and infirmity. Perhaps she lived, either in America or in France, at an address in someone else's name, so that no fixed address for Carmen was recorded.

Again, questions without answers. Two tentative scenarios might be floated, though very tentatively. In the first scenario, Carmen's identity remained American after 1960. She may have gone back to France for Hélène's funeral in 1963 but, if so, she then returned to New York, possibly still at 277 East 56th Street, and remained there until old age and memories of France took her back home on the road to Champcueil.

In the second scenario, something transformative happened to Carmen in 1956, either in her American life or to the family in France. Perhaps she had to leave the United States for unspecified personal or economic reasons. Perhaps the death of her last surviving parent led to long-drawn-out legal complications, including the sale of the family business and the home at 4 Rue de la Gaîté. As a result, US citizen or not, Carmen was dragged back by circumstances to her Parisienne identity. This may be linked to the reasons why Carmen spent eleven months in France in 1953-54. As so often with Carmen, the truth is that we do not know how near to the truth either of these scenarios might come.

The only fixed reference points are that Carmen died at Champcueil in 1982, on her eighty-second birthday, that her US social security number 132-22-6211 was terminated when she died, and that her last known postal address was PO Box 912, US Consulate, Paris.

One interpretation of these fragments of evidence might hint that Carmen's life from 1960 was mostly in America; why else would her mail be sent to the US Consulate, not to a fixed address in France? But it is not much to go on.

There is one final clue about Carmen, in the place where she died. Champcueil is a place with no known connections to her previous life. Why was she there? The answer may be found in the Hôpital Georges Clemenceau, a large nursing home and hospital. Built in the early 1930s as a sanatorium for the regional health authority, the 'Assistance Publique de Paris', the Hôpital Georges Clemenceau is still in operation in 2022. But for the restrictions of the Year of Covid, the records of the hospital might have been open to enquiries from a visiting English historian seeking proof that Carmen stayed there, for how long and what infirmities she suffered from. Even without such confirmation, by far the most likely explanation for Carmen being at Champcueil. is the Hôpital Georges Clemenceau.

Champcueil is a quiet place in a quiet countryside, yet conveniently close enough to Paris for commuters. With a grand historic church and its showy flying buttresses, Chanpcueil lies in a landscape of flat fields, rural villages and small towns like Étampes and Evry, near to slow-moving rivers like the Orge and the Essonne making their way to join the Seine. Just to the east of Champcueil is the pretty village of Barbizon, famous for its 'Barbizon School' of artists, like the landscape painter Jean Francois Millet. A few miles to the south is the great chateau of Fontainebleau and the low bouldered hills of the Forests of the King. In Champcueil itself nothing very exciting has happened since American troops stopped there briefly in August 1944, on their way to the Liberation of Paris. Champcueil seems an incongruous last stop for a posh girl from Paris who had travelled so far and wide in her active life.

Exactly when Carmen moved to Champcueil, or how long before that she had arrived back in France, remains unclear. Nor is it certain what ailments Carmen might have been suffering from, though dementia is one possibility and arthritis might be a prime suspect in the light of Carmen's long and strenuous sporting life. It is unknown whether there were surviving family or friends to save her from loneliness.

Carmen was now far away from the football fields of her youth, or her friends in Preston, or the tennis courts of Rochester, or her elegant address in Central Park West when she lived and worked in New York City. Did people in Champcueil know anything at all of Carmen's younger days? Were there mementoes to tell people that this old lady had been a champion javelin thrower, a famous footballer, sister to a film star and modern dancer, secretary to a rich and famous film actress?

Did other patients or their carers realise the old lady had crossed the Atlantic at least ten times, had met the President of the United States and worked at the United Nations? That she and her sister had been in the French Resistance? Was there a photograph in her room of the Fémina football team, or Carmen with Florrie Redford at Herne Hill in 1925, or Carmen in her athletic prime, on the high diving board at Blackpool's outdoor pool in 1938?

Perhaps Carmen was comfortable and well cared for. Perhaps she had happy memories to soften her last days. Wishing cannot make it true but, whatever Carmen's health or happiness, it was a subdued ending to a full, adventurous and amazing life. Such a life deserves to be remembered. Again because of Covid, going to find Carmen's grave was not possible. Nor is there much in the way of memorials to Carmen in France, Hélène has her books. Georges has his five films and the many arthouse photographs of his famous dance routines. Carmen is remembered, if at all, by the relatively few French people interested in women's football in the interwar years, or perhaps in Alice Milliat and women's athletics. There is, however, one evocative monument to commemorate Carmen Pomiès, though not in France.

In 2017, in a corner of Preston North End's football stadium, a fine memorial in pale granite stone was installed in memory of the Dick, Kerr Ladies team and all they did for women's football in Preston. Nearby is another stone memorial in honour of Preston's greatest-ever footballer, Tom Finney. On the stadium wall, high above Tom Finney, the Dick, Kerr girls stand in a line exactly as they did in a famous photograph taken during their epic season of 1921. Carmen is there.

The sun only rarely gets into the corner where the monument is situated. The girls seem somehow dimly lit and ghostly, rather like an old photograph album. The only flash of colour against the grey stone comes from their light-blue shorts and from the black marble plinth on which is carved their names and some of their great exploits. Leader of the pack is Lily Parr, holding a football. It's a shock to remember Lily was then sixteen years old. Behind Lily, the rest of the team stand like a chorus line, eyes to the right. Third in the line is Carmen Pomiès. Sixth is Florrie Redford. Alfred Frankland is not there, though perhaps he deserves to be remembered, too.

The monument is righting a great wrong, giving due acknowledgement to a remarkable slice of history that was for too long suppressed and forgotten. Well done to Gail Newsham and all who helped her campaign to bring the memory of Dick, Kerr Ladies back to life. Beyond that, however, the monument places Carmen Pomiès where she belongs, in her second football home. Perhaps one day there will be a fine memorial in France, commemorating pioneers of women's football like Louise Ourry, 'Mado' Braquemond, Andrée Gauckler, even the scandalous Violette Morris. If that happens, Carmen will belong alongside them, but she also belongs to Preston.

The girls in granite look out from Deepdale stadium, gazing over Tom Finney towards the green spaces of Moor Park. Those green spaces were where Carmen spent some of the happiest times of her life; training there in 1920 on the first French tour, and in 1921-22 when she was living in Preston as one of the team, playing a big match there in 1932 watched by a huge crowd at the Lancashire Agricultural Show, perhaps most of all just messing abut with her football friends like Lizzy and Margaret and Lily almost every summer during the 1930s. It's as good a place as any to remember the remarkable life of Carmen Pomiès.

Epilogue

What Happened Afterwards?

After Carmen died in 1982, there was no new generation to continue the story of the talented Pomiès family. The only surviving relative of her immediate family was her brother-in-law, Roger Joseph Henri de Morot de Grésigny, who died in July 1984. But Carmen and her siblings left their mark on history.

Carmen Pomiès faded away quietly in old age after the vibrant, adventurous course of her life until her sixties. Her career in women's football has been recorded in great detail, both in France and in Britain, with numerous photographs and match reports. Carmen's successes with Fémina can be traced season-by-season in the eight volumes of *Les Footballeuses* by Helge Faller. Carmen's close connections to Dick, Kerr Ladies feature prominently in Gail Newsham's book, *In A League Of Their Own!* Carmen's place in the history of women's football in Preston is also commemorated in the monument at Preston North End's Deepdale stadium, unveiled in 2017. Brief accounts of Carmen's life story can be found online at Football Makes History. Carmen is also remembered as one of three sisters to a famous brother with a lasting legacy in French cinema and modern dance.

Hélène Pomiès left a legacy of three books. She translated *Nouvelles Espagnoles* (Stories From Spain), edited by Jean Cassou and published in 1937. Hélène coordinated and edited *Danser C'est Vivre* (To Dance is to Live), published in 1939, which presents thirteen tributes to her brother Georges from people who knew him. The final chapter, by Hélène herself, is probably the most illuminating source of information about Georges and his sisters. Hélène's collection of stories about the French resistance in the Alps, *Du Sang sur la*

Montagne (Blood on the Mountain), published in 1947 reveals her literary style and atmospheric use of language, if not much about Hélène's personal life. All her books can be obtained from online booksellers in France. Little is known of Hélène's last years or how close she was to Carmen. Hélène died in May 1963, at Versailles.

Yvonne Pomiès is one of the most elusive figures in Carmen's story. Little is known about Yvonne, except that she was two years older than Carmen, that she was a talented pianist and that the three grieving sisters were together after Georges died in 1933. In November 1958, Yvonne, then aged sixty, married a man six years younger than herself, Roger de Morot de Grésigny. Yvonne died in February 1977 in Geneva.

Georges Pomiès gained an international reputation as an actor and modern dancer, even though he died young, aged thirty-one. He had leading roles in five films, including two directed by the great Jean Renoir, and is commemorated by numerous artworks and studio photographs as well as reviews of his memorable dance routines as dancer and choreographer. Among the tributes to Georges in *Danser C'est Vivre*, the 1939 book edited by Hélène, are vivid, affectionate pen-pictures of Georges by his celebrated dance partner Lisa Duncan and by Hélène. A retrospective assessment of the artistic legacy of Georges Pomiès the dancer and choreographer, by Pierre Driout, gives an impression of his aura:

> Georges Pomiès wrote in *Propos sur la Danse* in 1930 'Only Dance creates the individual. Dance is the most effective method of human evolution'. Who now remembers Pomiès? And yet his untimely death cannot detract from his talent. An unforgettable complete music-hall artist in his roles as mime, singer, dancer, actor and otherwise lover of Lisa Duncan, adopted daughter of Isadora, Georges Pomiès was a delight. He even embodied the Michelin Man!

Lisa Duncan (Liesl Milker), dance partner and girlfriend of Georges Pomiès, remained close to his sisters after Georges died. She contributed her personal recollections of him in *Danser C'est Vivre*. Born in Dresden in 1898, four years older than Georges, Lisa was already famous in her own right as one of the 'Isadorables', the six adopted daughters of the legendary Isadora Duncan. By 1939, however, Lisa was over forty. The style of dancing that made the 'Isadorables' cultural icons of the 1920s was seen as a historical curiosity. Lisa died in 1976.

Roger Joseph Henri de Morot de Grésigny married Yvonne Pomiès in Paris on 8 November 1958. Yvonne was then sixty, Roger fifty-four. Roger was the youngest of three brothers, from an aristocratic family whose titles went back to 1650. Roger died at Saint-Mandé, Val de Marne an eastern suburb of Paris in July 1984, seven years after Yvonne. He was Carmen's only living close relative in 1982.

Alice Milliat never achieved her great dream of winning full acceptance of women competing in track and field at the Olympic Games. Nor did she live long enough to witness the great breakthrough of women's football in modern times, though she did see women in France gain the right to vote in 1946. Alice Milliat died in 1957. After her death, she was belatedly celebrated by historians and journalists as the 'Suffragette of Sport'. The Alice Milliat Foundation was established in 2006 to carry on her quest for equality. In 2017, the role of Alice Milliat in promoting equality for women in sport took pride of place in a cultural exhibition in Paris devoted to Feminism and Women's Football in France.

Violette Morris died a premature death in April 1944, killed in a hail of bullets at the age of fifty-one when her car was ambushed by fighters in the French resistance. Violette's memory did not die well. Her reputation lived on as a scandalous woman with a very public lesbian lifestyle. Even more, her place in history was defined by her supposed role as wartime collaborator, denounced as the 'Hyena of the Gestapo', who eagerly participated in the torture of French patriots, and as a superspy who had passed vital military secrets to the Germans before 1940. Many books have been published about Violette, mostly sensationalised and unreliable. The French-American novelist, Francine Prose, wrote a fine historical novel *Lovers at the Chameleon Club: Paris 1932*, in which Violette is thinly disguised as 'Lou Villars'. It's a brilliant evocation of character, time and place but it also reinforces many lurid myths about Violette the collaborator. In recent years, a more realistic, less hostile picture of Violette Morris has been put forward by historians like Marie-Jo Bonnet, whose two-volume graphic book *Violette Morris: A Battre par Tous Moyens* (Winning by Any Means), uses a deceptively simple cartoon format to reveal the complexity of her character and her historical importance as sportswoman and feminist icon.

Madeleine ('Mado') Bracquemond married Eugene Jeannot, brother of one of her football friends and teammates, in 1930. Mado continued to play football at the top level; she scored the winning goal against Belgium in France's last international before the war, at Cherbourg in 1937. She died in 1981 at Antony, the suburb on the southern edges of Paris where she had her wedding fifty years before. The short silent film about Madeleine by Gaumont-Revue films, made in 1929, *La Femme et le Sport* (Woman of Sport) can be viewed online.

Jean Renoir was the famous son of an even more famous father, the painter Pierre-August Renoir. Born in Paris in 1904, Jean became one of the great directors in French cinema. Among his early films were *Tire au Flanc* (The Sad Sack) made in 1928, and *Chotard et Cie* (Chotard & Company) in 1932. Georges Pomiès had leading roles in both. In 1937, Renoir directed *La Grande Illusion*, regarded by critics ever since as one of the greatest films ever made. When France was defeated in 1940, Jean moved to the United States. As a supporter of the Popular Front in the 1930s, he would have been a target for the security forces if he had stayed. After the war, Jean Renoir made many films in America and Europe. He died in 1979 in Beverly Hills, California. In 2012, a lavish historical drama *Renoir*, set on the Riviera in 1915, told the story of the aged father and the young son, and of the women in both their lives, Gabrielle Renard, beloved nanny to Jean who was also Pierre-August's long-time model and lover, and Andrée Heuschling, model for Pierre-August in his last years.

Renée Saint-Cyr had reached a peak of fame by 1943 as one of the two outstanding leading ladies of French cinema alongside Danielle Dasrrieux. For a time after the Liberation, Renée lived under a cloud, accused of having enjoyed a life of comfort and privilege during the Vichy years while working for the German-controlled Continental Films. She was able to regain her place at the forefront of French cinema, starring in thirty-two films (usually as queen, duchess or countess) between 1945 and 1992. Her son, Georges Lautner, became a successful screenwriter and film director involved in the making of more than sixty films between 1958 and 2003. Several of them featured his mother in the cast. Renée Saint-Cyr died at Neuilly-sur-Seine in 2004, just before her one-hundredth birthday. Her grave is at the hilltop cemetery overlooking the sea and the Promenade des Anglais at Nice.

British Connections: Preston & Belfast

Florrie Redford was at her peak as a player from 1919 to 1925, when she was the greatest goalscorer in women's football, both in England and in France. Florrie played little or no football after emigrating to Canada in 1930. Her last match, soon after her return to Preston in 1938, was an anti-climax, a 4-0 defeat in Whitehaven. By then, aged forty and after many years away from the game, Florrie had lost the slender physique and athleticism that had once made her famous. After the war, Florrie spent much time caring for her mother who was in poor health. They moved to the Midlands, to Coventry, where Florrie married an older man, John Fairley. Florrie Redford Fairley died of heart trouble in January 1969.

Lily Parr remained a living legend of women's football until she retired from the game in 1950 after a playing career of more than thirty years. It has been claimed that Lily had scored 967 goals, though this number may have been inflated by dubious record-keeping. Lily also played cricket and hockey in the 1930s, with great success. Alongside her sporting career, Lily continued her career as a nurse and shared a home in Preston with her colleague and partner Mary. Lily Parr died in 1967 of breast cancer, possibly a consequence of her lifelong chain-smoking. The memory of Lily as one of the greatest-ever female footballers has been celebrated in books, such as *In a League of Their Own!*, Gail Newsham's history of Dick, Kerr Ladies and in newspapers and television documentaries. In 2019, a statue of Lily Parr was installed at the National Football Museum in Manchester. In 2017, a monument to the Dick, Kerr Ladies team was unveiled at Deepdale, the stadium of Preston North End. The monument is derived from a photograph of the team in their great year of 1921. First in line, holding the match ball, is Lily Parr.

Lizzy Ashcroft started her playing career with St Helens before joining Dick, Kerr Ladies in 1923. Her first meeting with Carmen was when she played for St Helens against DKL in an exhibition match at Port Erin, Isle of Man. Lizzy was an important part of the history of Dick, Kerr Ladies, especially in reviving the club's fortunes in the early 1930s, and became a special friend to Carmen. Lizzy's playing career ended in 1935 when she married Joshua Bolton but she continued to be closely involved with the game. Lizzy died in Preston in 1973. Her grandson, Stephen Bolton is a historian who has assembled a vast collection of evidence and memorabilia on women's football, and is author of several articles for Playing Pasts and Football Makes History. Steve is working on a book and a film about his beloved Granny.

Alfred Frankland was central to the rise and success of Dick, Kerr Ladies from its beginnings until his death in 1957. Perhaps it was for the best he did not live long enough to see Preston Ladies cease to exist in 1965. Without the organising abilities and flair for publicity of Alfred Frankland, the Dick, Kerr Ladies story might never have been fulfilled, nor recorded for posterity. His voluminous scrapbooks, stuffed with photographs, match reports and newspaper cuttings, have provided an essential starting point for later historians.

Margaret Thornborough was a fine player for DKL/Preston in the 1930s and a fine all-round sportswoman, good at cricket, hockey, tennis and bowls as well as football. Margaret was even more important off the field, as assistant manager to Alfred Frankland. Margaret was one of Carmen's closest friends, sharing the determination to keep women's football alive and kicking. Margaret was there in Belfast in 1932 to help the French tour; in 1934, she was there in London to greet the Belgians at Liverpool Street station, in 1945, she was there with Alfred Frankland to welcome Carmen back to Preston. Margaret's brother, Eli, was a professional player for Bolton Wanderers and Preston North End, and later for local clubs, Horwich RMI and Chorley. After Alfred Frankland died in 1957, Eli took charge of coaching and training.at Preston Ladies. In 1965, however, the club disbanded. Amid the social transformations of the Sixties, there were too few girls wanting to take up football. Margaret Thornborough's last years were clouded by dementia. In September 1994, she died at Whittingham, a place long associated with the story of Dick, Kerr Ladies.

Mary Ann ('Big Molly') Seaton shared several great moments in the football life of Carmen Pomiès, especially as rival captains in big matches between 'Ireland' and 'France' in Belfast in 1932 and 1936. 'Big Molly' was a local legend in Greencastle and North Belfast during her time as a player. Her name was remembered long afterwards, too, though few people actually had any accurate knowledge about her until the very recent past when Steve Bolton told her story, accompanied by evocative photographs of Molly and Carmen, in a newspaper article for the *Belfast Telegraph* and online articles for *Playing Pasts*. Mary Ann Seaton died in 1974. Her grave is in Greencastle, close to her North Belfast roots.

Other Fighters for Equality in Interwar Europe

Jenny Toitgans was an outstanding athlete and footballer who played many times against Carmen in France-Belgium internationals. Like the history of women's football in Belgium in general, Jenny faded to the sidelines of history after the Second World War. It was not until the 1970s that the Atalante club was reborn in Brussels. In *Avant Leur Temps* and *Le Grand Depart,* his two books on the history of Belgian football in the 1920s, Helge Faller has chronicled the atmosphere of the times and the roles of top players such as Jenny Toitgans and Françoise Desmedt.

Lotte Specht, the nineteen-year-old butcher's daughter from Frankurt-am-Main, had a brief moment of success in arousing enthusiasm for women's football in Germany in 1930-31. Lotte got thirty-five women and girls to take part in training sessions every Sunday but her dream was soon squashed by an anti-feminist backlash, led by her own father. Lotte's spirit of adventure was channelled instead into music-hall and cabaret as part of a comic duo singing and dancing its way round Germany, Austria and Switzerland. Lotte lived long enough to see the re-emergence of women's football in Germany before she died in 2002. An article in the *Süddeutscher Zeitung* in May 2010 told Lotte's story as a pioneer of *Damenfussball*. In 2014, a sports field in Frankfurt was renamed Lotte Specht Park. In 2020, Lotte was included in the collection of life stories on Football Makes History.

Brunilde Amodeo flourished briefly as a pioneer of women's football in Milan in the early 1930s. With her sister and their friends Rosetta and Nini, Brunilde led the way in many sporting activities, above all football, where she was centre-half and captain. But they were soon stifled by the regimented ideologies of women and sport in Fascist Italy. Brunilde married in 1938. Her daughter, Brunella, graduated as a civil engineer. Brunilde died in 2000, aged eighty-six, in Milan. An article about her, written by Marco Giani and accompanied by wonderfully evocative photographs, appeared on Playing Pasts, in 2020. At the same time, *Giovinette: Il Calciatrici Che Sfidarono Il Duce* (The Italian Women Who Defied Mussolini), a novel by the Corriere Della Sera journalist Federica Seneghini, presented a lively fictionalised account of the brief flowering of the women's game in Italy.

Edith Klinger led the way for women's football in Austria between 1935 and 1938, as a qualified referee with a talent for organisation. The women's game seemed poised for further expansion in Austria and Central Europe. But the historical context was not favourable. Conservative social and political movements in Austria fomented hostility to expressions of female equality. In April 1936, the *Anschluss* annexed Austria to Hitler's Third Reich snuffing out women's football along with much else. By the time Edith Klinger died in 1993, there had been a revival of women's football in Austria but few people remembered much about Edith or football in Vienna in her time. *Eine Klasse für Sich: Als Wiener Fussballerinnen einzig in der Welt waren* (When Vienna's Football Women were Unique in the World) by Helge Faller and Matthias Marschik, published in 2020, sets out in fascinating, well-illustrated detail the history of *Damenfussball* in Austria in the 1930s.

American Connections

Ardean Miller is still admired for his high-quality colour photography, especially his collection of images of the liberation of KZ Buchenwald in 1945. His three sons all followed him into careers as photographers, keeping their father's legacy alive for many decades through the photographic agency, Airstream.

The Democrat & Chronicle founded in Rochester NY in 1833 is still going strong. In recent years, it has frequently been at the top of the list of regional newspapers with the highest percentage of local residents who are readers, in print or online.

The United Nations Building still towers over Turtle Bay and the East River on the edge of Lower Manhattan, as it has done ever since its completion in 1951, just as Carmen Pomiès started her work there as a translator. Seventy years later, there is less innocent idealism about the United Nations and attitudes towards the UN in the United States are less generous and starry-eyed than they used to be. Even so, as home to the UN General Assembly and the Security Council, with its vast site, thousands of employees, its art collection, the Dag Hammarskjöld Library and daily tours for visitors, the UN Building remains a great landmark in New York City and in world affairs.

The 'Third Wave'; Reawakening Women's Football, c. 1970 to the Present

For a generation after the Second World War, women's football struggled to survive. In post-war England, twenty-six teams carried on playing but attracted little attention. Even Preston Ladies, with a great history going back to 1917, found it hard going; the club ceased to exist in 1965. There was a flurry of interest in West Germany, from girls enthused by the stunning victory of the men's national team in the 1954 'Miracle of Bern', but the DFB (German Football Association) was hostile to women's football and enforced an official ban from 1955. It was not until 1968-71 that a 'Third Wave' began to push women's football back up the agenda. Since then, the women's game has gradually achieved wider acceptance in the face of persistent obstructionism, The success of the 2019 Women's World Cup in France might be seen as a landmark on the long road towards true equality. Tracing the full story of the Third Wave is beyond the scope of this book but here are six milestones along that road:
Stade de Reims Féminines had a leading role in what Professor Laurence Prudhomme-Poncet has called *La réapparition du football féminin*. FCF Reims was formed in 1968 when Pierre Geoffroy, a sports journalist at the daily newspaper *l'Union*, organised two women's

teams to play each other at a sports festival. This sparked interest and reawakened memories of *Les Sportives Reims*, one of the teams of the 1920s competing against rivals like Fémina and En Avant! The rise of Stade de Reims was matched by a similar resurgence of women's football in Strasbourg and Bas-Rhin. In 1973, Stade de Reims made a tour of Ireland that was reminiscent of French tours made by Carmen Pomiès in the 1920s and 1930s. In 1974, Stade du Reims became one of twelve founder members of the new Division 1 Féminine. For a time, Stade de Reims were the outstanding team in France, winning five league titles between 1975 and 1982. After that, the team went into decline. Division 1 Féminine also endured hard times until it was reorganised in 1992. But women's football in France had got back to where it had been before 1933. Since 1992, the existence of a national professional league in France has enabled the rise of new elite clubs like Olympique Lyonnais, winner of fourteen French league titles in a row from 2006 and of five consecutive European Champions League titles. In recent times, Stade de Reims has made it back to Division 1. A sign of the growth of the women's game by 2020 is that the Reims squad contained fifteen French players, two each from USA, Ukraine and Cameroon, and one from England, the Netherlands, Portugal and Costa Rica. The story of FCF/Stade de Reims was highlighted in an exhibition about Feminism and Women in Sport staged at the Centre Hubertine Auclert in 2017.

The Unofficial Women's World Cup in Mexico in 1971 was organised to take advantage of the huge public interest aroused by the men's World Cup in 1970, won by Brazil. There was positive momentum behind the tournament, In England, a new Women's Football Association was formed in 1969. In Italy, the FFIGC (Federazione Femminile Italia Giuoco Calcio) staged a 'world championships' in Rome in 1970, sponsored by the Martini Rosso drinks company. In October 1970, the DFB lifted its ban on women's football in West Germany. In 1971, the English FA at last rescinded its 1921 ban outlawing women's football from all grounds recognised by the FA. On the other hand, there was intense official disapproval for the 1971 Mexico City tournament, from FIFA and from national associations including the English FA. Outside Mexico, the press and broadcast media took little notice. Despite the official indifference in Britain and most of Europe, the *Campeonato de Futbol Feminil* was a big success in Mexico. Six teams competed, representing six countries: Mexico as host nation, Argentina, Denmark (who had won the unofficial tournament in Italy in 1970), England, France and Italy. Martini-Rosso paid for all travel, accommodation and football kit. Attendances at the matches were enormous. 80,000 watched Mexico play England in the group stage. 112,000 watched the final at the Azteca stadium between Mexico and Denmark. Denmark were the winners and received a civic reception at Copenhagen Town Hall when they got home.

The 'England' team was mostly players from Chiltern Valley Ladies, coached by Harry Batt, a bus driver from Luton who had been a fighter with the International Brigade in the Spanish Civil War. Batt's reward for his enterprise was to be banned by the FA for daring to call his team 'England'. Many of Batt's players were teenagers, including thirteen-year-old Leah Caleb. In 2019, at the time of the Women's World Cup in France, there was a reunion for the team that had gone to Mexico nearly fifty years before. They got far more attention in 2019 than they ever did in 1971. The unofficial World Cup of 1971, therefore, demonstrated the huge potential for the growth of women's football. Equally, it demonstrated the tenacity of the forces of opposition blocking its advance. The story of Harry Batt's impact on the women's game is well told in a 2022 book by Jean Williams, *The History of Women's Football*.

'Das Wunder von Taipeh' 1981. Ten years after the unofficial Women's World Cup in Mexico, another such tournament was staged in Taiwan. In 1975, the Asian Ladies Football Confederation had organised an invitational tournament in Hong Kong, won by New Zealand. From 1978, this tradition was continued every three years by the China Taipeh FA; the last such event took place in 1987. A few national associations took the tournaments seriously and sent representative national teams. Most associations resolutely refused to give approval. Any team choosing to compete did so as an individual club side. In 1978, the winners in Taipeh were Stade Reims of France. HJK Helsinki were runners-up, the Republic of China and Dallas Sting of the United States came third and fourth.

In 1981, West Germany was represented, unofficially, by Bergisch Gladbach 09 from North Rhine-Westphalia. Bergisch-Gladbach Women were far and away the best team in West Germany, winning nine national league titles between 1977 and 1989, along with three cup finals. They dominated the Taipeh invitational tournaments, too, winning in 1981 and again in 1984, even though there was no support, only obstruction, from the DFB (German Football Association). In their first triumph, in 1981, Bergisch beat New Zealand in the final. Republic of China and Il I BUL, a club side from Oslo in Norway, were third and fourth. At the time, these tournaments made little direct impact but in the longer term, they led to mounting pressure on FIFA to consider an official Women's World Cup.

In 2019, in a new era when the DFB had begun to give official recognition to women's football, a documentary film *Das Wunder von Taipeh* (its English title was We Wanted More) was produced to celebrate Bergisch-Gladbach's victory in 1981. The women who had been involved in 1981 enjoyed the experience of reuniting for the film but many of them remained critical of the lack of any official support at the time. The film was released in January 2020, timed to coincide with the fiftieth anniversary of the lifting of the ban on women's football in West Germany. Its title, *Das Wunder von Taipeh* is a conscious echo of *Das Wunder von Bern*, the 2003 film celebrating West Germany winning the FIFA World Cup in Switzerland in 1954.

Football, Feminism and Film. Popular culture often plays an important role in reflecting social change; sometimes, popular culture can even help to influence and accelerate social change.

Prevailing social stereotypes can be reinforced or challenged by the visual images of magazines, advertising, television and the cinema. In the case of women's football, there has been a long history of such images ridiculing women's football as either an amusing oddity or a danger to the social order. In *Gregory's Girl*, a lovely film directed by Bill Forsyth in 1981, Dorothy, the girl of young Gregory's dreams is both unattainable and exotic because being a female footballer in 1980s Scotland was weird. At the end of the 1980s, *The Manageress*, a six-part BBC TV series, starred Cherie Lunghi as the impossibly beautiful Gabriella Benson, female manager of a men's professional team in Lancashire. Again, the situation was seen as a fairy story; as if it could never actually happen.

Bend It Like Beckham, a film directed by Gurinda Chadha in 2002, was different. The central character, Jasminder ('Jess'), is a Bangladeshi girl who really wants to play football. In the happy ending to the film, Jess flies off with her friend Jules, to take up sports scholarships at an American university. This outcome was plausible, in tune with reality. Along the way, *Bend It Like Beckham* addressed real social issues, about migration and diversity, about the generation gap between Jess and her socially conservative parents, about homophobia, about jealousy between friends. Gurinda Chadha's kindly, optimistic view of multiracial Britain reflected a new mood that reached a peak at the time of the London Olympics in 2012. Perhaps above all, it presented a young girl's determination to play football as something that was both possible and to be applauded. Social developments since 2012, post-Brexit and post-Trump, might suggest the optimism of the film was overdone or premature.

In *Mustang*, a French-Turkish film directed by Deniz Gamze Ergüven in 2016, the heroine, twelve-year-old Lale, is not yet a football player. Living in a village near the shores of the Black Sea, Lale is a passionate fan of the local Super Lig club Trabzonspor. Her love of football becomes a battlefield on which Lale's rebellious sense of female independence clashes with her ultra-conservative family and their view of her pre-ordained destiny as submissive wife and mother. At the end of the film, Lale runs away to faraway Istanbul, helped to escape by her friend and fellow Trabzonspor fan, a long-haired young truck driver. What happened to Lale afterwards, and how much football might have shaped her life, remains an open question. Just like *Bend It Like Beckham*, the story of Lale revolves around serious themes about women in society and the revolutionary implications of women and girls taking up a 'man's game'.

The Climb to Equality in 2017 was literally a climb. Thirty-two women from all over the world trekked for days up the highest mountain in Africa, Mount Kilimanjaro, to play a symbolic game of football at 5,700 metres, higher than any game of football in history. It was a proper match too, eleven-a-side, FIFA rules and a full-sized pitch with a surface of volcanic ash. The game had a propaganda purpose, to raise awareness of issues of gender equality in sport and show the world that the time had come for an Equal Playing Field. The idea was the brainchild of Laura Youngson, backed by her friends Erin Blankenship and Maggie Murphy. They got willing support from the authorities in Tanzania and from footballers of twenty countries, including Lori Lindsey from the United States, Petra Landers from Germany and Yasheen Shabsough from Jordan. To maximise publicity, Equal Playing Field made a deal with media company BeIN to produce a sixty-minute documentary video directed by Ben Jacobs. (The video can be found on Football Makes History.eu). It's an inspiring story, reminiscent in some ways of 'propaganda matches' in the interwar years, when special one-off events and tours were staged in the hope of spreading enthusiasm for women's football. The perennial problem with that approach has always been that the impact soon fades without some kind of structure for continuation. In the case of the Climb to Equality, the power of the internet and the presence of high-profile players from professional leagues has enabled a lasting legacy that promoters of the 1920s such as Alice Milliat and Alfred Frankland could only have dreamed about.

The FIFA Women's World Cup, 2019, hosted by France, was the eighth tournament after the inaugural World Cup in China in 1991. Earlier world tournaments had been unofficial, with relatively little coverage in the press or mainstream media. The UEFA Women's Championship began in 1984, dominated by Germany and the Nordic countries. By 2013, Germany had won eight times out of eleven. Sweden reached the final four times, Norway six. The 2011 World Cup, hosted by Germany, was something of a breakthrough, with 49,000 spectators watching Japan win an exciting final against the United States in Frankfurt. In 2015, the United States defeated Japan 5-2 in the final at Vancouver in Canada. By the time of the 2019 tournament in France, women's football was moving to a new, higher level. Backing from FIFA was more enlightened, many of the players were competing in professional leagues and the twenty-four nations at the finals had a genuinely worldwide reach, six from Australasia, six from the Americas, three from Africa and nine from Europe.

Perhaps above all, there was intense media coverage of the event. Attendances were high at games involving France; crowds at group stage matches averaged about 17,000. Although France was knocked out in the quarter-finals by the United States, 53,000 watched the semi-final between the USA and England, 48,000 watched the Netherlands v Sweden. 58,000 saw the USA defeat the Netherlands in the final at Lyon. The overall global TV audience was estimated at 1.2 billion.

What Carmen Pomiès might have thought about the World Cup in France if she had been there to witness it can never be known. It is likely that she would have been greatly impressed by the technical quality of the football – the intricate passing of the Japanese, the organisation and physicality of the English and the Dutch, the ruthless efficiency of the Americans. Carmen would also have been amazed to see the flawless green pitches the football was played on, so different from the mudheaps of her own day. But it's possible Carmen's response might have been to ask an angry question: 'Why did it take so long to get this far?'

Following in Carmen's Footsteps: Six Fighters for Equality

Carmen was a noble fighter for women's football and equality but saw the women's game suppressed and marginalised in 1939 and 1940, as the Second World War began. By the time the women's game started to come back to life in the 1970s, Carmen was an elderly lady watching from the sidelines. Women's football did not really break through until after Carmen's death. Most great achievements, however, are made by people standing on the shoulders of those who went before.

Here are six remarkable women who have taken leading roles in the ongoing battles for equal rights through football. More can be found about five of the six, Petra, Megan, Nadia, Stephanie and Ebru, from their life stories on the Football Makes History website. Hope Powell has told her own story in *Hope: My Life in Football*, her autobiography first published in 2016. Carmen would have recognised all of them as comrades fighting for the same cause.

Petra Landers was part of the revival of women's football in Germany almost from the beginning. An athletic, fiercely competitive defender, Petra joined Germany's best women's team, Bergisch-Gladbach, helping them to win their nine league championships in thirteen years from 1976. Petra was in Taiwan in 1981 for the 'Miracle of Taipeh', when Bergisch-Gladbach won the unofficial world club championship for women. In 1989, she was part of the German team that won the UEFA Nations Cup. After retiring from the game as a player, Petra came back as a coach and campaigner for equality. At the age of fifty-four, Petra was up for the challenge of playing at altitude near the summit of Mount Kilimanjaro in the 2017 Equal Playing Field match. Petra has made numerous visits to Lusaka in Zambia, to inspire young African girls in the townships and to train a new generation of African coaches. But Petra has never quite forgiven the male-dominated DFB (German Football Association) for its patronising, negative attitudes towards women's football as it began its rise. Her withering expression as she showed her audience in 2020 the elegant, wildly inappropriate coffee set that was presented to the players who won the UEFA trophy for Germany in 1989 is hard to forget.

Hope Powell faced many forms of discrimination from an early age. Brought up by a Jamaican-British single mother in Peckham, a tough area of South London, Hope knew all about economic inequality and racial prejudice. Hope also learned about domestic violence; by the age of seven, she was defending her mother against her violent partner. When she began playing football, Hope learned about class discrimination, too, because she quickly recognised the not-so-subtle differences in the way working-class girls were treated by the coaches as compared with girls from a middle-class background. Quiet in manner but fiercely determined, Hope had the resilience and leadership qualities to make it as a football player. She shone in professional league football, was selected for England and soon made captain. In 1998, after sixteen years as a player, Hope Powell then moved on to be coach of her national team for fifteen years before going on to be a leading administrator and educator with the PFA (Professional Footballers Association). She then went back to her tracksuit self, as manager of Brighton & Hove Albion in the WSL. Almost since the day she was born in 1966, Hope Powell has been sticking up for all kinds of equal rights.

Megan Rapinoe was born in California in 1985. She started football early, at the age of three, because she idolised her older brother. By the age of seventeen, Megan was good enough to be playing n the WPSL (Women's Professional Soccer League) but began to reach her peak some years later after a university sports scholarship at Portland, Oregon. Though undeniably talented and skilful, what made Megan special was leadership and the winning mentality. For some years her career was blighted by serious knee injuries but from 2011 Megan was a key component in the United States women's team as it surfed a wave of success. The USA reached the final of the World Cup in

2011, won the gold medal at the London Olympics in 2012 and the World Cup in Canada in 2015. Megan was captain of the team that won the World Cup in France in 2019; she also won the Ballon d'Or Féminin. But Megan did not achieve fame just for football. Spiky and outspoken, she was also a lightning rod for controversy. Though much admired as a role model for women and girls, she was also the target of a culture war on social media attacking her same-sex relationship with basketball star Sue Bird, as well as her fiery persona on the football pitch. This led to a furious row on Twitter with President Trump who ostentatiously announced he would not be inviting the USA team to the White House. Megan's response was uncompromising and divisive. The fight for equality cannot always be accompanied by politeness.

Stephanie Frappart made a symbolic statement of female equality in sport when she was the referee at the head of an all-female team of officials for the EUFA Super Cup final between Liverpool and Chelsea in Istanbul in August 2019. Watched by thousands inside the stadium and by millions on worldwide television, Stephanie Frappart and her assistants, Manuela and Michelle, had a near-flawless game, receiving lavish compliments afterwards from Liverpool manager Jürgen Klopp. Demonstrating calm authority over twenty-two famous men who have big egos and even bigger bank balances is about as powerful an assertion of equality as can be imagined. Nor was this a one-off occasion. Stephanie began officiating at men's professional matches in France in 2011, when she was twenty-eight, was part of the FIFA panel of referees at the 2015 Women's World Cup in Canada in 2015 and then took charge of the 2019 Women's World Cup final in Paris. In March 2021, she became the first-ever referee of a men's World Cup qualifier, between the Netherlands and Latvia in Amsterdam. Along with Bibiana Steinhaus, referee for many matches in the Bundesliga, and Sian Massey-Ellis, assistant referee in the English Premier League, Stephanie Frappart has broken through one of the hardest 'glass ceilings' anywhere in the world of sport.

Ebru Köksal was born in Istanbul in 1968 and grew up with an intense love of sport, including water polo and football. Aged eight, however, Ebru was told by doctors that she had advanced scoliosis of the spine, a condition that would make sporting activities impossible for the rest of her life. She played lots of sports anyway, including social football, but made her career in economics, international relations and investment banking. When she was working with Citibank in Istanbul, one of Ebru's clients was the elite men's football club, Galatasaray. The directors of the club were so impressed they made Ebru CEO in 2001. From there, she moved to administrative posts at the top levels of European and world football before becoming Chair of Women in Football. A vivid public speaker, usually holding a football in both hands as she wows her audience, Ebru is a powerful voice for equality and an inspiration to women and girls wherever she goes.

Nadia Nadim was born in Herat in 1988. When she was twelve years old, her father, a general in the Afghan National Army, was murdered by the Taliban. Nadia, her mother and her four sisters fled abroad, via Pakistan, to seek asylum. After a long, hazardous journey across Europe with little idea of where they were going, they found themselves in Denmark where they could begin a new life. Nadia decided she wanted to play football and joined Aalborg B52. She discovered she was extremely good at the game. By the age of twenty, Nadia was a goalscoring winger playing for Denmark's national team. Soon, she was courted by leading professional clubs in the United States, first Sky Blue New Jersey, then Portland Thorns. Then she returned to Europe, to play for Manchester City and Paris Saint Germain. In her spare time, Nadia studied medicine at Aarhus University and is now a qualified reconstructive surgeon. She speaks multiple languages. Perhaps surprisingly, Nadia's use of English is not only fluent but colourful, often littered with swear words. Unsurprisingly, Nadia Nadim is a charismatic role model for girls all over the world.

What Happened Afterwards?

Past and Present

Historians are always seeking ways to connect the past with the present. Petra, Hope, Megan, Stephanie, Ebru and Nadia have had lives distant from Carmen by two generations at least; they could never meet or know each other in real life. But connections exist. Carmen and Petra Landers would recognise in each other the sheer love of the game that drove them on. They also shared the passion and pride that went with playing for teams, Fémina in the 1920s and Bergisch-Gladbach in the 1980s, who won everything in sight year after year. Hope Powell came from a social background utterly different from Carmen's but they shared the steely resolve that marks out captains born to lead. Perhaps Carmen's view of Megan Rapinoe might have been ambivalent, seeing something of the turbulence that Violette Morris had left in her wake. As with Violette, there would be great respect as well.

In Carmen's time, it was always men who refereed the big matches. Seeing the calm authority with which Stephanie Frappart has controlled major finals, both men's and women's, would have been even more impressive in the interwar years than it is more than it is now, eighty years later. As for Ebru Köksal, Carmen fought many bruising battles in committee rooms herself and had experience of the ways in which Alice Milliat operated. Carmen knew how much the politics of football mattered.

Perhaps Nadia Nadim might come closest of all to Carmen. Both had fathers who collided with war and dictatorship. Football took both of them on travels far and wide across Britain and Europe. Both for a time at least, lived and worked in America. Significant differences, of course, separate these six women from Carmen and her times. Even so, it is permissible to believe that all six would have regarded Carmen Pomiès as a kindred spirit. Any time a man declares, as Gabriel Hanot did in 1923, 'football is not a game for girls', their answer would be a trenchant 'Why not?'

Appendices

Carmen's Football Diary
[with thanks to Helge Faller]

1920

15.02.1920	First official match for Fémina, 3-0 v En Avant (Championnat de Paris et France). Carmen played left defender, as in most of her early games
29.02.1920	Second official match for Fémina, 3-0 v Academia
21.03.1920	Played for Fémina in the Championnat play-offs, 0-1 v En Avant
11.04.1920	Played in the FSFSF Cup Final, 1-2 v En Avant
22.04.1920	Carmen was chosen to take part in the first training session to select the French squad for the forthcoming tour to England
30.04.1920	Carmen played left defender at Deepdale, Preston, 0-2 v Dick, Kerr Ladies
01.05.1920	Carmen played in Stockport, 2-5 v Dick, Kerr Ladies
05.05.1920	Carmen played in the third match, 1-1 v DKL at Hyde, east of Manchester
06.05.1920	Carmen played in the last match, 2-1 v DKL at Stamford Bridge, London
11.07.1920	Carmen came second in the javelin competition, FSFSF Championnat de France d'Athlétisme, Paris (distance 35.17m)
17.10.1920	Played midfield for Probables v Possibles in FSFSF selection-match for 'France' to play v Dick, Kerr Ladies on their forthcoming tour

24.10.1920	Played for France 5-0 v Rest of France in selection-match
31.10.1920	Carmen played left midfield, 1-1 v Dick, Kerr in Paris. 22,000 watched
01.11.1920	Carmen played in the second match, 0-2 v DKL at Roubaix
06.11.1920	Carmen in central midfield 0-6 v DKL, in Le Havre
07.11.1920	Carmen in left midfield for the last game, 0-2 v DKL, in Rouen

1921

09.01.1921	Carmen played for Fémina in the final of the Coupe d'Encouragement in Paris, 4-4 v En Avant
30-01. to 10.04.1921	Carmen played for Fémina in at least 3 of 6 matches in the Championnat de Paris. Fémina came second and did not qualify for the national finals
01.05.1921	Carmen played for Probables in selection-match for the tour of England
17.05.1921	Carmen played central midfield 1-5 v DKL at Longton, Staffordshire
18.05.1921	Carmen played at Fartown, 1-0 v Huddersfield Ladies
19.05.1921	Carmen played in Stoke, 3-1 v Stoke Ladies
21.95.1921	Carmen played in Plymouth, Devon, 1-0 v Plymouth Ladies
26.06.1921	Carmen competed in the Championnat de Paris d'Athlétisme Third in 1000m (3min 45.2); third in Javelin (31.49m)
03.07 1921	Women's Olympiad, Monte Carlo. Carmen 4th in 1000m; 3rd in Javelin
29.07.1921	Carmen joined Dick, Kerr Ladies in Preston

08.08. to	
18.02.1922	Carmen played twelve matches for DKL (She was the third French player to do so, the first was Louise Ourry)
26.12.1921	Carmen's last known match of that season, 3-1 v Fleetwood

1922

1922-23	Fémina came 2nd in the Championnat de Paris and did not reach the national finals; they also lost in the semi-finals of the Cup
05.04.1922	Carmen played midfield for 'France', 1-2 v Plymouth Ladies
06.04.1922	Carmen played in Exeter, 0-0 v Plymouth Ladies
07.04.1922	Carmen played in Falmouth, Cornwall, 0-0 v Plymouth Ladies
24.09. to	
07.11.1922	Dick, Kerr Ladies tour of North America; 9 matches, all against men. Carmen played as goalkeeper in every game.
17.12.1922	Carmen's first match after the US tour, 1-0 v En Avant. Carmen scored her first goal in an official match. The game was the first Florrie Redford played for Fémina.

1923

21.01 to	
04.03.1923	Fémina won four of five matches in winning the Championnat de Paris Carmen scored seven of the nineteen by Fémina
04.03.1923	Carmen played in the 'scandal match' v Olympique. It was abandoned five minutes early (Fémina leading 2-1)

	after the Laloz twins, playing for Olympique, joined their brother in beating up the referee
11.03.1923	Fémina won the French Cup Final by default; Olympique refused to play claiming they had too few players after the Laloz twins and Violette Gouraud-Morris had been suspended after the 'scandal-match'
11.03.1923	Fémina played a friendly match instead of the final, 0-1 v Les Sportives
25.03.1923	Carmen played for the Probables in selection trial for the France team
15.04. 1923	Carmen scored twice as Fémina won the Championnat de France, 4-0 v Les Sportives de Reims
29.04.1923	Carmen in midfield for 'France' in Paris. 0-1 v Heys Brewery Bradford
30.09 to 10.23	Scandal in Lisbon. Carmen and Florrie Redford were in a squad of twenty-six Parisian players touring Portugal, accused of 'immoral behaviour' with Portuguese men. Alice Milliat imposed long suspensions on twenty-four players. Carmen and Florrie were the only players not suspended

1924

11.23 to 27.01.1924	Fémina won Groupe A in the Championnat de Paris. Carmen scored five of Fémina's thirty-three goals in the group
06.01.1924	Fémina eliminated from the Cup, 0-1 v Les Cadettes de Gascogne. Carmen wrote several letters to explain this totally unexpected defeat (She claimed Fémina had been forced to field five reserves, but Les Cadettes had fielded three). Carmen was seen as a bad loser

17.02.1924	First full women's international, Belgium v France. (Top clubs including Fémina refused to send players in protest against the FFSF)
12.04.1924	Fémina threatened to boycott the championship but decided not to
27.04.1924	Carmen scored for Fémina in winning the Championnat, 4-2 v Clodo
29.10.1924	Fémina led a breakaway from the FFSF in protest against Alice Milliat
18.11.1924	Fémina opted out of the Championnat de Paris after only two matches
28.12.1924	Fémina and Les Cadettes formed a new federation (UFSFS) to set up the Championnat de la Ligue Parisienne. Many players left Fémina

1925

Carmen appointed captain of Fémina after the previous captain, Simone Chapoteau, left the club. (Chapoteau later joined Nova Fémina). The 'Chapoteau Affair' was symptomatic of the turmoil in the FFSF and top French clubs at this time.

19.04.1925	Fémina won their own championship in a play-off, 4-0 v Cadettes
11.05 to 27.05.1925	Carmen captained Fémina on a nine-match tour of England, Scotland and Ireland v Dick, Kerr Ladies. Results: W1, D2, L6. Carmen scored six goals. She also played goalkeeper in the match at Dumfries).

1926

11.04.1926	Carmen's first full international, 1-0 v Belgium in Brussels-Molenbeek

04.05.1926	Carmen won the French Cup with Fémina, 1-0 v Clodo after extra time
06.06.1926	Carmen won a third Championnat de France (after 1923 and 1924) 1-0 in Paris v Les Cadettes

1927

10.04.1927	Carmen's second international, France 1 Belgium 2 in Paris. Her friend Jenny Toitgans scored both goals for Belgium
24.04.1927	Carmen's fourth Championnat de France, 1-0 v Les Cadettes in Paris

1928

24.01.1928	Carmen elected one of three vice-presidents of Fémina
01.04.1928	Carmen's third game for France 4-2 v Belgium in Brussels-Schaerbeek. Carmen captained France for the first time and also scored a goal
22.04.1928	Carmen won her sixth Championnat de France 4-1 v Dunlop in Paris

1929

03.03.1929	Fémina won the championship again. Carmen was second-top scorer with fourteen goals) in the tournament
14.04.1928	Carmen scored three goals in a 6-0 win over Belgium in Paris
26.05.1929	Carmen won her sixth national title with Fémina 3-0 v Dunlop in the final Carmen scored the third goal (all three came in extra time)

03.11.1929	Only international club match by Fémina between 1925 and 1932, v Atalante of Brussels in Paris. Fémina won 3-0; Carmen scored twice. Other matches v Belgian teams were planned but did not materialise.

1930

06.04.1930	Carmen's fifth international 4-0 v Belgium in Antwerp
18.05.1930	Fémina got a lucky draw, 1-1 v CASG de Marseille, in the league final
25.05.1930	In the replay v Marseille in Sochaux, Fémina were 1-2 down but won 4-2. Carmen scored a goal in the comeback, to make Fémina champion again

1931

07.01.1931	Carmen resigned as Fémina vice-president; but the club decided that Carmen should be re-appointed at the next annual general meeting
22.03.1931	Carmen's sixth international; captain and centre-forward in 4-0-win v Belgium in Douai. Carmen scored the first goal
12.04.1931	Fémina won an eighth national title in Montbéliard, 1-0 v Les Cadettes

1932

03.04.1932	Carmen's seventh international, 0-0 v Belgium in Brussels, the third time Carmen captained France. She played central midfield

10.04.1932	Carmen and Fémina won their ninth (last) Championnat de France 4-0 v Dunlop in Valenciennes. Carmen scored the fourth goal
30.07. to 05.08.1932	Carmen captained Fémina (plus guest players) on a tour of England (v Preston Ladies, (two defeats) and Northern-Ireland, first in Belfast, then in Bangor). Carmen was injured in the first game and did not play in Bangor

1933

09.04.1933	Carmen was probably captain of France again, 3-1 v Belgium in Roubaix.
28.05.1933	The FFSF abandoned women's football and cancelled the finals of the Championnat de France and the play-off in the Parisian Championship
05.08. to 12.08.1933	New tour to England: games in Preston, Salford, Hull, York, Buxton and Harrogate. Fémina won v Terry's Athletic Club in York, 5-1, but lost to Preston Ladies in the rest. (The result of the Buxton match is unknown). Carmen was injured at Hull and had to retire from the game at half-time
15.08.1933	French women's football clubs formed their own federation (FFFF)
07.19.1933	Carmen's brother Georges died in a sanatorium at Dreux, Eure-et-Loir, not far from Chartres

1934

22.04.1934	Fémina won the inaugural FFFF league title, 2-1 v Dunlop

Carmen Pomiès

11.08.to	Belgian women's team arrived in London for their first tour in England.
	Players from Atalante and En Avant were in the squad, most played for Belgium in the 2-0 win over France in Paris in April. The Belgians played Preston Ladies in Halifax, Bolton, Tredegar in south Wales, Morecambe, Accrington, New Brighton and Widnes with a famous 2-1 win in Bolton.
18.08.1934	Carmen had a key role as organiser, translator and go-between
16.08.1934	Carmen was one of three French players for the "Anglo-French' team v Preston Ladies at the Royal Lancashire Show, Garstang. She got three goals
04.12.1934	Fémina defaulted all matches v Dunlop in protest against Violette Morris

1935

01.08. to	A French selection (not the national team) toured England and Wales. Seven games v Preston Ladies at West Ham, Coventry, Pontypool, Chester, Liverpool, Leyland and Barrow-in-Furness. (W1, D1, L5).
13.08.1935	Carmen was captain of 'Team France' and scored twice during the tour

1936

12.04.1936	Carmen's ninth (and last) international, 3-1 v Belgium in Paris. Carmen scored all three goals
29.05. to 07.06.1936	Carmen captained a French touring team against Preston Ladies in South West England. Carmen

	scored seven goals on the tour. Preston won at Southsea, Ryde (Isle of Wight), Bristol, Kettering and Southampton. At Yeovil in Somerset, a French/Preston XI won 3-0 v Yeovil Ladies.
31.07. to 11.08.1936	Carmen was captain and team manager of a French tour of Northern and England, with matches v Preston Ladies at Ripley, Blackpool, Bacup and Nelson. In Belfast, 'France' won 4-1 v a Northern-Ireland XI

1937

31.01.1937	Carmen's last French championship match. She scored the winning goal. The league season in France ended in chaos, many matches cancelled
28.07. to 11.08.1937	Carmen was team manager (not a player) of the French tour of England. A weak squad, containing many high-school girls played nine matches at Birmingham, Nuneaton, Wilmslow, Wakefield, Rochdale, Haslingden, Bolton, Pontypridd and Blackpool. (No wins and many heavy defeats)

1938

18.03.1938	Violette Morris sensationally acquitted of murder, due to self-defence
17.06. to 29.06.1938	Carmen was part of the last French tour to Britain before the war. This time, Carmen was again a key player but handicapped by injuries. She missed at least two games, at Cheltenham and Fleetwood.

	At Workington and Macclesfield, Carmen played but struggled with injuries.
19.11.1938	Florrie Redford's last-ever game, Preston 0 Whitehaven Ladies 4

1939

01.03.1939	Carmen presented a petition on the future of women's football to a Fémina Sports meeting. Her petition was rejected by the club Bureau
03.09.1939	France and Britain declared war on Germany after Poland was invaded.

Carmen's Travels

Date	Event/source	Comment
1922	Sailed from Liverpool by SS *Montclare* with Dick, Kerr Ladies football tour	Canadian Pacific Passenger list
	In the US, Index to Alien Arrivals at Canadian Atlantic and Pacific Seaports	Occupation given as 'teacher' Address listed as Preston
22/9/1922	Border Crossing from Canada into the United States.	Canadian border crossings list
09/10/1922	Arrival in Liverpool from New York by White Star SS *Adriatic*	Passenger list Occupation given as 'secretary' Address listed as Preston
4/7/1941	In the US, Border Crossing from Canada to the United States, near Niagara Falls?	The United States was still neutral in the war at this time. No evidence has yet come to light about Carmen crossing the Atlantic to North America and back again
19/4/1946	Arrival in New York City from Le Havre, SS *Desirade*	Soon afterwards, Carmen settled in Rochester in upstate New York
19/4/1946	Resident Alien's Border Crossing Registration Card, New York NY	Destination address 964 Winton Road North, Rochester NY

Date	Event/source	Comment
1948	US City directories	Carmen's address listed as 176 Akron St, Rochester NY; occupation 'stenographer'
13/10/1948	Sailed to France with French Line SS *De Grasse*	Passenger list, occupation 'secretary'
11/1948	Return to the United States	Ship not known
1951	US City Directories	Address: 1050 East Avenue, Rochester, NY; occupation: 'office secretary'
1953	US City Directories	Carmen's address: 45 West 76th St, Central Park West, Manhattan, NY
19/5/1953	Sailed from New York to Boulogne by SS *Veendam*	Holland America Line passenger list
21/4/1954	Arrival back in New York from Le Havre by *SS Liberté*	French Line passenger list (After a stay in France of 11 months)
1954	Alien Registration Form	No. 6274111 POMIES Carmen Charlotte Marianne
1954	Petition for Naturalisation	Filed in NY; residence: NY; Title and location Court: NY Southern District No. 621237
17/5/1954	Certificate of US Citizenship	New York City No. 7320827
16/8/1956	Flight from New York to Paris by Air France 7879/0815 Lockheed Super Constellation	Passenger list states 'American' Why did Carmen fly on this occasion, not travel by ship as usual?

Carmen's Travels

Date	Event/source	Comment
1957-58	Possible return journey to the United States?	Not known
1957-58	Possible journey back to France?	Details not known
1960	US City Directories	Address: 277 E 56th St Manhattan, NY
22/10/1960	Sailed from Le Havre to New York by *SS Flandre*	French Line Passenger and Crew list
??	Return visit(s) to France?	Not known
1982??	Final return journey to France	Not known when or why.
29/9/1982	Died in France	Champcueil, Essonne (south of Paris)
10/1982	Death recorded in US Social Security Death Index	SSN: 132-22-6211 (issued before 1951 in NY)
10/1982	Last postal address PO Box 912, US Consulate, Paris, France	Does this last known postal address at the US Consulate in Paris indicate that Carmen had no fixed residence in France and had only recently returned from the United States?

Afterthought: Awkward Questions

In the life story of Carmen Pomiès, something is surprisingly absent. Carmen was a lively, confident, sociable, team-spirited woman with a gift for friendships. Yet there is scarcely a hint during her long life of anything about love and relationships. This leads once again to unknowns. The significant gaps in the evidence relating to Carmen's life outside sport leave room enough to hide any number of relationships. Carmen may have had one or many love affairs. On the other hand, maybe she didn't. We just do not have the evidence to judge.

Speculation without much evidence to go on can be a dangerous business. When first researching women's football for Football Makes History, Marcel Put and Chris Rowe composed a feature article on the close friendship between Carmen and Florrie Redford. As in the Prologue to this book, we used the 'captains kiss' at Herne Hill in 1925 as a starting point, That moment might have been no more consequential than any handshake or greeting before kick-off; the point of the story was that for Carmen and Florrie it was a moment in a long and special friendship. Unwisely, we posed a speculative question, 'was this a love affair?' Posing this awkward question got us into a bit of trouble. Female historians with a special interest in Florrie, Carmen and the history of Dick, Kerr Ladies made their objections known to us. We were happy to re-edit the article as they requested.

Two different strands of the history of women's football were coming into conflict. From our twenty-first century perspective, shaped by countless seminars about diversity and discrimination, a presumed same-sex relationship would be something not only to accept but to celebrate. There was no sense nor any intention of intruding on sensitive personal issues. As we learned more, however, about prevailing trends on social media, the counter-arguments came into focus.

Lily Parr, for example, got a lot of public attention when her statue was unveiled at the National Football Museum in Manchester. This public attention was not only about football. Lily was adopted as an icon for LGBT activists. The intentions of those who followed this line were benign, in tune with contemporary ideals of anti-discrimination and equality. Others were dismayed. They wished to see Lily Parr celebrated as a great footballer, not as an icon of Gay Pride. (As far as we can tell, Lily, who lived quietly in Preston with her long-term partner Mary, would have hated it). In 2005, Hope Powell, coach of the England women's national team and a noted campaigner for acceptance of diversity, commented: 'There's always been that stereotyping of female footballers as butch, dykey and unattractive, so maybe it's just best left alone'.

Perhaps that is the way it should be with Carmen and Florrie. It was a long time ago, in a different age when behaviour and attitudes were very different from today. Historians do not have a divine right to know everything. The details of relationships should be nobody's business except for the women involved. Perhaps it would be best to call out the misogynists who express prurient, outdated attitudes but otherwise leave the awkward questions about lesbianism and women's football behind a door marked Private and Personal. But that is easier said than done.

Firstly, part of the historical record is that a number of female footballers in modern times have openly acknowledged their same-sex partners, By 2021, the number of professional female footballers to do this numbered more than forty, Hope Powell and Megan Rapinoe among them. The situation in men's football is very different. The most high-profile player to 'come out' so far has been Thomas Hitzlsperger, and he did so after retiring as a player. It seems to reflect the frightening intensity and intrusiveness of public scrutiny, especially on social media.

In 2019, Megan Rapinoe was at the centre of such scrutiny after leading the United States to an impressive victory in the Women's World Cup. Her vigorous assertion of equal rights for women and same-sex relationships led to a brief but very hostile Twitter War with President Trump, who announced he would not invite the USA team to the White House to celebrate their triumph. In return Megan Rapinoe let it be known she would be less than disappointed to miss out on meeting Donald Trump in person. It was an indication of how, in the twenty-first century, LGBT rights are on the front line of culture wars about diversity and social inclusion. Women's football is part of this.

In twenty-first century France, the story of *Les Dégommeuses* illuminates vividly the ongoing battles that have still to be fought for women's football and equality. *Les Dégos* (literally, 'The De-gummers') was formed in 2012 to promote social inclusion through a football club that welcomed lesbians, trans-women and refugees – all those who felt excluded from mainstream women's football. By football matches, travelling exhibitions and jazzy online presentations by articulate and uncompromising activists like Suzette Robichon. *Les Dégos* soon carved out an influential niche in France's sporting arena. A wide-ranging exhibition on the history of women and sport in France staged at the Centre Hubertine Auclert in 2017 highlighted the importance of *Les Dégommeuses,* alongside the Midinettes, Alice Milliat and FCF Stade Reims, in promoting equality. When France hosted the Women's World Cup in 2019, *Les Dégos* seized the opportunity to broadcast its inclusive agenda to a national audience. The combative mentality of *Les Dégommeuses* has no patience with the idea 'leave well alone'.

Secondly, for the last 140 years, women in football have faced a tidal wave of hostility and denigration from people, not only men, who see football .as undesirable or even 'unnatural' for women. This backlash has frequently weaponised the accusation, direct or implicit, 'they're all lesbians'. Addressing this issue is an essential part of the history of women's football because the fear of independent women has been part of the social history of twentieth-century Europe.

In *Women and Football. A Contradiction,* their contribution to *Gender, Sport, Politics*, edited by J.A. Mangan in 2013, Gertrude Pfister, Kari Fasting, Sheila Scratton and Benilde Vazquez offered a trenchant analysis of this fear and its stifling impact in the 1920s:

> The success of single women in public life threatened the status quo. Independent women were accused of sex hatred and pilloried for preferring their own sex to men. Amid a wholesale effort to revive marriage and [ideals of] delicate womanhood, single women were covertly and overtly attacked.

The authors were writing about anti-feminism in the special circumstances of Europe after the First World War but their analysis could be applied to many other contexts. The thesis of *Male Fantasies,* a 1984 book by the German social scientist Klaus Theweleit, asserted that fear of women was a paramount motive for many of the men who joined the SA in Germany in the 1920s and 1930s. In Theweleit's view, the ranks of marching, macho SA men in brown shirts who provided the background noise for Hitler's rise to power were desperately clinging together for security and reassurance as much as they were expressing male dominance. The same might be supposed of noisy gangs of male football fans the world over. Since 1984, many historians have challenged Klaus Theweleit's interpretation as too extreme but his analysis of the driving force of fear behind misogyny carries a ring of truth.

That fear was especially powerful in the interwar years, not only among right-wing ideologues. There was great anxiety about the social impact of the Great War and its appalling casualties. Many observers were alarmed at the prospect of 'a generation of mateless women' and warned of by the harmful effects of low birth rates. So there was both fear and urgency behind recommendations to 'revive marriage and protect delicate womanhood'. Such thinking was particularly influential among Church leaders. It was fertile ground for the opposition and ridicule so often directed against women's football.

Thirdly, fear has affected women, too. Fear of seeming 'unwomanly' remains an issue for young girls in football. In *A Game for Rough Girls?* Professor Jean Williams analysed the factors that can cause girls to drop out of a game they enjoy and are good at. Among the factors she identified were pressure from socially-conservative parents, perceived problems in acquiring or keeping boyfriends, the multitude of other leisure activities in modern society and culture, or peer pressure accentuating the fear of being 'different' from other girls. The stereotyping Hope Powell talked about in 2005 has proved tenacious. True equality is still some way off.

There is also the powerful 'magnetic field' of motherhood. One of the finest female footballers of modern times, Fatmire Alushi, fled with her family from war-torn Kosovo to Germany when she was five years old. Fatmire grew up to be one of the finest players in the Women's Bundesliga and wrote her autobiography, aged twenty-one, in 2009. Fatmire married Enis Alushi, like herself a Kosovar-Albanian refugee. She missed out on playing in the 2015 Women's World Cup because she was expecting their first child. At the time, Fatmire was determined she would resume her playing career but when the time came in 2017, still aged only twenty-eight, she decided family came first and decided to retire from the game.

There are many different ways to achieve equality but it is worth noting that the fight for equality through women's football needs men as well as women, such as brothers, boyfriends and husbands. Men like Alfred Frankland, or the male coaches like Bob Holmes and Eli Thornborough, who helped Dick, Kerr Ladies, or Frank Zanazzi who coached at Plymouth Ladies. Male journalists like

Levi Wilcox in Philadelphia in 1922, or Willi Schmieger, who supported *Damenfussball* in Vienna in the 1930s. Men like Monsieur Bessoneau, who enabled the purchase of Stade Elisabeth as a home for women's football in Paris. Perhaps even the men at the English FA who decided, albeit fifty years too late, to rescind the infamous ruling of 1921. Perhaps, too, the many men of the present time who were born in a different era but have slowly learned to move away from the outdated attitudes they absorbed in their youth.

So it is not easy to follow the line that sex, gender, love and relationships are 'just best left alone' when it comes to women and football. These issues have been significant since the 1880s and 1890s when pioneers like Helen Matthews and 'Nettie Honeyball' first launched women's football. The fight for equality requires dissecting and challenging the old myths.

Yet perhaps it is possible to avoid straying from these big themes of social and cultural history into unwarranted and intrusive speculation about individual lives. While there is a natural curiosity to know more about the friendship between Florrie Redford and Carmen Pomiès, there is no right to know more than we know already. They were best friends. They shared life-changing experiences in France, England and America. They were talented, independent young women. They both happened to be wonderful footballers. That's enough.

Find Out More: Books

Hélène's Books:

Cassou, Jean (ed) & Pomiès Hélène (tr), *Nouvelles Espagnoles* (Stories from Spain), Paris 1937

Pomiès, Hélène (ed), *Georges Pomiès: Danser C'est Vivre*: (To Dance is to Live), 1939

Pomiès, Hélène, *Du Sang sur la Montagne* (Blood on the Mountain), Paris 1947

Women's Football in Carmen's Times

Brennan, Patrick, *The Munitionettes: A History of Women's Football in North East England During the Great War*, 2007

Faller, Helge, Les Footballeuses II Season 1919-20

Faller, Helge, Les Footballeuses III Season 1920-21

Faller, Helge, Les Footballeuses IV Season 1921-22

Faller, Helge, Les Footballeuses V Season 1922-23

Faller, Helge, Les Footballeuses VI Season 1923-24

Faller, Helge, Les Footballeuses VII Season 1924-25

Faller, Helge, Les Footballeuses VIII Season 1925-26 (all in German)

Faller, Helge, *Avant Leur Temps* (Before Their Time): L'histoire du Football Feminin Belge 1921-25, 2018

Faller Helge, *Le Grand Départ* (The Great Journey): Football Féminin en Belgique, 1925-28, 2019

Faller, Helge & Marschik, Matthias, *Eine Klasse für Sich: Als Wiener Fussballerinnen einzig in der Welt waren* (In a Class of their Own: When Vienna's Football Women were Unique in the World), 2020

Jacobs, Barbara, *The Dick, Kerr Ladies: the factory girls who took on the world*, 2004

Newsham, Gail, *A League of Their Own!*, 2021 (3rd edition).

Prudhomme-Poncet, Laurence, *Histoire du Football Féminin au XXth Siècle*, 2003

Rey Javi, Galic Bertrand, Kris & Bonnet Marie-Jo, *Violette Morris: A Abattre Par Tous Moyens* (Winning By Any Means), 2 vols, 2018

Tate, Tim, *Girls With Balls: The Secret History of Women's Football*, 2013

Women and Football in General

Collins, Tony, *How Football Began: A global history of how the world's football codes were born*, 2019

(FIFA), *The Official History of the FIFA Women's World Cup: the story of women's football from 1981 to the present day*, 2019

Mangan, J.A. (ed), *Sport in Europe: Politics, Class, Gender*, 1999

Powell, H, *Hope: My Life in Football*, 2016

Williams, Jean, *The History of Women's Football*, 2021

Williams, Jean, *A Game for Rough Girls?*, 2007

Williams, Jean, *A Beautiful Game: International Perspectives on Women's Football*, 2003

The Historical Context

Atget, Eugène, *Paris*, 2016

Beevor, Antony & Cooper, Artemis, *Paris After the Liberation*, 1994

Gildea, Robert, *Fighters in the Shadows: A New History of the French Resistance*, 2015

Horne, Alistair, *Seven Ages of Paris*, 2018

Jackson, Julian, *France, the Dark Years 1940-1944*, 2001

Macmillan, James, *Twentieth Century France*, 1992

Rousso, Henry, *The Vichy Syndrome*, 1995

Sardo, Michael, *A Tribute to New York City in the 1950s*, 2001

Find Out More: On Screen

Football Makes History (footballmakeshistory.eu)
The Lives section contains 100 + football life stories. Twenty-two are of women, including Carmen Pomiès, Alice Milliat, Violette Morris, Florrie Redford, Lily Parr, Brunilde Amodeo, Stephanie Frappart, Edith Klinger, Ebru Köksal, Petra Landers, Nadia Nadim, Megan Rapinoe and Molly Seaton. Stories and Videos include *The Incredible Life of a French Footballer,* and *The Climb to Equality*

Playing Pasts. The Online Magazine for Sport and Leisure (www.playingpasts.co.uk)
Among features on women's football in the interwar years are:

'The Forgotten Pioneers: International Women's Football in the Interwar Period', Parts 1-4, by Helge Faller

Other articles on women's football in the interwar years include:

'And then we were boycotted: New discoveries about the birth of women's football in Italy' by Marco Giani

'Edith Klinger: Austria's first female referee & Viennese women's football 1935-1938' by Cherardo Bonini

'Lily Parr: amateur cricketer, hockey player and footballer' by Steve Bolton

'Molly Seaton: legendary Irish Woman Footballer, Talented Pioneer and Iconic Figure' by Steve Bolton

'Women's football in interwar Scotland: Sadie Smith and the legendary Rutherglen FC' by Steve Bolton & Fiona Skillen

Donmouth.com
A website compiled by Patrick Brennan, author of the Munitionettes. It has splendid Galleries of photographs related to the early history of women's football.

Society for American Soccer History (www.ussoccerhistory)
'The Dick, Kerr Ladies come to Philadelphia', 1922
'Dick, Kerr Ladies in Washington DC', 1922
British Pathé newsreel
'Football: Women's International Football at Herne Hill 1925'

DVD

Chotard et Cie, directed by Jean Renoir, 1932. Comedy film set in the markets of Paris in the 1860s, starring George Pomiès

La Symphonie Fantastique, Continental Films 1942. Historical drama about the French composer Berlioz, starring Renée Saint-Cyr

Laissez-Passer (Safe Conduct), directed by Bertrand Tavernier, 2002. The story of French cinema under German occupation and the Vichy regime

Bend It Like Beckham, directed by Gurinder Chadha, 2002. Romantic drama about a Bangladeshi girl in West London who wants to play football

Mustang, directed by Deniz Gamze Ergüven, 2016. French-Turkish film about five sisters rebelling against social conservatism

Das Wunder von Taipeh (We Wanted More), directed by John David Seidler, 2019 . Documentary celebrating the German women who won the unofficial world cup.

Newspaper Acknowledgements

Manchester Guardian match report on England-France, May 1920, re-issued in 2020. Courtesy of *The Guardian*

Report on the FA ruling against women's football, December 1921. Courtesy of *The Daily Mirror*

Newspaper reports from Washington DC, Fall River and Philadelphia on the Dick, Kerr Ladies tour of North America in 1922. Courtesy of the Society for American Soccer History.

Letter to the editor from Neal Ascherson about violence in Paris, 1934. Courtesy of *The Guardian*.

Carmen's letter from Spain, 1941, and report on Carmen in Preston, 1945. Courtesy of the *Lancashire Evening Post*

Features on Carmen's years in Rochester NY from *The Democrat & Chronicle*: Pour le Sport, May 1947, Carmen Seeded No 1, April 1948, From Underground to UN skyscraper, October 1950. Courtesy of newspapers.com

Index

Action Française 4-5, 99, 108
Air France 152-7
Alushi Fatmire 204
Amodeo Brunilde 107-8, 172-3
Antony 168
Ascherson Neal 98
Ashcroft Lizzy xiv, 38, 91, 93, 99-102, 164, 170

Barcelona 17, 68
Baker Josephine 8
Belfast 79-81, 85, 92-5, 103, 171
Belgium 1934 tour 99-100
Belgium 1939 tour 110-1
Bend It Like Beckham 178
Bessoneau Julien 21-2, 205
Blackpool 29, 91, 109-11
Bolton Stephen xiv, 170-1
Boultwood Jessie 36, 43-4,
Bracquemond Madeleine 23, 29, 36, 42-4, 72, 77, 91, 164, 168
Brennan Patrick xvi, 18
Bridgett Len 67-8
Bridgett George Arthur 67-8
Bridgett sisters 67
Brulé sisters 7, 23

Casablanca 115
Champcueil 153, 161-3
Choltitz Dietrich von 131
Climb to Equality 179
Clune Henry 120-2, 141-4
Cohen Sir Benn Jack 78
Continental Films 124

Daily Mirror 40
Darrieux Danielle 122-3
Das Wunder von Taipeh 176-7
Deepdale 20, 24-6, 28-9, 163-4
De Gaulle Charles 130-6, 158-9
Dégommeuses Les 15, 202
Democrat & Chronicle xvii, 59, 139, 173
Dick, Kerr Ladies xv, xix, 19-39, 42-5, 46-61, 69, 75-82, 90-5, 99-103, 170-1
Dick, Kerr Ltd, 19, 62
Drôle de Guerre 115
Dublin 80
Duncan Isadora 6-7, 88-9
Duncan Lisa 6-7, 89, 96-7, 109, 166-7
Dreyfus Affair 3-4, 99,

Exposition Universelle 2-3, 11

Fairley John 169
Faller Helge xiv, 67, 72, 95, 108, 172
Fall River xvi, 54
Fallon Pat 121-2, 126, 144-5,
Fatherland Front 108
FCF Reims 15-6, 174-5
Fémina 10-3, 21-30, 42-3, 62-75, 82-4, 109
Football Association xx, 39-41, 48, 62, 75
Football, Feminism & Film 177-8
Football Makes History xii, 181
Franck Paul 109
Frankland Alfred 19-29, 35, 45-61, 76-82, 92-9, 112, 116, 164, 170-1, 204
Frappart Stephanie 183, 185

Garstang 100
Gauckler Andrée 100-2, 164
Gaudriot Henry 138
Geli Bertrand 94,
Goebbels Josef 123-4
Gouraud-Morris Violette, see Morris Violette

Hanot Gabriel 62, 90, 185
Harding Warren Gamaliel, President 53
Harris Jenny 50, 65

Henie Sonja 85
Herne Hill xix, 62, 77-81
Hey's Brewery Bradford 42, 65, 69
Hôpital Georges Clemenceau 162-3

'Isadorables' 7, 89

Kell Alice 26, 47-9
Kent Cecil 41, 77-8
Kiki 'Queen of Montparnasse' 7
Klinger Edith 107-8, 173
Köksal Ebru 184-5

La Femme et le Sport 84, 168
Laloz sisters 42, 65-6
Lancashire Evening Post 116-9
Landers Petra xiv, 179, 181-2, 185
Laval Pierre 104, 131
Le Havre 1, 34
Le Petit Journal 73
Liberté 152
Lisbon Scandal 69-71

Manchester Guardian 30-2
Maquisards 127-9
Matthews Helen Graham 16, 205
Maurras Charles 4-5, 99
Midinettes 13-5, 202
Milker Liesl see Duncan Lisa
Miller Ardean 133-4, 138, 143, 173

Index

Milliat Alice xiii, 9-12, 15-6, 21-7, 32-3, 63, 66, 69-75, 83-4, 167, 179
Moor Park, Preston 25, 92, 164
Morot de Grésigny, Roger de 158-60, 165-7
Morris Violette xiii, 11-2, 33, 37, 42, 65-6, 70-1, 83-6, 100, 105-6, 132-3, 164, 167-8
Mustang 178-9

Nadim Nadia 184-5
New Bedford xvi, 53-54
New York City 49-50, 146-9, 154-5, 159-61
Newsham Gail xvi, 76, 164

Olympiad Féminines 11-2, 37
Olympique Scandal Match 65-6, 70
Ourry Louise 22-3, 29-33, 74, 164

Parr Lily xiii, 27-9, 34-8, 50-2, 60, 91-2, 101-2, 164, 169-70, 201
Pawtucket xvi, 50
Pétain Philippe 104, 115, 131
Plymouth Ladies 36, 42-4
Pomiès Adèle (née Guignard) 1-9, 151, 156
Pomiès Charles 1-9, 135-6, 151, 156
Pomiès Georges 1-9, 88-90, 96-7, 109, 166,

Pomiès Hélène 1-9, 47, 97, 105, 109, 113, 119, 128, 135, 146, 156-8, 164-5
Pomiès Yvonne 1- 7, 156-8, 165
Powell Hope 181-2, 185, 201
Prudhomme-Poncet Laurence 20, 90, 104
Put Marcel xiv, 200

Rapinoe Megan 182-3, 185, 202
Redford Florrie xiii-xx, 26-9, 34-8, 40-61, 62-75, 91, 109, 137, 164, 169, 200-5
Renoir Jean 2, 89-90, 97, 168-9
Renzulli Pete 55
Robey George 77
Robichon Suzette 15, 202
Rochester NY 38, 47, 59, 112-4, 120-1, 136-46
Rumsfeld Donald 153
Ruth Babe 51

Saint-Cyr Renée 38, 89, 109, 121-4, 133, 146, 151, 169
Schmieger Willi 107-8, 205
Seaton Mary Ann ('Molly') 81, 93-4, 103, 171
Spanish Civil War 104-5, 119
Specht Lotte 85-6, 172
Stade Elisabeth 21
Starace Achille 107
Stoke Ladies 44-5, 67-9, 75
Swartenbroeks Armand 17

213

Tavernier Bertrand 123-4
Thomas Marjorie 110-1
Thornborough, Margaret 91-2, 99, 116, 164, 171
Thornborough, Eli 171, 204
Toitgans Jenny 82-3, 172

United Nations 144-8, 174
Unofficial Women's World Cup 175-6

Vercors Rising 128-9
Vichy regime 98, 112, 115-9, 125
Vichy Syndrome 134
Villaplane Alex 106, 128, 131-2

Washington Post 52
Washington Stars 50-4
Washington Times 51
Whittingham Hospital 171
Wilcox Levi 55-8, 205
Williams Jean xvi, 204
Wilson Woodrow, President 8
Women's World Cup, 2019 180
Women's World Games 87-8, 100

Zanazzi Frank 43, 204